FRIDAY NIGHT FIGHTER

FRIDAY NIGHT FIGHTER

GASPAR "INDIO" ORTEGA
AND THE GOLDEN AGE OF
TELEVISION BOXING

Troy Rondinone

UNIVERSITY OF ILLINOIS PRESS

Urbana, Chicago, and Springfield

Library of Congress Control Number: 2013933248

For my Parents, Jeff and Rochelle
And for Indio

Contents

PART III. THE HARDEST GAME

Illustrations

Acknowledgments

Though many people have helped me create this book, without my having met Gaspar Ortega by chance in 2005, this project would simply not exist. So first and foremost, I would like to thank Indio for sharing his amazing story with me. Gaspar's family has also been a wonderful help. Special thanks to Ida, Michael, Rene, Gaspar Jr., Martha, Gaspar Benitez Jr., Torito, Sapo, Fausto, Felix, Lupita, Eulala, and Cathy.

I also would like to thank the boxers I have spoken with—Hardy "Bazooka" Smallwood, Tony DeMarco, Carmen Basilio, Emile Griffith, Joe Miceli, Bill Tate, Chico Vejar, Ramon "Kid Irapuato" Perez Pazuelgo, Jose Luis Diaz, Bernardo "Gordo" Zuniga, and Manuel "Jilguerillo" Cruz. Thanks as well to Ben Rendon, Joe Cortez, Victor Bernal, and Raymond Solis.

The University of Illinois Press has provided much insight and guidance. Thanks to Willis Regier for his patience. Also, I deeply appreciate the insights of the sports historians who have read and commented on drafts of this project—thanks to Randy Roberts, Russell Sullivan, and Gerald Early.

Many thanks to friends and family who helped me at different points along the way—Luis Rodriguez, Xochitl Mercado, Raul Mercado, Dr. Alan Miller, Brenda Sullivan Miller, Sandra Lopez Egan, Dr. Bruce Calderone, Michael T. Carter, Byron Nakamura, Julian Madison, and Josh Zeitz all played wonderful, helpful roles. Thanks to my supportive colleagues in the History Department of Southern Connecticut State University. Thanks especially to those who shared their stories with me—Joseph Rondinone, Rochelle Rondinone, Jon Purmont, Brenda Sullivan Miller, Dr. Harold Levy, Bob Jirsa, Chuck Hasson, Milton Hernandez, John

O'Connor, Bob Hink, Gil Clancy, Bert Randolph Sugar, LeRoy Neiman, and Carlos Santana.

I also appreciate help that I received from folks at institutions that keep the past of boxing alive—Rick Kaletsky, Henry Hascup, Jeff Brophy, and the people at the Papers of Jack Barrett collection at the Brooklyn College Archives. Thanks also to the library staffs of Southern Connecticut State University (especially Alba Reynaga) and the Yale Sterling Library.

Finally, I would like to thank my immediate family. My children, Sophia and Catalina, never fail to cheer me along in whatever I do. My brother David has always been in my corner. And my wife, Kathleen, has gladly endured hearing me talk about boxing for years now. Her insights and help are evident to me on every page of this project.

I would like to dedicate this book to my friend Indio. He has taught me much more than proper jabbing techniques and how to snap punches. I would also like to dedicate the book with love to my exceptional parents, Jeff and Rochelle Rondinone. I have always wanted to better understand their experiences growing up as Baby Boomers. I hope I got it right.

Boxing Lessons

From the street, the building looked condemned. Murky windows and weather-blasted bricks overlooked a dismaying frontage of ragweed, dandelions, and broken cement. A chain-link fence off to the side surrounded an empty parking lot. No sign, marker, or any other evidence of human life availed itself. A desperate Google search for a boxing program had brought me here, to this post-Apocalyptic community center.

I got out of my car. I walked through a rust-colored door and down a short flight of stairs that opened into a dank basement hallway. My inner voice grew testier. Was the boxing workout better imagined than lived? Was this place really a suitable substitute for the expensive, well-appointed gym in my own cozy suburb, with its air-conditioning and televisions? And what *was* that smell?

The boxing room itself was long and narrow. It lay snug against the length of the front of the building, brightened by buzzing fluorescents and ground-level half-windows. Three well-abused heavy bags hung from the ceiling like tired sides of beef, drifting about on short chains attached to steel hooks. Overhead tiles sagged under a history of mold and neglect. A small ring squatted at the far end, edged by a motley assortment of jump ropes, gloves, and weights. A loud, jarring electronic bell marked time as a couple of kids whacked away at the bags. A poster of Britney Spears holding a Pepsi adorned one wall. Others featured fading bills for local fights, young tough guys posed opposite each other, eyes fixed, gloves at the ready. And then the smell—or rather, *first* the smell—all old sweat and mold. On a later visit, I'd notice the photocopied clippings of Rocky Marciano and a young boxer from Mexico taped near the far door.

An old man approached me. He was thin and bronze-skinned and stately, with ramrod straight posture and tight, close-cropped hair. He seemed very tall, though he couldn't have been more than five-foot-ten. His gaunt, creased face sported wire-framed glasses and a faint black mustache set over a wide, toothy grin. "You need help?" he asked, grinding a stick of gum. His rough, accented voice sounded like a fist diving through a bag of gravel. I explained that I was here to learn how to box and that I had no experience. I spoke quickly, cutting myself off after what seemed like a long string of apologies. The old man clutched my hand with his big, leathery paw and told me to come back the next day with hand wraps (long strips of cloth used to support and protect bones and tendons in the wrist and hands), the longer the better. He asked if I knew how much it would cost. I told him no. Twenty dollars a year, he beamed. He also told me that his name was Gaspar "Indio" Ortega, and that he had been a contender once.

On the first day of my training I learned some hard lessons. I discovered that merely holding my hands up, with or without gloves, and pumping the air for three minutes straight was nearly impossible. I learned that I could not jump rope continuously for even ten seconds. I learned to inhale deeply and slowly to avoid passing out when the room began to spin. I found that punching properly is neither natural nor easy. I got light-headed. I got sick to my stomach. Sometimes, I'd just stare at the heavy bag, hands dead at my sides. Luckily for me, Gaspar was patient. He might shove the back of my head down to illustrate chin protection or laugh at my weak punches, but he always paid me the greatest of care, as though my learning to box was his highest priority.

In time I learned other things. I was surprised to discover that my tolerant trainer had been, once upon a time, a bona fide American celebrity. I got my first clue when I told my father (who is no boxing aficionado himself) that I was learning how to box from an old ex-pro named Gaspar.

"Ortega?" he asked.

Fighting under the ring name "Indio" (or Indian), my teacher had been on prime-time network television many times, more than almost any other boxer in history. He had battled the biggest names in the sport in the late fifties and early sixties, in its most important arena, before an audience of millions. He was featured in the *New York Times*, *Ring Magazine*, and a slew of other periodicals. Parades were thrown in his honor just across the border from San Diego.

As the lessons passed and my body adjusted itself, I started asking the old pugilist questions about his life. I wanted to know why he had been famous, what it had felt like. I also wanted to know what had happened to that fame. As we talked, a larger question came to mind: what had happened to boxing? Sure, the sport still exists. But not like in the past glory days. It's not on network TV anymore. It's no longer a regular, highlighted feature of most sports sections in the big papers. It's not the hot topic of discussion in office lunchrooms on Mondays. Thinking about this made me realize that I had happened upon a big, interesting, and largely untold story. My trainer was a living artifact of a forgotten golden age of boxing in America.

I'm an academic historian, the sort of person who spends his time in libraries and archives, excavating a long-dead past. Quite unintentionally, I had uncovered an important chapter of our history that was lost but not entirely forgotten. The makers of that history are still among us; we just don't know it. It did not take long for me to recognize my luck. My research agenda was about to change.

I began by taking inventory of what I already knew. Television, "the idiot box" as my dad called it, suddenly became important in the 1950s. In the receding shadow of World War II, this new invention webbed together millions of children into an emergent culture of abundance. Families gathered nightly in front of the flickering, black-and-white screens of their newly purchased Philcos and Admirals, watching the same shows that everyone else watched. Television viewing was both a national bonding experience and an intergenerational one; parents and children sat together in their family rooms inside the new stucco palaces sprouting up on former farmlands across the country. The high-minded complained about cultural degradation; the high-minded were ignored. This history has been told. What I did not realize was that the sport of boxing helped birth our collective addiction to this electronic distraction.

Among the most popular offerings in the early days of TV was a program called *Gillette Cavalcade of Sports Friday Night Fights*. Compared with today's top shows, the *Cavalcade* was something completely and utterly different. To grasp the difference, we must understand what the term *popular* once meant. In 1955, approximately 20 percent of the country (not just the population with televisions) tuned in to watch the fights on Fridays.[1] Compare this to the megahit show *American Idol*, which is currently watched by about one percent of Americans regularly. There was no channel surfing with remotes back then, no taping shows to watch later, no TiVos or digital recorders, no internet rebroadcasts or YouTube clips. The evening came and families huddled together in front of big wooden cabinets and watched the same thing, a one-off event, something that could be discussed later.

Boxing shows were on TV regularly—nearly every single day of the week for a while—but Friday night represented something special. It was the night of the main event. Every Friday night my grandfather would let my dad stay up, and they would watch the fights together. Dad would sit on the floor in his pajamas while Grandpa watched from his favorite chair, tossing back drinks and pulling smoke from his pipe. It was one of their few real bonding experiences.

As I continued my investigation, I was amazed to discover that academics had yet to examine the show. My father's generation certainly remembers it. Many of his cohorts have sung the theme song to me as though it was on last night. Some even tooted, "Look sharp, feel sharp!" just the way Sharpie the Gillette Parrot would screech it. Yet historians have skipped right over it. Or worse, they have consigned it to a footnote of "popular culture." And at least one popular history of America in the 1950s does not deal with boxing at all.[2] I hope to help correct this.

What follows is an attempt to redirect our attention to the squared circle that captivated America as it came into its most prosperous years. Telling this story requires going back to a time when boxing mania reigned supreme. This was a period when even elementary schools boasted boxing teams; when the *New York Times* regularly printed fight results on page one; when boxers were walked on as guests on big TV shows like *Ed Sullivan's Toast of the Town*, *The Steve Allen Show*, and *Masquerade Party*; when fighters were closely attended by Hollywood's A-List and dated models and starlets; when even presidents eagerly sought their company.

The Friday Night Fighters epitomized a new epoch for our country. They represented the dream of every man who saw himself as a maker of his own destiny. Alone and nearly naked, TV boxers faced off against one another in bright rings and performed a kind of live drama on a stage with no props and no backdoor. They counted on their skill and will to get them through, and though they were often immigrants and outsiders, their struggles were internalized in homes across America. Hands balled into fists and swatted the air. Grown men cursed, cheered, and lectured at tiny figures moving across tiny screens in large lacquered cabinets. Children propped themselves up on their elbows or sat in laps and listened intently while fathers discoursed on the proper techniques of unarmed combat. Families paused between rounds to discuss the fight, even recording their own scores on cards provided in the newspapers.

Understanding this story also requires that we dive beneath the happy surface of this seemingly placid era. In darkened living rooms, we find veterans living with nightmares born in the viscera and muck of the battlefields of Europe and the Pacific. For many of these men, the ritual of blood combat is familiar, if unremarked upon. Then there are the boxers themselves, a diverse group whose integration into Anglo-American living rooms mocks the nation's lived experience of de facto and de jure segregation. Most ominously, behind the klieg lights, crime lords are pulling the levers, making decisions that would shock the fans. And just before the curtain lowers, there will be an act of unspeakable brutality: a televised killing.

To borrow a phrase from historian Peter Laslett, this is a tale about a world we have lost. Rediscovering it is to understand why a poor kid from Tijuana could compete with *The Twilight Zone* for TV ratings; it is to find an America of deep paradox, both optimistic about the new abundance and fearful of nuclear holocaust and internal subversion, a nation astride the world yet wary of the heights. It is a lost moment when the Greatest Generation and the Baby Boomers sit together, happily watching the fights.

It will not last. Soon, tensions will escalate. Parents will shake their heads and wonder what happened to the closeness and simplicity of the fifties. Children will see their fathers as dinosaurs yet to be informed of their own extinction. And TV boxing, that agent of bonding and manhood education, will be increasingly seen not as entertainment but rather as evidence of anachronistic barbarism staining American civilization. The boxers themselves, the heroes of Friday nights, will tumble into oblivion and poverty. But for one historical moment, all is well. The boxers are on top, and the two generations are at peace, counting the blows and cheering their man.

I trained with Gaspar at the community center for about a year until the place finally succumbed to mold and had to be relocated. We moved temporarily to a local martial arts studio and then to a newly appointed community gymnasium near the original location. In time, Indio and I fell into something like a routine. I'd train once or twice a week, and on Friday afternoons we'd meet to sip tea and talk about his life as a boxer. For a man struck in the head thousands of times, Gaspar proved to have a remarkably lucid memory. He could tell me in what round he knocked a man to the canvas back in 1956, how it felt when that man got up and struck back. He could recall moments of great triumph and of great pain from half a century ago. He remembered how the woman who became his wife looked when she walked to school in the morning, while he stared from a high apartment window in Spanish Harlem. Without such memory, this story could not have been told.

And so, after countless training sessions, thousands of practice rounds, hundreds of cups of tea, and many additional interviews with other boxers, fans, fight folks, and family members (along with a good bit of traveling), I present to you a lesson learned. This is a journey along a less-traveled path of our postwar history through the experiences of one remarkable boxer.

A good place to start is the beginning of the end. It is 1961, Los Angeles. A fighter sits atop a massage table and has his hands wrapped with tape.

FRIDAY NIGHT FIGHTER

INTRODUCTION

Fight Night

It is Saturday, June 3, 1961. Gaspar "Indio" Ortega sits patiently, his eyes looking at nothing in particular. Legendary trainer Freddie Brown carefully draws long strips of white gauze around his hands. A tough Lower East Side Jew whose flattened nose and ever-present cigar describe a life lived in the fistic world, Freddie Brown has seen it all. He was once a cut man (a person in the boxer's corner who applies Vaseline and other treatments to the face during a fight) for Rocky Marciano, and he prides himself on keeping his boys safe and on top. His attention to his charges is famous. "He was like my baby sitter," Gaspar would later tell a reporter.[1] Once, back in 1952, Brown had helped clear out Marciano's eyes during a controversial fight with Jersey Joe Walcott after his man complained that a substance on Walcott's gloves had blinded him. After a good rinsing, the eyes cleared and Marciano came away with the victory. Brown was always right there to help.

Gaspar splays his fingers and then makes a fist as the cloth winds its circuit. The knuckles on one hand have been flattened flush along the ridge of his fist due to years of improper jabbing, and Gaspar now recognizes the importance of correct protection. Though only twenty-five years old, he has been boxing professionally for eleven years and has fought close to one hundred professional fights.

Down in the belly of Los Angeles's Olympic Auditorium, the crowd cannot be heard, but it can be felt. There are eighty-five hundred fans in the seats, counting down the minutes until the main event. They are from Tijuana, San Diego, Los Angeles, New York. They chant, "Indio! Indio! Indio!" They chant, "Viva Mexico!" and "Tijuana!" There are Mexican flags flapping about, sombreros in laps and on heads. A local youth band is probably already playing bullfight songs in the stands. Spanish is more likely to be heard here than English.

Freddie Brown finishes wrapping. Gaspar checks his hands and then glances at the clock. Forty minutes to seven. He slips off the table and continues his prefight ritual. He secures his cup and tugs at his trunks. He fidgets with his trademark white boxing shoes, a color first made popular by a Cuban boxer named Kid Gavilan. Then he stretches, slowly at first, touching his toes, rotating his torso, shaking his feet to get the blood moving. The stretching begins to resemble fighting now. The head bobs side to side and the torso bends low in the maddening, twisting way that has frustrated opponents for years. The hands come up and the fists tighten. Jabs snap out like pistons, elbows push forward hooks and overhands, locking briefly before repeating imagined punishment. The head moves; the feet dance. Gaspar's tall, lanky form casts blurry shadows against a concrete wall.

A boxing commissioner, whose sole job at this moment is to ensure that Gaspar's men don't apply extra hand wraps or give him anything "special" to drink, stands nonchalantly off to the side. Nobody talks. Gaspar doesn't speak much English, and he doesn't feel like chatting anyway. When the commissioner does speak, it will be a brief exchange:

"Gaspar, you know the rules?"

"Yah."

"I know I don't have to tell you anything."

Gaspar tries his best to focus, but it is difficult tonight. This week's training did not go as planned, and the pressure on him is intense. Earlier in the day, after he had taken his usual post-weigh-in walk, he had gone back to his hotel room to rest, but sleep would not come. His manager, Nick Corby, didn't help things when he repeated what seems to have become his mantra: "You're the only Mexican fighter who has raised up Tijuana into the clouds. Do NOT let her fall!"

This night, Gaspar understands, will define his life. It is the night of his first and, considering his age and experience, possibly last shot at the world welterweight title. Unlike the ungainly carnival of belts, divisions, and "contenders" that would develop in later years, at this point in history there was only one champion in each division, and there were far fewer divisions. There was only one major promoting company and only one key recognizing body. There was a deeper, wider talent pool; fighters had to battle many more opponents to get into position to challenge the top. The audience was also much, much larger, making the fights much more significant. In short, reaching this moment meant that Gaspar had already outclassed literally thousands of other fighters, men who had also dedicated their lives to the slim chance of ring glory.

A proverbial dark horse, Gaspar Ortega grew up poor and fought his way out of the dusty streets of Colonia Morelos, Tijuana, traveling from utter obscurity to international celebrity in the space of a few short years. He is a Friday Night Fighter. At breakfast tables, water coolers, subway stations, restaurants, and bars across America and south of the border, Indio is the topic of lively conversation. Along with the others in his elite cohort—such as Jake LaMotta, Carmen Basilio, Tony DeMarco, Chico Vejar, Benny "Kid" Paret, Willie Pep, Emile Griffith, Kid Gavilan, and Dick Tiger—Gaspar Ortega is a part of the fabric of popular television culture and hence of American life.

The Friday Night Fighter occupies a particular niche in the history of sports. The sudden rise of television, and boxing's almost symbiotic relationship with it, created an intense demand for fighters for the small screen. From boxing clubs across North America and the Caribbean, a cohort of poor, tough young men became instant celebrities. While a few appeared to have been chosen as much for TV appeal as anything else, most Friday Night Fighters were gifted men who struggled to the top of a very deep pool of talent. For these fighters, television provided a chance at celebrity that otherwise would likely not have existed. Further, they represented a remarkably diverse group of TV stars considering the solidly white offerings that the networks mainly served up. Their passage from utter obscurity into the nation's living rooms was as remarkable as it was fleeting. The mob, the critics, and television's voracious need for a continued stream of fighters all combined to stain this cohort and nearly capsize the sport itself. Boxing would survive, but the phenomenon of the Friday Night Fighter would not.

By the time Gaspar got his title shot in 1961, the nation had been transfixed on TV boxing for almost two decades. Ever since Gillette Safety Razor first brought boxing to prime time during World War II, Americans had watched literally thousands of televised battles. Boxing shows dominated the programming schedules in a way that is hard to understand today. In the very earliest days of network television, boxing accounted for close to half of all programming. In some important markets, such as New York City and its environs, fights were broadcast live six nights a week by the mid-1950s.

There were a variety of reasons for this fame. For starters, the sport had an ongoing popularity dating back at least to the days of John L. Sullivan. In the late 1800s, the "Boston Strongboy" liked to announce to packed halls, "My name's John L. Sullivan, and I can lick any son-of-a-bitch alive." His cultlike celebrity kept the country fascinated. By the turn of the century, Sullivan was, according to historian Elliot J. Gorn, "perhaps the nation's most famous citizen."[2] Into the twentieth century, infamous boxers like the unapologetic, "unforgivably black" Jack Johnson and the "white hopes" that he generated kept the world's eyes focused on the squared circle. Wrote novelist James Weldon Johnson in 1915, "there is not, perhaps, a spot on the globe where Jack Johnson's name is not familiar."[3] Then came Jack Dempsey, the fighter who pulled in the first million-dollar gate, in front of ninety thousand fans. Dempsey earned more money than Babe Ruth. His rematch with the "Fighting Marine" Gene Tunney in 1927 reached some 50 million people over the National Broadcast Company radio network, on top of the 104,000 fans who showed up to watch in person at Chicago's Soldier Field.[4] Dempsey epitomized the modern sports pop-culture hero. He endorsed products, starred in movies, and worked the stage on the vaudeville circuit. He got plastic surgery and became an international icon. The next big fighter to entrance the country, Joe Louis, would represent the United States in an ideological contest with Nazi Germany. Louis captured the first million-dollar gate since Jack Dempsey and sold war bonds in World War II. As a black man, he was far more widely known and respected by white America than any other member of his race. After Joe Louis, on came "The Rock," Rocky Marciano, a man who crushed all opponents and in 1956 retired as boxing's only undefeated champion.

While the famous heavyweights drew much attention to the sport, they were only the tip of the spear. Boxing was everywhere in the culture. In backyards and basements, in youth centers and public schools, in boxing clubs and YMCAs, punching bags and roped-off rings seconded the sport's popularity. On Friday nights, folks across the country would go out to watch local favorites take on new challengers at fight clubs, venting their emotions in smoky auditoriums. When television arrived, it formed a symbiotic relationship with the sport. Two figures on a blank canvas translated well onto the ghostly black-and-white screens of the crude sets pumped out by General Electric and Motorola. Like the fight-club audience, the home audience was also heavy with veterans, men who might also have found familiarity in a competition characterized by brute force and clear, simple rules. But most Americans could see the appeal of boxing's simple morality play in an uncertain atomic world.

The night of Gaspar's title fight was important for many people, especially south of the border. In Tijuana, parades were held in his honor, issues of sports magazines dedicated to him. Tijuanans knew what Gaspar's parents did for a living, how his father wore his mustache, and what sort of Indian his mom was. They knew about his wife, Ida, and their young children. A cross section of Mexican sports writers had just carried out a lively discussion of Gaspar's pugilistic merits versus those of his opponent, Virgin Islander Emile Griffith. They had found Indio to be the better of the two men.

For U.S. fans, this matchup also promised to be an especially good fight. Emile Griffith had only recently won the belt, and he was an unlikely champ. Griffith had begun boxing late in life, after his Manhattan hat factory boss had noticed his remarkable physique one day. If you knew Emile, you knew this was an odd call. Musculature aside, Emile's big smile and easygoing personality did not suggest the makings of a ring battler. But Griffith humored his boss, a man who happened to be a failed fighter himself and who trusted his instincts. Griffith proved to be such a natural that within three months, he was entered in the New York State Golden Gloves Tournament. He almost won. A year later he did win, and then he went pro.

Emile Griffith shot to the top of the game like a bolt of lightning. Following a nearly unbroken string of easy wins, he had taken on and defeated Gaspar Ortega at Madison Square Garden a year earlier, in 1960. The fight proved to be Emile's ticket to the big time. He went on to defeat ring legends like hard-hitting Florentino Fernández and the bullish Luis Manuel Rodriguez. He was hailed by many as the next great boxer, a "sensation," the "most talked about" fighter of the day. In April 1961, he knocked out welterweight titleholder Benny "Kid" Paret to become the champion of the world. He was now set to face Gaspar again, in this, his first title defense.

Why fight Gaspar? For starters, Griffith's first victory over Indio had been by way of a split decision, and the bizarre scoring had stirred some controversy. While two judges and most fight reporters scored the fight heavily in favor of Griffith, referee Harry Ebbets, the man who watched the fight from the closest vantage point, scored it just as lopsidedly in favor of Gaspar. Who was to say another fight wouldn't also result in an exciting, controversial finish? Plus, Gaspar had also beaten Benny "Kid"

Paret when Paret held the title, two months before Griffith had taken it from him. Unfortunately for Indio, that battle had been a nontitle affair. Now Griffith had the belt, and Gaspar wanted it badly. Finally, and perhaps most importantly, West Coast boxing promoter George Parnassus had worked an agreement to get Griffith to fight the Indian in front of a huge home crowd in Los Angeles. Boxing was moving west in 1961, and Parnassus was the person perhaps most responsible for this shift. There was a good deal of money to be made off of a Mexican boxer in Southern California. Parnassus hoped that this evening, Gaspar might become Mexico's first welterweight champion.

The fact that this title fight is on a Saturday, not a Friday night, is indicative of something troubling for the sport. Ratings are respectable, but they are down and have been for a while. Like a cloud, a convergence of negatives is gathering above TV boxing. Overexposure, the rise of newer, more dynamic sports (like professional football), and novel, multiple-camera technologies that have made baseball easier to follow have detracted from the boxing's early cachet. Ever since NBC dropped the show and ABC picked it up as the *Saturday Night Fight of the Week* in 1960, moving it to the less-desirable time slot, many have been foretelling the show's demise. Plus, Tennessee senator Estes Kefauver's ongoing public crusade against corruption in boxing has already dragged a number of shadowy characters into the light, including pro boxers who admitted to participating in fixed fights. Many now rail that this is no sport at all but a con, a scam.

Still, there are enough people out there to keep the show on the air. Enough fathers who sit with sons (and even daughters and wives) and keep track of the rounds, enough bar owners who know how to fill a tavern with paying weekend customers (payday is Friday, after all), enough fans who need this release. Enough to let the TV execs know that this show can still sell advertising time.

At ten minutes to seven, a man comes into Gaspar's dressing room and signals that the time has come. The TV schedule is unforgiving, so the Indian and his crew move fast. He has already put on the thick, colorful, serape-style robe that TV announcer Don Dunphy will dreamily describe as a "composite of every Mexican sunset that ever was." A towel is wrapped snugly around his neck below his crew-cut head. He strikes quite a figure. His high white shoes contrast with the black-white-black stripes at the top of his socks. White block lettering reads INDIO ORTEGA across the bottom left side of his black trunks. The word MEXICO is spelled in black lettering down white vertical stripes on the sides.

A small detail of security men lead them out into the hallway. Manager Nick Corby follows, then Gaspar. Freddie Brown paces behind, along with Whitey Bimstein, a world-famous cut man carrying the buckets and ice and Vaseline. Down the corridor, through the doors, and up the aisle the retinue trots. The crowd is already a steady white noise. The corridor opens to intense light and bright sound. The walls of the Olympic loom high above, ten thousand seats steeply climbing into rowdy balconies. Mariachis fill the air with bright trumpets, plaintive violins, and deep *guitarrones*. The house lights have not yet been dimmed to make the ring sharply visible for the TV cameras. The fans, flags, and sombreros are all clearly visible to Indio. He tries not to think about them.

The platform comes into view. Ring announcer Jimmy Lennon is already there, looking sharp in one of his stylish trademark tuxedos, milling about with referee Tommy Hart and some other folks. Jimmy is the house announcer and uncle to the famous singing group the Lennon Sisters, who will have their biggest hit, "Sad Movies (Make Me Cry)," later in the year. Jimmy's got some notes in his hand that he will refer to when the mike drops down from the rafters. His Spanish accent is pretty good, and he uses it to nice effect when announcing contenders in this city.

The distance to the ring is now only a matter of feet. Like many other Friday Night Fighters, Gaspar grew up in a part of what folks had recently begun calling the Third World. His Mexican hometown, just a few hours' drive south of Los Angeles, might as well be on another planet. His journey to Olympic Auditorium has been a saga unto itself, a remarkable passage against the odds. During many of his TV appearances, Don Dunphy tells the home audience that Gaspar has been a bullfighter, a soldier, a cowboy. The truth is even more remarkable, because it is so improbable.

Gaspar Ortega is a Friday Night Fighter. He and his fellow heroes of the small screen, though forgotten today, are worthy of historical study and of our respect. For the most part, they were top-rated battlers, men who competed in a sport far more competitive than, and far different from, what we know as boxing today. The fog of historical amnesia has enveloped the once-bright rings that these men made glorious. It is time to let some light back in.

PART I

Gladiators of the Age of Contentment

"World War Two had certainly
made everybody very tough."

Kurt Vonnegut,
Slaughterhouse-Five (1969)

"Compared to boxing, nothing else
comes over television so bad so good."

Harper's Magazine,
August 1956

CHAPTER 1

"And the Winner—Television!"

Understanding the incredible success of TV boxing in the middle of the twentieth century first requires tracing the sport's crooked path to respectability. What we now know as boxing was born in the late 1800s, when the adoption of the Queensberry rules ended the old bare-knuckle days of limitless rounds, neck choking, no weight classifications, and muddy deaths. The new rules imposed uniformly sized rings, three-minute rounds, standardized judging, weight categories, and padded leather boxing gloves. In addition, by outlawing seconds "or any other person" from the ring during the fight, the Queensberry rules seemed to demand that everything be on the level.

The new structure fit in well with Progressive Era concerns regarding social regulation and masculine regeneration. America was changing dramatically in the decades between the end of the Civil War and start of the First World War. Millions of non–English speaking New Immigrants from southern and eastern Europe poured into America's ports. The workplace became more regimented and impersonal. Technologies reshaped entertainment, communication, and transportation, at once atomizing old communities and uniting the consumer public into a single mass of shoppers. Many men, in particular, felt dehumanized, numbered, and emasculated by these changes. Dominating one's household was more difficult when you had to punch in and kowtow to a foreman all day. In his autobiography, Theodore Roosevelt praised the manhood-molding powers of boxing as a cure for the physical degeneracy that accompanied an unstrenuous life indoors. "I do not like to see young Christians whose shoulders slope like a champagne bottle," he explained.[1] The new Queensberry rules placed this invigorating activity in line with Progress and Discipline, two saviors of a troubled age.

But regulation did not simply transform backroom brawling into a respectable activity. State legislators inevitably found the sport problematic. For example, New York's Frawley Law of 1910 held that no verdict would be determined at the end of a fight, but rather that the referee would present his decision in the next day's papers, alongside the views of sports reporters. This was aimed at preventing gambling. It did not work. Shady types hovered around the ring, making money outside the purview of authorities. Laws aimed at "taming" boxing never really challenged its essential, uncivilized aspects, either. The Walker Law of 1920, which legalized boxing in New York (it had been outlawed in 1917) and set the stage for boxing's acceptance everywhere, also prevented cops from breaking up fights for brutality, creating instead state-licensed officials to do this. The violence remained even as the rules became more formalized.[2]

Beyond the problematic, Paleolithic nature of the sport, the very structure of boxing invited trouble. It is a contest between only two players, so teams and all of the groupthink, coaching, and league formation found in other sports have played no part in its historical progress. Theodore Roosevelt himself complained in 1913 about "the crookedness that has attended its commercial development."[3] Worse, the law often seemed to conspire with the criminals. The Eighteenth Amendment, ratified one year before boxing became legal in New York, banned the sale of alcohol and created an industry of bootlegging. By the end of Prohibition, cash from booze had boosted organized crime considerably. Boxing, the "red light district of sports," was a lucrative arena in which hoods invested.[4]

By the 1940s, a single Mafia family (or *borgata*, Mafia slang for "gang") had managed to dominate the fight racket. Led by a hit man named Frankie Carbo (known as Mr. Gray in the fight world), the Lucchese *borgata* skimmed a good deal of money off the sport, typically by "convincing" managers to hand over a percentage of a fighter's winnings.[5] When boxing came to television, the mob did not leave. In fact, it skimmed more money than ever. What the home audience did not know (but might have suspected) was that Gillette *and* the mob brought them the *Friday Night Fights*.

In the end, there would be lots of blame to go around to account for why TV boxing declined and went off the air. The criminal element obviously had something to do with it. So did the inevitable on-air ring fatalities and the ironic damage wrought by television itself. But for a time, the sport of boxing had a bright shining moment in American culture. A new invention, television, had everything to do with this.

Forget the de luxe, crystal clear, HD, flat-screened, multichanneled televisions sitting on our walls like ever-changing paintings. Early televisions were at worst a joke, at best a novelty. Their success, interestingly, had much to do with boxing. It began with a world war and a razor company.

Two and a half months after D-Day, the in-house promoter of the most famous boxing venue in the world developed a new idea for pulling in revenues. Madison Square Garden's Mike Jacobs made a deal with the Gillette Safety Razor Company to stage a fight every Friday evening for a year. Filmed by TV crews mainly at the Garden proper (to be moved elsewhere when another event usurped the fights), these contests would be shown live at 10 P.M. Eastern Standard Time via the Mutual Broadcasting System, which had an average hook up to over two hundred stations in the eastern United States and twenty-seven more in Canada. For the inaugural battle, Jacobs and matchmaker Nat Rogers arranged a bout between featherweight champion Willie Pep and ex-champion Chalky Wright.

The significance of this first Friday Night Fight was not lost on the sportswriters. Explained Jack Cuddy for the United Press, it marked the "tallest order . . . in sports history," legitimizing boxing as "a year-round entertainment of national appeal." Considering the very limited amount of airtime available in these early days of the new medium (television had first been introduced to the public at the 1939 World's Fair), the decision to program boxing was made with the utmost calculation. Ed Wilhelm, the radio executive handling the Gillette account for the Maxon Advertising Agency, saw it this way: Gillette had been sponsoring fights from the Garden since 1941 with great success. Perhaps more importantly, he recognized "something new—that there is a basic boxing audience." It did not matter to this group "who is fighting and where it is held if they can be sure of getting such a broadcast at a certain time every week." A large, built-in audience meant a safe, constant supply of customers.[6]

Gillette was a logical choice for a TV deal. Its first promotion had been the Baer-Braddock upset of 1935, an event that would become legend when reports of the stunning result transformed Braddock, the hard-luck longshoreman, into "Cinderella Man," an instant Depression-era celebrity. Gillette itself did not reap much benefit from the fight, however, and it didn't go back to promoting boxing until the summer of 1941, when it sponsored the radio broadcast of the first, dramatic Joe Louis–Billy Conn matchup. That fight proved a tremendous commercial success, getting a rating of 56.4, the highest of any radio program up to that time. That same year, someone at Gillette devised the title Gillette's Cavalcade of Sports to describe its sponsored sporting events. The name conjured up visions of a grand procession of athletic contests, a bounteous, bumptious celebration of physicality. By the 1950s, *Cavalcade of Sports* and *Gillette* were synonymous terms. In the years to come, Gillette's regular boxing broadcast on the radio, featuring Don Dunphy's distinctive lisp and staccato, phrase-turning coverage, placed legions of eager listeners at the ringside in their own homes.

Even with radio broadcasts selling mountains of razors, the move to television was not without real risk for the company. In a time when a single sponsor typically incurred the entire production costs of putting on a TV show, Gillette decided to funnel much of its advertising budget into a new, largely untested technology. In 1944 there was no certainty that television advertising dollars would actually pay off. In the first place, there were not that many TV sets in existence. They were expensive and reserved for better-to-do Americans who might not even enjoy prize-fighting. Perhaps more dauntingly, radio did not seem ready to yield even a minute of airtime to another technology. Radios were extremely popular (most households had at least one), and by the 1940s it was usurping everything from books to newspapers to board games. There seemed to be no room for something new. And besides, televisions were hardly "better." The screens were small and the view was often hazy. Images might "roll over" or "flutter." "Snow" and "ghosting" could make the tiny spectacle frustrating.[7] On the broadcasting side, lost signals were a regular, maddening occurrence. Additionally, the demands that the novel machine made on all of one's senses seemed far too exacting. During the 1939 World's Fair, one journalist dismissed the contraption altogether as too stultifying for the dynamic American lifestyle, noting, "People must sit and keep their eyes glued on a screen; the average American family hasn't time for it."[8]

Gillette's genius lay in being one of the first companies to recognize the potential of this questionable new medium and in taking the calculated risk of featuring it as a centerpiece of its advertising campaign. The company grasped early on that television offered an entirely new way of bringing attention to a product. It was one thing to view a still image in a magazine, or read a print testimonial in the newspaper, or listen to a salesman pitch the virtues of the razor on the radio. It was something of an entirely different order to provide potential customers with all three at once, for them to watch the product literally dance before their eyes in their own living rooms.

Boxing and television had met before. In the late 1920s, inventor Philo T. Farnsworth experimented with adapting filmed sequences of a Dempsey-Tunney fight for television broadcast. In August 1931, the CBS station WZXAB broadcast a fight from New York to a lucky few. By 1938 a few more fights had made tentative TV broadcasts. In March 1939, England broadcast the Eric Boon–Arthur Danahar championship fight of Great Britain for the first "big screen" television viewing at a theater for paying customers.[9] In April 1939, NBC got in on the action, broadcasting an exhibition match between Lou Nova and Patsy Perroni. Six weeks later, the first professional match was televised from Yankee Stadium, a bout in which Lou Nova defeated Max Baer.[10] Sadly, these broadcasts were of poor quality, in large part due to lenses that could not zoom in satisfactorily and capture a useable image. Investment continued, and in May 1941, RCA broadcast a championship fight from Madison Square Garden to fourteen hundred viewers at the New York Theater with a decisively more efficient system. Then came World War II, and America's technology resources were diverted elsewhere. But the proposal had been accepted, the wedding already arranged.

When Mike Jacobs made the deal with Gillette for a year of *Friday Night Fights*, the scope of this cycle of telecasts was to be unprecedented. The premier battle, set for Friday, September 29, 1944, would be the first widely broadcast fight in history. The matchup between Willie Pep and Chalky Wright seemed a safe bet for a lively battle. Pep was a young scrapper from Hartford, Connecticut, with an impressive 78-1 record, a man whose speed earned him the nickname "Will o' the Wisp." Albert "Chalky" Wright, a solid puncher who had held the title until Pep took it from him in 1942, was considered among the best boxers of all time in his class. Although his real age was elusive (sportswriter Jimmy Cannon remembers a manager seeing Chalky's gray stubble and telling him, "Go down and get a shave. . . . They'll pick up your [boxing] license you look so old. You could be your own father."[11] Writing just before the 1944 bout, Jack Cuddy referred to him as the "Methuselah of Maul"[12]), Wright still hit hard and moved well. Pep would remember him as the hardest puncher he ever faced.[13]

The Pep-Wright fight reached between six thousand and seven thousand sets on the East Coast, a considerable audience considering the technical limits of "national" broadcasting in this era. Mike Jacobs, always angling for the best possible publicity, touted the fact that this fight would be shown to injured veterans recovering in hospitals from Philadelphia to Schenectady, New York.[14] Pep was a military veteran himself, and this fact also was not missed by Jacobs. Gillette's boxing radio announcer Don Dunphy gave the blow-by-blow as the two boxers, who were surprisingly easy to follow given the primitive quality of the technology, danced across the screen. Pep proved the better fighter and took the fifteen-round decision.

TV boxing worked. The two figures cut a distinct outline against the white box of the ring. Dark gloves highlighted the trajectory of the blows. The arena audience was blacked out, leaving the ring centered in such a way that it was impossible to miss the action, which was captured in a single frame by a stationary camera. And the sport was simplicity itself. The rules were clear-cut and the competition apparently transparent: two men, with nothing up their sleeves, punching away at each other in a small, closed environment. It was perfect.

Success for the show struck hard and fast when televisions began to sell in great numbers after the war. Perhaps an especially important moment happened on the evening of Wednesday, June 19, 1946. Gillette and NBC hosted the much-anticipated Joe Louis–Billy Conn heavyweight title fight at Yankee Stadium. Via coaxial cable, NBC had the bout broadcast to New York City, Schenectady, and Philadelphia, and with a one-time agreement with the DuMont network, to Washington, D.C. The press was abuzz over the invitations sent out to government luminaries to watch the fight on twenty-one TV sets at the Hotel Statler in D.C. Among those who accepted the invitation were the secretaries of commerce, agriculture, and the interior; the directors of the post–World War II Reconversion Program and the Office of Price Administration; and assorted generals, presidential secretaries, and aides (Truman, unfortunately, declined due to previous commitments); and even a Supreme Court justice. Wrote the *New York Times*, "Top-hat Washington will be at the ringside—by television."[15]

According to one historian, 140,000 viewers tuned in to watch the 1946 Louis-Conn rematch on TV. Exclaimed the *Philadelphia Daily News* afterward, "The winner—Television!" Another reporter predicted that "this is the kind of event that'll make people buy televisions."[16] With the Brown Bomber's help, boxing became a main feature of early television.

In 1946, boxing (along with a smattering of other sports programming) accounted for nearly 40 percent of all television programming—granted, this represented only three hours and forty-five minutes of a nine-and-a-half-hour schedule, but impressive it was.[17] Reminiscing many years later, former NBC director Harry Coyle noted, "What some people forget is that television got off the ground because of sports. Today, maybe, sports need television to survive, but it was just the opposite when it first started. When we put on the World Series in 1947, heavyweight fights, the Army-Navy football game, the sales of television sets just spurted."[18] Boxing sold TVs in a way that almost nothing else could. People would walk down the streets of their hometowns and boxing would literally stop them; business owners figured, what better way to sell the new product than to face TV screens outward in their storefront picture windows? Folks would stop and watch the fighters banging away, thinking about having that device in their own house. Some shopkeepers set up magnifiers in front of the screens to make the boxers easier to spot, making them seem literally to jump out of the sets and onto the sidewalk.

By 1955, two-thirds of American households had television sets, and approximately one-quarter of these were tuned in regularly to boxing.[19] This meant somewhere in the neighborhood of 17 million people (if two people per household watched) viewed the average TV fight. If one skews viewership strongly for males, this might mean one-quarter or more of all men in the country regularly watched boxing matches on television. According to a 1955 Newsweek article, "If the rating services are accurate," a grand total of some 50 million viewers watched the four major boxing shows each week.[20] Add to this the many working-class men who didn't own sets but who filled the bars to watch on Friday nights, and one gets a sense of show's huge audience.

And then there were the big fights. The televised battle between Chuck Davey and Kid Gavilan in 1953, for instance, captured 67.9 percent of the national audience, which might have amounted to some 30 or 40 million viewers.[21] Today, such ratings as a percentage of the population rival the Super Bowl. If measured in terms of people who owned televisions, it represents an even larger number. And this was no fluke event. A televised Marciano fight three months later gathered even more viewers. It is no stretch to say that perhaps a majority of shaving-age American men watched the biggest fights on TV.

From its newfound toehold in the public imagination, Gillette went on to monopolize virtually every major sports event for the next quarter century. Clever advertising kept the company one step ahead of the competition. Starting in 1945, the company adopted the logo "Look Sharp, Feel Sharp." Then came a catchy jingle, sung by the Sportsmen Quartet. During the 1952 World Series, the second-ever Series broadcast out to California (and sponsored, of course, by Gillette), viewers first heard the jingle set to a big-sounding march. Composed by Mahlon Merrick (the musical director for Jack Benny's show), the Gillette march took the country by storm. Within a few years, "Look Sharp" could be heard everywhere from Boston Pops concerts to college half-time shows. And then the second whack of the advertising one-two punch: the cute mascot. Sharpie, a cartoon parrot decked out in a jacket, bow tie, and feathered fedora, asked cartoon men lathered in shaving cream, "How're ya fixed for blades?" According to Gillette historian Gordon McKibben, Sharpie was "almost as well known for a while as Donald Duck and Mickey Mouse."[22]

The catchphrase, the jingle, the music, the bird. It was money well spent. Starting in 1954, the vice president for corporate planning, Paul Fruitt, correlated Nielsen data and found that between 1948 and 1953, as the transnational coaxial cable network was established, Gillette sales increased precisely as more houses received the *Cavalcade*. By the late 1950s, Gillette's share of the shaving market had risen to over 60 percent, a dramatic increase from the 16 percent share it had held in the Depression years.[23] With no question of the efficacy of TV advertising, money poured forth; by the mid-1950s, the company was spending 85 percent of its ad budget on the *Cavalcade of Sports* and watching its profits soar.[24]

Mike Jacobs's dominance was extensive (the area near his ticket agency, between Broadway and Eighth Avenue, was known as "Mike's Beach" or "Jacobs Beach"), and he had a good run. But it was not destined to last. He had become unpopular by 1946, considered a monopolist over the fight racket and described in *Life* magazine as "an aging former ticket speculator with badly fitting false teeth, the beady eyes of a gambler and the slightly stooped, jerky way of walking."[25] By 1947 his health was in decline, and on December 5 of that year, Jacobs's trump card, Joe Louis, got pummeled soundly by Jersey Joe Walcott in Camden, New Jersey. Although the judges still awarded Louis the victory (Louis himself had supposedly conceded defeat to Walcott before the announcement was made), everyone who witnessed the match knew that Louis's boxing days were numbered. Planning for his retirement, Louis formed Joe Louis Enterprises, Inc., which put four leading contenders (including Walcott) under contract, allowing the Brown Bomber to gracefully retire his belt and share in the profits with the new titleholder. Getting the organization off the ground proved difficult, however, and Louis had to sell his contract rights to a pair of investors named James Dougan Norris and Arthur Wirtz. Norris and Wirtz created a new organization and called it the International Boxing Club (IBC).

The IBC gave Joe Louis $150,000 and a 20 percent share in the organization. The offer was a lot less than Louis had originally asked for, but the Brown Bomber was in no position to bargain. By this point, he owed over one million dollars to Uncle Sam in unpaid taxes. Jacobs, now without a champion and seriously ill, had few options left. Norris let Madison Square Garden know who the new boss was, after which the venerable institution bought out Jacobs's remaining interests and assigned them to the IBC. Jacobs was officially yesterday's news. The Garden had been losing money since 1947 (ironically resulting in part from declining attendance due to the cameras brought into the arena by Jacobs himself), and Jacobs had little power to counter the IBC's hand. His health never recovered, and he died in 1953.

The IBC proceeded to control the sport of boxing to an unprecedented degree. For the first five years of its existence, the club controlled thirty-six of the forty-four championship fights in the United States, including all of the heavyweight and middleweight title bouts. Jim Norris became president of Madison Square Garden, the IBC of New York and Illinois, and the IBC's parent company, the Chicago Stadium Corporation. He bought out the Tournament of Champions, CBS's boxing subsidiary that promoted the popular *Pabst Blue Ribbon Wednesday Night Fights*, and then required contenders to grant the IBC exclusive promotional rights to title matches under pain of excommunication. Controlling just about every major boxing venue (including leases on the Polo Grounds, Yankee Stadium, and the St. Nicholas Arena), Norris gave boxers little choice. Overnight, and in true monopoly fashion, Norris and his Octopus ruled the fight game.

By this point, TV boxing was so inescapable that comedian Red Skelton could joke, "The Monday fight, scheduled for a Tuesday this Wednesday, has been postponed till Thursday and rescheduled for Friday this Saturday because Sunday's a holiday." A look at the *New York Times*'s "On Television This Week" listings page for the week of January 20–26, 1952, tells the story. Boxing programs are listed for every single day of the week (though on Sundays, just *Kid Boxing* is on). Often, several different fight shows compete in a single evening. Golden Gloves matches are broadcast Monday through Thursday. Gene Smith fights Corky Gonzalez on the *Pabst Blue Ribbon Fight* broadcast from Washington on Wednesday night. Johnny Saxton fights Livio Minelli at the Garden for the *Gillette Friday Night Fight*. Saturday has boxing from Ridgewood Grove. There are also *Boxing News* shows on Monday, Tuesday, and Thursday, not to mention a good deal of *Sports News* broadcasts throughout the week that might also cover boxing. If one adds in the local networks, still more boxing is to be found.[26] With only three major national networks (and one lesser one, for a time) and programming that did not carry twenty-four hours a day, boxing wasn't merely one of countless entertainment options. It was one of a few. Low production costs (around twenty-five hundred dollars per program in the early years)[27] and easy translation to the small screen also helped.

But this still begs the question: Why boxing? Why not wrestling or roller skating or basketball? (These were also popular, but to a much lesser degree.) To begin with, it needs to be understood that we are talking about a sport that was much different from what it is today. Start with the weight divisions. Today there are seventeen. Back then there were eight. Today there at least eight "legitimate" world-ranking organizations (with four or so "major" ones and numerous minor ones). In the 1950s, while individual states had boxing titles, only the New York State Athletic Commission (NYSAC) wielded "world" power, with some power shared with the National Boxing Association (formed in 1921 to counter New York's influence and provide a sense of uniformity and order). And thanks to TV, both of these bodies were in the thrall of a single organization, the International Boxing Club. Considering there were also more boxers around competing for these limited belts, and that the average fighter battled many more opponents, the upshot was that most fighters had a long, narrow, and incredibly rough road to the top.

While there are many more ranking organizations today, boxing is ironically far less popular now. In December 1955, for instance, just about anyone on the street could tell you without hesitation that Rocky Marciano was the heavyweight champ. He could also probably tell you that Sugar Ray Robinson was the middleweight titleholder. And it went without saying that Friday night was fight night in America. Today, most folks couldn't name even one of the half-dozen or so boxers who claim the heavyweight title, let alone the multiple leaders in any of the other divisions. One reason for this is a simple matter of math. In the fifties, television was a novelty with few channel options, and every major television station showed boxing. Today, no major network schedules the sport; one must seek it out on cable or pay-per-view. A viewer might find one channel in three hundred that shows boxing. Going beyond the numbers, it is important to realize that in the 1950s, boxing was popular in its own right. Fight coverage in the sports pages ranked behind only baseball. Big fights made the front page. Today, one struggles to find even a small paragraph about an upcoming match in the local papers.

Perhaps nothing drives home the difference between then and now as does a remarkable 1949 *Life* magazine cover. Titled "Five-Year-Old Boxer," there is depicted a large image of a child, close-up, wearing leather boxing gloves. He has a Norman Rockwell innocence and an unforgettable, determined smirk on his lips. The accompanying article tells the story of Joe Clark, a cop and "former fighter himself" who teaches boxing lessons in the afternoons "for the small fry." The article notes that "one of his 9-year-old protégés last year honored his coach by winning the Glendale Silver Mittens championship in the fleaweight division." Addressing safety concerns, it is noted that "in 11 years no boxer has suffered more than a nosebleed."[28]

The fact that one of the most popular TV offerings of the fifties was a blood sport deserves pause. Watching the old footage, you can actually hear the *tut-tut-tut* sound of a man's gloved fist hitting his opponent. This was real. To understand the mass allure of this sport at midcentury, it is essential to place boxing in context. Millions of soldiers—killers, now, many of them—had recently come home. But home was not the same.

CHAPTER 2

"The Regular Friday Coaxial Bloodbath"

World champion Carmen Basilio once defeated Tony Demarco after Basilio had broken the bones of his hand early in the fight. He just continued punching with his shattered fist. When questioned later about how healthy his boxer would be to defend his title, Basilio's manager dismissed concerns. "There is nothing wrong with Carmen's right hand," he said. "Yes it's a little sore, but Carmen's a tough guy and can deal with the pain." Carmen was certainly a "tough guy." But he was no anomaly. He was a product of his age.

The quality of ruggedness that made Basilio so admired—and Gaspar Ortega, too—was a trait fetishized throughout America in the 1950s. A broader program to "toughen" up young men at home and project strength overseas permeated the culture. Republican senator Joe McCarthy, whose crusade to rid America of the Communist menace defined the era, constantly challenged the "effete" eastern liberals who put America in a "position of impotency." For Joe and many other Cold Warriors, the battle against Communism was a battle for manhood. "Soft" intellectuals, homosexuals, and left-wingers (and the three were often imaginatively combined) made the country "weak" in its battle against Soviet aggression. America needed to resist all forms of feminine softness. As McCarthy once told reporters, "If you want to be against McCarthy, boys, you've got to be either a Communist or a cocksucker."[1]

But toughness came at a cost. In the first half of the 1940s, parents had been forced to wait anxiously for letters home, fearing the worst. Film audiences saw moving picture images of the dead or dying, be they Marines bobbing in the tides of Tarawa or Japanese sailors gunned to pieces in their lifeboats on the Pacific. The whole society was deluged with dehumanizing Orwellian hate messages against evil Germans and apelike "Japs." Then in 1945 came the cathartic rush of atomic energy unleashed on a mortal foe, followed by the Pandora-like terror of the possibility of similar weapons finding their way home in the bellies of long-range Soviet bombers. A new awareness descended. By 1955, nearly half of all Americans believed that another world war would soon end all humanity.[2]

World War II and the Korean War had returned men bruised and shocked from the experience. Although "neuropsychiatric hospitals" under the Veterans Administration appeared after the war, most veterans were loath to voice their fears and loneliness. Veteran suicides mostly went unrecorded in the press. One that did make the front pages tells us more about spectacle than about postwar distress. On January 26, 1947, a "despondent veteran" named David H. Gordon Jr., as reported by the *New York Times*, told another soldier who happened to be on the Empire State Building's observation tower with him, "I'm going to jump." Then, over he went. He plunged eighty-six floors before ricocheting off a projection on the building and slamming into a tourist standing on the sidewalk.[3]

War damage remained, even if invisible to the eye. World War II veteran and novelist William Styron recalled, "Our generation was not only not intact, it had in many places been cut to pieces."[4] Over one million Americans had been killed or wounded in the war, a vast and awful number.[5] For Styron, the war had "unhinged" the "cosmos." "I think most of us were in a way subtly traumatized . . . not only by what we had been through and by the almost unimaginable presence of the bomb, but by the realization that the entire mess was not finished after all: there was now the Cold War to face, and its clammy presence oozed into our nights and days."[6] Returning veterans found that the world was not as they had left it; people had changed, life had gone on without them.[7] Post-Traumatic Stress Disorder (PTSD) was poorly understood and not talked about back in those days. The term itself did not even exist yet. Rather, veterans who returned dealt with their memories by submerging them. My grandfather, a wounded veteran of the Battle of the Bulge, would sometimes wake up to find himself strangling his struggling wife in the dark of the night.

Despite the devastating silence of the veterans, new sounds filled the households of millions. A baby boom began nine months after the soldiers started returning. The children of World War II entered a new America, one quite unlike that of their parents. The breadlines and empty stomachs of the Depression years were gone. After a brief downturn and a tempestuous strike wave, the postwar economy thrummed to life. Thanks to the GI Bill, housing on a mass scale finally became a reality.

In these houses, one room came to symbolize the comfort and security to be found in a tough new world: the *family room*. A term first coined in 1946, the family room was designed to be a sealed capsule of family togetherness, where parents and offspring could come together after dinner and relax in the isolated safety of their atomized neighborhoods. Here they watched television. In fact, the television became so associated with this room that in 1950, *Better Homes and Gardens* used the phrase *family-television room* to describe it.[8] The year 1960, the same one that saw the majority of Americans owning a home for the first time, also found almost 90 percent of households owning at least one television set, watched by the average person an incredible five hours a day. Children were especially susceptible to the cathode tube. As early as 1955, the typical American child had already watched five thousand hours of television, staring at the screen three-to-four hours a day.[9]

It is important to understand how new this was. A decade earlier, very few had televisions and dreadful economic uncertainty was still the norm. The new American landscape would be pioneered by autonomous, affluent nuclear families living in a Cold War world of material contentment and military containment.[10] Inside their family rooms, a generation of children watched the larger world reveal itself on tiny black-and-white screens. Isolated from the crowded urban cores in which their parents had grown up, these children played in (relative) material abundance and yet possessed the unacceptable knowledge of potential nuclear obliteration.

Strangely, fear is not the emotion that the Boomers first mention when thinking about their Cold War childhoods. These were also halcyon days. It is almost as if in reaction to the strange combination of anxiety and plenty, the adults wove a dream-cocoon around their young. Author Bill Bryson humorously remembers, "Happily, we were indestructible. We didn't need seat belts, air bags, smoke detectors, bottled water, or the Heimlich maneuver. We didn't require child-safety caps on our medicines. We didn't need helmets when we rode our bikes or pads for our knees and elbows when we went skating."[11]

The Cold War reawakened the cultural icon of the armed father-protector. The Soviet threat could not be removed by a simple military invasion or a bombing run. Mutual atomic weaponry had ended that possibility. So a revitalized emblem of Americana, the Western gunslinger, returned. Like the boxer, the gunslinger spoke to a new desire for a purer moral world of redemption through straightforward violence.

Facing hostile Indians, deadly outlaws, or citified criminal master-minds, the gunslinger knew the score and accepted his fate, as Gary Coo-per's Marshal Will Kane famously did in *High Noon* (1952), when a terri-fied town failed to oppose evil. Cultural historian Richard Slotkin notes that in the Western, resolution typically comes in the form of a "singular act of violence."[12] A final, cathartic shootout, and the bad man is no longer a problem. Although the Western genre had deep roots, stretching at least back to James Fenimore Cooper, the Cold War gave it special resonance.

Westerns were big. By the late 1950s, early Western shows like *Hopalong Cassidy*, *The Gene Autry Show*, *The Roy Rogers Show*, and *The Lone Ranger* were superseded by "adult" Westerns, new prime-time offerings that dis-tanced themselves from earlier children-oriented fare, introducing adult themes and products (like cigarettes) to the home audience. Soon, adult Westerns dominated every network's prime-time market. Thirty different Western series marked the 1957–58 season (the first year that Westerns beat comedies in the ratings wars). By 1959 a TV exec could quip that "a network that ran nothing but Westerns from 7 P.M. to midnight would, in time, capture the entire viewing public." Importantly, these shows were not only watched by adults; an estimated one-third of viewers were under sixteen. Westerns provided brutal, popular family fare.[13]

TV boxing followed along Western lines. Though sometimes the iden-tity of the "villain" was unclear, the image of two men going mano a mano drew the mind to an appealing, if imagined, yesteryear of settling an issue with combat. Lest the moral of the moment be lost, one preacher exorted fathers to use the teachable moment that was Carmen Basilio's welter-weight title match against Johnny Saxton in 1957. "You fathers," preached the Right Reverend Samuel H. Lowther from the pages of *Boxing and Wrestling* magazine, "hold up this man, Carmen Basilio, as a model to your children. Your boys will be indelibly impressed by the fact that a 'fighter,' strong and almost impregnable, depends wholly on God for the success of life's work." Basilio had annihilated Johnny Saxton on a televised *Friday Night Fight*. After pummeling away at will, a solid left hook to the head had sent Saxton to the mat in the second round. Saxton looked so shaky struggling to get up that the referee had ended the match. Basilio was not surprised; he had known the end was coming since the first round, when he'd delivered a particularly terrific left to Saxton's head. "I could see it in his eyes right then," he told reporters, "that he wasn't going to last, but I was swinging so much that I had to pace myself." After obliterating his foe, Basilio took a knee in prayer. For the Reverend Lowther, this display was "the most effective and dramatic sermon of contemporary times." He dubbed Basilio the "Evangelist of the Ring."[14] In godly combat there existed a glorious parenting message.

President Eisenhower loved Westerns, and he loved boxing as well, having boxed for fun as a youth. In June 1953, Ike posed with Rocky Marciano (along with other sports icons) at the White House. The next day the papers ran the photo of the commander-in-chief holding Rocky's fist up, admiring it with a smile as Joe DiMaggio looked on. This was an age of killer-fathers and dreaming little boys, and boxers were gunslingers.

In 1954 *Ring* magazine noted that while ordinarily, "Mom and the kids" pick out what to watch on TV, on "title fight night" dad is "as firm and unyielding as the Rock of Gibraltar." Besides, "womenfolk who at first resigned themselves to watching bouts, now in many cases have edged the old man out of his favorite spot in front of the set at the opening bell."[15] Escaping the smoky clubs and beer-drenched arenas, boxing had penetrated the family sanctum, had become wholesome fare.

I talked to a lot of folks who remember watching the fights as kids, starting with my dad. His own father, a man I barely knew, would sit on his leather chair and bark at the screen between sips of Ballantine Ale. Mom went to bed, leaving "the men" (my dad, born in 1947, was seven years old when he started watching boxing with the old man) alone in the family room. There they would watch, my dad on the floor in his blue cotton pajamas with the pocket on the shirt. No toys or other distractions were allowed, and my dad wasn't allowed to talk during the rounds.

Grandpa was a World War II vet who had fought in the Battle of the Bulge. He had volunteered because he was too old to be drafted, and when they assigned him to a clerk's position, he'd lobbied for the infantry. His transfer request was granted, and he went across the Atlantic to go "kill Krauts," and he did, though he never talked about it. He returned with a two inch-square scar across his knee, where a German bullet had brushed by during a charge. He had marched on with blood crusting on his shin and filling his boot and did not see a doctor for two full days. He never took the time to apply for a Purple Heart. My own memories of Grandpa when I was a kid of four or five are sharp and angular; he looms and tells me to sit on the couch and not touch anything. I was terrified of the old man.

Sitting in the family room and watching the *Friday Night Fights* represented father-son time for my dad. I asked him if Grandpa's war experiences might have made boxing more attractive, with the violence element. He told me that he thought it might. "My father got what he needed out of it, I got what I needed." Grandpa would tell the boxers to "stop dancing" when they weren't punching enough. He would look at my dad and tell him, "Now watch the head. When it snaps back you know he got hit good." Grandpa was teaching my dad how to be a man. It was an education of violence. Grandpa got the satisfaction of punishment handled out deftly and instantly, with skill and cold calculation. My dad got time alone with his pop, just the two of them.

Jon Purmont remembers that on Friday evenings, you could walk down the street and see the glowing lights of the cathodes casting out of the darkened living rooms fronting carefully kept Connecticut yards. Jon would watch the fights with his father—mom and the sisters usually didn't hang around. He and his dad would marvel at "exotic" Kid Gavilan's sweeping bolo punch. They'd talk between rounds about their fighter's progress or scoot into the kitchen for another soda in-between rounds. Across the street, Jon could sometimes see the neighbor kid and his dad watching the same show.

Bob Jirsa watched with his dad in their one-bedroom Oak Park (a suburb of Chicago) apartment. Propped up on a pillow tossed on the living room's compact floor, Bob learned a lot from his policeman dad on Friday nights: "I learned a lot of profanity." Dad, who was usually three-sheets to the wind by the time the fights began, would holler at their ten-inch Zenith along with his two buddies, "shady characters" not on the police force. Bob's dad would inevitably get excited, calling all of the black fighters "niggers." He and his pals always rooted for the white guy if a mixed-race fight was on. If there were two black fighters, they'd have to weigh the individual merits of the combatants before choosing one.

Chuck Hasson started watching with his father in 1955 in Philadelphia's suburbs. His pop was an Army vet who had served in the Pacific and who never talked about his experience except occasionally with his buddies over a few beers. Chuck was born in 1946, and his dad let him stay up on Fridays. Other nights, Chuck and his brother would sneak out to the top of the stairs to watch the fights. Dad knew they were there, but he didn't say anything. "Today nobody knows what's going on" in boxing, Chuck explains. "Back then guys on the corner knew all the top ten contenders." Neighborhood kids boxed each other in the street and then took their beefs into the local clubs. Benny Paret was a "great favorite" of Chuck's, although "Gaspar was a mainstay. He had much heart and guts. Everybody would root for him."

John O'Connor watched with his dad in New Haven, Connecticut. His dad used the TV fights to educate his son about the Sweet Science. Dad boxed amateurs at a local stockcar track at Savin Rock where they put up a makeshift ring. He would sign up after work sometimes on Fridays and when called would box for a "prize" watch, which would be sold later for $25 to be recycled for the next week. It was quite a thing to be allowed to stay up late and watch TV with dad. "It started as young as I can remember." When boxing went off the air, "I was very disappointed. It was a thing we did together. And I learned a lot. . . . It was my time with him." Dad would smoke cigars while they watched. "The next morning, the house smelled like burnt rope. Even now when I see a cigar I think of Friday night."

Across the country in Texas, young Milton Hernandez marveled at the "elegant" Ortega, a fearless and bold model of Latino musculature, tearing up opponents. For Milton, watching Gaspar was a real treat. Of course, Milton had lots of other heroes, too. He loved the *lucha libre* (Mexico's popular, acrobatic professional wrestling) performers who sprang across local rings in masks and capes.

South of the border in Tijuana, a recent arrival from Autlán de Navarro named Carlos Santana watched the fights with his brother and dad first on neighbors' sets (through the window) and then later on a new black-and-white television. He marveled at the hometown fighter who "looked so pretty when he fought," with his flattop and striking Mexican features. "We knew he was from Tijuana. We claimed him because he represented us." For young Carlos, who saw Gaspar on TV for the first time when he was only eight years old, seeing a Mexican, especially a Mexican from Tijuana, was transformative. "He did teach me certain things were available on a worldwide arena."[16]

Out in Berkeley, California, Bob Hink watched the *Saturday Night Fight of the Week* on ABC (the *Friday Night Fights* moved networks and time in 1960) with his dad, a World War II veteran who had served on the staff of General Omar Bradley. His parents had gotten divorced when he was young, and some of his fondest memories involved spending Saturdays with dad and then watching the fights with the old man and his grandparents as day turned to night.

World-famous painter LeRoy Neiman also enjoyed watching the fights, on TV or at the Garden he loved to haunt. "I used to watch the Friday

Night Fights a lot . . . along with so many boxing fans during the 1960s. Gaspar Ortega was a swift, flashy and tenacious fighter. He fought Kid Gavilan, the great Cuban boxer, twice and having learned from his first defeat to Gavilan, won in their second encounter."

In written memoirs, one occasionally finds evidence that Gillette's show was etched into the brains of the Boomer generation. Most of the recollections are pleasant. Dad would let you have a sip of beer while you watched. A local bartender without a TV made a funny sign: "WE DON'T HAVE TELEVISION BUT THERE'S A FIGHT HERE EVERY NIGHT." A young boy would sit in awe of his grandpa's uncanny ability to call a fight better than the commentators could. Another son would be amazed that "as the bout wore on, the winner always seemed to be listening to my father, while the loser seemed to pay him no heed." Then there's the girl who watched her dad while he watched the fights. He was a traveling salesman, home at last on Friday, screaming at the television and flicking ashes from his cigar. The girl used the fights as an opportunity to "figure out what and who the heck this man is who dominates the rhythms of the household and my mother's mood." Another girl was told to turn her head while dad turned down the volume—not because of the violence, but rather due to the sinful beer and cigarette commercials in between the rounds. Some memories are less pleasant. "Your father decided what station you would watch," wrote one man. "You watched boxing whether you liked it or not." Some memories are horrifying. Gillette's show begins and dad is already drunk. He demands another beer from mom, who is tired and refuses. Dad gets up and grabs her by the hair and starts hitting her. The son tries to push dad off, and so dad comes after him instead. Mom pleads with her boy, "Please don't interfere."[17]

One cannot help to speculate about the impact of the *Friday Night Fights* on famous Americans. Scanning biographies and autobiographies, it's possible to catch a glimpse here and there of the influence of the show. Thirteen-year-old Barbra Streisand crawled across the living room floor on Friday nights, knowing that her emotionally abusive stepdad would rage at her if she obscured his view of the TV for even an instant. Motivational speaker Jack Carew watched the fights with his dad and found an educational experience. The jingle "Look Sharp, Feel Sharp, Be Sharp" told him all about having the message of "Positive Contact. . . . Looking sharp is your appearance. Feeling sharp is your attitude. Being sharp is your energy." Future senator John McCain and his Naval Academy roommates chipped in to purchase a contraband TV so that they could watch the fights secretly in their room. They hid the set in a crawl space, waiting for Friday night. A young Dick Cheney watched the show with other neighborhood families on a new TV at a neighbor's house in College View, Nebraska, in 1949. Actor Burt Lancaster enjoyed the show for "the ambiance of the thing," pleased at how it reflected "the seamy underbelly" of sports. Future heavyweight champ Joe Frazier watched the fights on TV and discovered hope: "We admired Rocky Marciano and those white fighters, but lookin' at the black fighters, men that made it all the way, there was your hope, your chance, right in front of you!"[18]

Perhaps it is in the small, simple memories, mostly left unwritten, that one finds the show's truest significance. Purdue's successful football coach Joe Tiller has a short passage early in his memoir. "My dad was a very introverted, silent, but strong person. He didn't say much, but he loved the fights. If I could sit still on the couch, I'd get to watch the fights with him, which was a very big deal to me."[19] This is what the fights meant for many boys. It was a bridge that closed painful distances. Writes poet Ronald Wallace,

> Out in the kitchen, my mother never understood
> our need for blood, how this was as close as we'd get
> to love—bobbing and weaving, feinting and sparring.[20]

Boxing was universally recognized as a man's sport, but much was made of the fact that women watched it on TV, too. In fact, the gentler sex had been watching boxing for decades before television was even invented. Jack Dempsey, the definitive pugilist of the Jazz Age, once remarked, "It's no longer enough to have speed and a good right arm to be the favorite. You have to be good-looking, now that ladies go to the fights."[21] Women were originally courted to help make the sport "respectable," thereby opening the way for new sources of middle-class cash. (Baseball boosters, it should be noted, had been trying to do the same thing since the early 1900s). But how could one make a blood sport appealing to the "delicate" gender? For many fight folks, this simply required adding a dimension of romance. Before Dempsey, much was made of heavyweight "Gentleman" Jim Corbett's dashing good looks. An 1893 photo of Corbett catches his classical Grecian face in partial profile, revealing the tautness of his muscles, the smooth shine on his boxing boots, the Elvis-like pompadour. Boxing writers in the 1950s made much of the looks (or lack thereof) of the Friday Night Fighters. Be it the "handsome" Vince Martinez, or the "dreamboats" Chico Vejar and Chuck Davey, reporters often gestured explicitly to what they considered to be of interest to women viewers. Chico Vejar even started taking acting lessons and landed a few small roles in movies like "World in My Corner" (1956).[22]

One 1954 *Ring* magazine piece, written by a woman, addressed the allure of TV boxing for the female viewer. Explained Joan Loubet, the sport appealed to women on several levels. For starters, it "keep[s] her guy home and happy instead of tearing out to boxing matches." More wickedly, strapping young boxers tapped into a woman's hidden, primitive desires. "Way deep down," Loubet writes, "there has always been the attraction for the virility of the fighting male. Call it a leftover from cave-men days, or an echo of crusaders in armor, clashing swords in tourney combat, or plain old fisticuffs for a man's woman as wagons crossed the frontier. There's something about the flailing fists and bodies beautiful that stirs the female bosom." There was also the bonding aspect. As more women watched the fights and talked about them with each other, they began to feel "safety in numbers." "You get to know the names and the faces and the blows and pretty soon you get to looking forward to it . . . especially since Laura and Connie and Dot do too."[23]

Such reflection should give us pause to consider the deeper cultural processes at work. Ever since the early years of the twentieth century, writers celebrated the virtues of primal masculinity, the hidden kinship between modern "civilized" man and his distant, club-swinging ancestors, even his kinship with the still-living "lower" races of Africa. Tarzan, a fantasy of the civilized-white-man-as-primitive, was an incredibly popular Hollywood staple throughout the 1950s in television and in film. First conceived by Edgar Rice Burroughs in his 1912 book *Tarzan of the Apes*, this character marked an ideal of masculinity that prized atavistic violence over the alleged "effeteness" of modern civilization. The Ape Man was compelling at a time when postwar economic transformation increasingly put men in a position of replaceable cog in the corporate machine. Interestingly, the first movie Gaspar ever saw was a Spanish-subtitled *Tarzan* flick he snuck in to watch in a Tijuana theater at age ten.[24]

Primitive Man also represented a reaction to the ongoing, potentially threatening presence of women in formerly all-male domains of work and social power. Popular portrayals of cavemen thumping women over the head and dragging them off echoed the dream of the unbound, naked, virile hunter. Shucking the feminizing bonds of middle-class boredom and taking what rightfully belonged to him appealed to the Organization Man's inner Neanderthal. Popular culture pushed the dream. In the

1949 film *On the Town*, Jules Munshin drags actress Ann Miller by her hair across a floor in a dance scene. She looks perfectly delighted by this. Singing the song "Prehistoric Man," she explains: "Modern man is not for me, the movie star and Dapper Dan/ Give me a healthy Joe from ages ago, Prehistoric Man." Other expressions of the fear of feminine power were less humorous. Philip Wylie's book *Generation of Vipers* (1949) bitterly railed against the power of mothers to squelch young male virility.[25]

Although it is important not to paint with too broad a brush the unabashed celebration of the Cold War caveman—witness the pop-cultural wink represented by the popular *Flintstones* cartoon—the allure of the dominant, violent male was unmistakable. As modern critic Susan Faludi points out, males were trained from childhood to protect the home; girls, to cultivate the nest. Boys were instructed to prepare for possible combat with Communist invaders. Girls were taught, among other things, "to hone their fallout-shelter decorating skills in home ec classes." Movies, books, magazines, radio programs, and television shows all celebrated female delicacy and homemaking skills alongside scenes of justified male violence, typically in the form of bravely defending the home against the forces of evil. America became obsessed with threats to female virtue. A bevy of new sex-crime laws (despite the actual postwar decline in such crimes), the rise of vice squads, and J. Edgar Hoover's obsession with moral purity reinforced the sentiment with the power of law.[26]

Such times bred a deep sense of anxiety over female boxing viewership. Was TV boxing making women less feminine, threatening their purity? To be fair, this debate had been raging long before the advent of television. Promoter Tex Rickard, who courted women customers for the big Dempsey fights, perhaps is responsible for getting the debate started. In the 1919 bloodbath between Dempsey and the giant Jess Willard, in which Willard's face literally shattered under Dempsey's blows, the press reported how a woman in the front row had screamed, "Get me one of the big guy's teeth!" Many feared that letting women watch matches would reduce them to an animal state, a shameful, degenerate position. More than one 1950s commentator noted women in tears watching brutal fights or expressed shock that "men, women, and children who are banned by law from entering a fight club in New York until they are eighteen years of age make up family groups that almost nightly watch fights on the television."[27]

But many others believed that the integration of the gentler sex into the audience was a good thing. It seemed to complete boxing's passage from primitive blood contest to legitimate sport. As John Lardner wrote in 1953, "the final, complete merger of boxing and respectability—universal suffrage, it might be called—came only with television."[28] By 1955, *Ring* magazine's annual TV Fights edition included an article titled "How Women Score TV Fights" and featured the cover image of a man watching the fights with his wife and child. Like her husband, the woman, who is dressed in a sensible dress and done up with makeup and neatly parted hair, is watching with a clenched fist just as the TV boxer strikes his opponent.[29] Watching the fights was also an education for women. It taught them, many men hoped, to revere the power of the independent, tough male defender.

Cold War hypermasculinity combined with lived war memories to provide a potent cultural milieu in which boxing found a comfortable place. Though it is difficult to prove that war "made" TV boxing popular, a few facts suggest linkages. This was truly a generation of soldiers. An astounding 80 percent of the men born in the 1920s became veterans.[30] It is entirely possible that this unprecedented wave of warriors coincided with the absolute height of boxing viewing in America is sheer coincidence. But this fact, combined with much anecdotal evidence and a cultural backdrop of gunslinging violence, suggests a connection. Whether it be the cover story of *Life* magazine featuring a five-year-old "fleaweight" boxer, military veterans like Willie Pep and Carmen Basilio and Hardy "Bazooka" Smallwood entering the ring, the enthusiastic core of veterans who watched the fights, or the ongoing dialogue about women and the "caveman" allure, boxing and war experience cannot easily be separated.

Within this martial context, televised boxing struck a winning formula. As Western screenwriters and directors recognized, audiences were anxious to witness the spectacle of Good versus Evil, a spectacle made all the more relevant in an era in which the two superpowers did not battle directly. However, what Westerns couldn't do was completely transport the audience into that reality, because it wasn't completely real. In boxing, it was. These men were really doing damage. For a generation of Boomers, many early, happy family memories involved sitting in the living room with one's parents, watching two sluggers beat the hell out of each other.

CHAPTER 3

The Friday Night Fighters

For Friday Night Fighters, the new age of television meant grand opportunity. As broadcasts expanded in the postwar years, fighters discovered that a main event fight in Madison Square Garden equaled instant national celebrity and a big pile of cash. In 1944 Willie Pep and Chalky Wright each received $400 for their premier TV fight. By the early 1950s, boxers pulled in $4,000 per fight, plus a percentage of the gate. For big fights, they received $15,000 plus gate. At the time, this was a good deal of money. The standard $4,000 TV payout was nearly $500 more than the median annual salary for a white adult male in 1955 and over double the yearly income of a male person of color. Regular TV boxers might net from $40,000 to $60,000 a year, or over ten times the American average annual wage. Champions could make a good deal more than that. Sugar Ray Robinson, who earned $4 million over the course of his career, cleared $50,000 alone for his TV match against Gene Fullmer at the Garden in January 1957. (This title fight, shown on ABC, was blacked out in New York and Philadelphia to ensure a big gate.)[1]

To make it on TV, a boxer first needed to be in New York. Some migrated internally, arriving from the red dirt roads of the Deep South, the rangy farmlands of the Midwest, or the urban outposts of the West. For others, home was the cane fields and ghettos of the Caribbean or the desert metropolises of Mexamerica. Still others crossed the Atlantic, originating in Europe, Asia, even Africa. In a way, the Friday Night Fighters symbolized New York immigration. The first Friday Night Fight, after all, was between the son of poor Sicilian immigrants (Willie Pep was born Guglielmo

Papaleo) and an African American who had been born in Durango, Mexico. To use another illustration, a list of the top ten welterweight contenders from February 1, 1959, includes two Mexicans (Gaspar Ortega being one); a Cuban; a West Indian; an Italian American; a Latino; three African Americans; and Ralph Dupas, a dark-complexioned white man previously claimed by the Mafia to be "colored" in order to prevent him from fighting for a mob-owned belt under Louisiana's segregated boxing rules.

While New York had it all, all was not peaceful, nor even particularly welcoming, for the Friday Night Fighters. The country was still sharply segregated in the fifties; and while Jim Crow rule still governed Dixie, the South did not corner the market on racial discrimination. Housing covenants prevented nonwhites from purchasing houses in middle-class suburbs across the nation. Within the major metropolises, segregation existed by fact if not by law. As Malcolm X would later say, "ultra-liberal New York had more integration problems than Mississippi."[2] Indeed, within this remarkably heterogeneous space existed remarkably homogeneous neighborhoods. On Gaspar's densely peopled block, most residents were Puerto Ricans.

But the Friday Night Fighters made an impact beyond their neighborhoods, and one worth noting. In the 1950s, boxing shows, among the most popular programs on television, marked the arrival of people of color into countless white, middle-American households. Television collapsed comfortable racial distances, bringing brown and black people into white living rooms. TV not only inaugurated a shift in spending patterns and entertainment choices (in 1955 alone, fifty-five movie theaters went out of business in New York City; radio and book sales plummeted; libraries emptied), it also compromised racial divides. True, most of the fare was indeed white: *Ozzie and Harriet* and *Leave It to Beaver* presented a polished-beyond-recognition ideal of racial homogeneity, and programs like *The Amos and Andy Show*, which featured African American actors, reinforced ugly stereotypes. But sports shows were different, and they were widely watched.

Baseball, America's most popular sport, started to look more like America in the 1950s. Back in 1947, Jackie Robinson took the field for the Brooklyn Dodgers, breaking the color line in modern Major League Baseball. As the 1950s wore on, team after team began to integrate (though on a very small scale numerically). Boxing, America's second favorite sport, presented a different, much-accelerated version of this process. Perhaps because of its shoved-aside yet undeniably entrenched place in society, prizefighting had long provided opportunities for nonwhites.[3] In the nineteenth century, African Americans and other "outside" groups (such as the Irish) fought before large, Anglo crowds. Blacks even held the belts in a number of weight divisions by the start of the twentieth century. But this did not mean the sport completely escaped the larger culture. In the heavyweight division, the racial divide was closely policed. John L. Sullivan would challenge all comers but with one caveat: "all fighters—first come first served—who are white."[4] He prided himself on never having fought a black man. When African American Jack Johnson challenged the current white heavyweight titleholder in 1908, John L. cried, "Shame on the money-mad champion!"[5] When Johnson won and then refused to play the role of "safe negro," dating and marrying white women, dressing in the latest European styles, and even getting driven about by a white chauffeur, this was more than white America could take. Accused of violating the Mann, or White Slave Traffic, Act (he had crossed a state line with a white woman with whom he was not married), Johnson fled to Europe in 1913. His later loss to white Jess Willard in Cuba closed the door on black contenders until Joe Louis came along in the 1930s.

But despite its troubled history, boxing in the fifties was far ahead of all other major American sports in terms of racial integration. Put another way, if baseball looked more like America, then boxing looked more like New York City. Cubans, Mexicans, Africans, Dominicans, West Indians, Puerto Ricans, Argentines, Brazilians, Panamanians, Venezuelans, "ethnic" whites, and African Americans all walked into the rings and family rooms of middle-class white households. Thinking back on his postwar childhood, African American scholar Henry Louis Gates Jr. recalled, "What interracial sex was to the seventies, interracial sports were to the fifties. Except for sports, we rarely saw a colored person on TV."[6]

This did not mean that boxing represented a magical raceless utopia. Boxing's history tells us that a big part of the "integration" of boxing involved fans' desire to see racial combat, and more particularly, *inter*-racial combat.[7] One of the most famous boxing rivalries of the age was between the black Sugar Ray Robinson and the white Jake La Motta. They fought six times from 1942 to 1951. Robinson won every fight but one. Folks who sat up and watched the *Friday Night Fights* with their parents, including my father, tell how their dads thrilled at interracial fights, often shouting racist epithets at the darker figure on the screen. One man who grew up watching the fights with his dad and his dad's friends explained that when black fought white, the white guy automatically was the guy you rooted for.

Still, boxing provided a space that had not hitherto existed in America. Malcolm X recalled with a sense of pride that "the ring was the only place a Negro could whip a white man and not be lynched."[8] It should also be noted that Joe Louis, a little less than a decade before Jackie Robinson first put on a Dodgers uniform, captured a truly interracial fan base. When he battled Hitler's favorite boxer, the German Max Schmeling, in Yankee Stadium in 1938, he was depicted in the press as representing not *black* America, but America.[9]

The Friday Night Fighters also taught middle America that boxing was not just black and white. As different groups of immigrants arrived, the ring reflected, to a remarkable degree, their current social status. In the nineteenth and early twentieth centuries, Irish and Irish-descended boxers dominated boxing. Some boxers even made their names "Irish" in order to earn instant fight credibility. Vincent Morris Scheer, a New York Jew, became Mushy Callahan. Ugo Michelli from Florence, Italy, fought as Hugo Kelly.[10] Then came the Jewish boxers, led by Barney Ross (born Dov-Ber Rasofsky) and Benny Leonard (born Benjamin Leiner). According to one account, in the 1920s and 1930s approximately one-third of all professional boxers were Jewish.[11] Keeping with tradition, some goyim started adopting Jewish-sounding ring names. Italian Samuel Mandella, for instance, became Sammy Mandel.[12] Soon even nonpracticing Jews, such as Max Baer, donned the Star of David just to scare opponents.

As Jews left the ghettos and Italians came to hold sway in the inner cities, the face of boxing changed again. By the 1930s, Italian immigrants dominated the ring, with the Irish and the Jews comprising the second and third largest groups, respectively. But the wheel kept turning. The most famous boxing son of Italian immigrants, Rocky Marciano (born Rocco Marchegiano), entered the ring just as African Americans began to dominate the sport. The ascent of black boxers had less to do with any recent arrival (though a relatively recent mass migration out of the South did have something to do with it) than with the changing opportunities following the pathbreaking rise of Joe Louis, coupled with the relative decline of white "ethnic" boxers. The First World War and the draconian Immigration Act of 1924 resulted in a sharp reduction of new immigrants from eastern and southern Europe, resulting in a dwindling pool of inner-city Italian Americans. But just as African Americans came to dominate the ranks (by 1948, nearly half of all professional boxers were black, according to one study)[13], another group began to make its presence known in the ring. They came from south of the border.

Latino boxers had a long history in the American fight scene. Boxers like "Mexican Joe" Rivers (born Jose Ybarra in Los Angeles in 1891) and Solomon "Solly" Garcia Smith (another Angelino, whose mother hailed from Mexico) had paved the way early in the twentieth century. By the Depression, more Mexican pugilists were climbing up through the ranks, typically at the lighter weights. In 1934 Alberto "Baby" Arizmendi, who fought in the Garden on several occasions, became the first Latino New York State Athletic Commission (NYSAC) World Featherweight Champion. He was born in Tamaulipas, Mexico, and eventually moved to California, even joining the U.S. Navy. In the 1940s, Juan Zurita took the boxing world by storm, making the cover of the June 1944 edition of *Ring* magazine and winning the National Boxing Association Lightweight Title the same year. He fought in the Garden once, and lost. In the 1950s, perhaps the most popular boxer in Mexico was a feisty bantam named Raul "Raton" (The Mouse) Macias, who won the North American championship in 1954 in Mexico City before a crowd of sixty thousand. By the 1950s, Mexicans represented the third-highest number of boxers if ranked by national origin or race.[14]

As a Mexican boxer, Gaspar Ortega occupied a more liminal space in America's racial order. Latinos and Latinas had been introduced to the white public in the very earliest days of film. Usually, they were cast as "greasers" (in such memorable epics as *The Greaser's Gauntlet* [1908] and *The Greaser's Revenge* [1914]). They were depicted as violent, loud, uncivilized, and frequently incompetent. As Hollywood expanded its market into Latin America in the 1920s, American films toned it down a bit ("greasers" stopped appearing in the titles, at least, if not in the films). By the Depression years, President Franklin Roosevelt's Latin American Good Neighbor policy influenced Hollywood's treatment further, and soon a Latin American expert was hired to help make sure potential audiences would not be offended so much as to hurt sales south of the border. World War II had an even deeper impact than 1930s reforms. With Europe cut off from the film market, Hollywood courted Latin America as never before, often including token Latinos within the melting pot units depicted in war films. While separating out Mexican from broader U.S. cultural depictions of Latinos is not always simple, it is clear that after World War II, Mexicans in particular seemed to embody a more threatening place in the popular imagination—Operation Wetback, an effort to stop illegal immigration from Mexico in 1954, for instance, associated Mexicans with illegality.[15]

Stereotypes governed the characterization of all Latinos in popular culture at midcentury. Famous Mexican actresses Dolores Del Rio and Lupe Velez appeared on the silver screen as sensual seductresses or frivolous types. And while actors such as Ricardo Montalban and Duncan Reynaldo proved that Hollywood could indeed cast Mexican-born actors in positive roles, more often than not Latino actors remained buffoons or villains. Or they could be both, as in Mexican character-actor Alfonso Bedoya's portrayal of a bandit leader in John Huston's film *Treasure of the Sierra Madre* (1948), with his infamous line, "Badges? We ain't got no badges. We don't need no badges. I don't got to show you no stinkin' badges!"

And this was when Latinos made any appearances at all. As one study of television between 1955 and 1964 finds, just "one in fifty" characters was Hispanic.[16] Desi Arnaz (a white-complexioned Cuban) and the Cisco Kid were exceptions to the more general rule of Latino invisibility at midcentury. Interestingly, the 1950s and early 1960s also saw a few films about Mexican American boxers, such as *The Ring* (1952) and *Requiem for a Heavyweight* (1962), where actors portrayed sympathetic, if flawed and stereotyped, roles. *Requiem for a Heavyweight*, starring the Chihuahua, Mexico–born actor Anthony Quinn, in particular sounds an empathetic note as a washed-up, punch-drunk fighter named Mountain Rivera gets exploited by those he counts on.

Latino boxers seemed to occupy a higher rung in the racial order than blacks did in the post–Jack Johnson boxing era. Jack Dempsey, for instance, refused to fight a black person but was willing to battle "The Wild Bull of the Pampas," Luis Ángel Firpo of Argentina. While Firpo often was described in subhuman terms—Grantland Rice called him "the Argentine Plesiosaurus" and newspapers designated him "this modern monster man," a fighter who "snorted" his rage when punched hard— Firpo was deemed an acceptable challenge to Dempsey in the 1920s.[17]

Mexican boxers were also acceptable challengers, though they were served up to the public in a condescending manner. When Alberto "Baby" Arizmendi defeated Freddie Miller to gain the featherweight crown in 1933, for instance, one reporter noted that the "bustling little two-fisted battler from Mexico, can fight worth his weight in gold but he has a terrible time 'rasslin' with the English language so he doesn't worry about 'technocracy' or the low price of wheat."[18]

The increased presence of Mexican boxers in the 1950s seemed to provide ever more opportunities for condescension, especially when these fighters were victorious. Rudy Garcia (who had in fact been born in Los

Angeles, California) was "Boxing's Two-Fisted Tamale" and a "Red-Hot Mexican Slugger."[19] When Mexican Lauro Salas defeated Jimmy Carter for the World Lightweight title in May 1952, *Time* magazine reported that while Carter early on "outclassed the work of the bumbling, brawling little Mexican," Salas, who "shuffled around" the ring during the fight, won by decision. The victory, explained the popular news magazine, was marked by a "hysterical scene" in which the reporter noted that Salas exclaimed, "'I ween the chompanship of Mexico!' After being reminded that he was now world champion, Salas amended his boast by a preposition: 'I ween the chompanship *for* Mexico!' Then, for almost two solid hours, the un-skilled little gamecock refused to settle down." Salas seemed determined, *Time* concluded, to "tell the whole world how he became the first Mexican fighter ever to win an undisputed boxing title."[20]

Often poor, often nonwhite, often immigrant, the Friday Night Fighters made their impact in ways that most outsiders never could. But television was not merely expanding the popularity of their sport. It was changing it.

The TV audience wanted more than mere combat; it wanted a back-story, and this was provided by promoters, announcers, reporters, and the boxers themselves. Friday Night Fighters (or more likely their managers) knew that they needed a hook to provide the audience entrée into their journeys. This early experiment in reality television quickly congealed into something of a farce for the dyed-in-the-wool fan. The peerless John Lardner dissected the Friday Night Fighters in a 1953 *Saturday Evening Post* article. Welterweight Chico Vejar was the "handsome, dark-eyed boy" whose management made it known that he was "trying to improve himself" by "studying dramatics in his spare time." When Vejar first ap-peared, in fact, women across the country sent letters to NBC asking if he was married. Billy Graham was the "martyr, constantly wronged by the judges." Chuck Davey was the (white) man in white, with his "blond curls" and "college degrees." Brooklyn-born Paddy DeMarco was the "bad boy, inclined to butt, but cute in his impishness." Frenchman Pierre Lan-glois was the exotic romantic lead, with locks that drifted "over his eyes, [and who] likes girls." Eugene "Silent" Hairston was the "courageous deaf mute," a man whose childhood bout with spinal meningitis left him with-out hearing but not without heart. Then there was Jake "The Bronx Bull" LaMotta, the guy you loved to hate, but whom you had to respect for his sheer toughness. He played the role of "brave villain, a sneerer."[21]

The TV audience demanded backstories. Wrote Lardner, a "prize fight has story appeal—what Hollywood for years has called 'human interest.' . . . The history, nationality, looks, and special characteristics of the fighters are more interesting to many people than the athletic phase of a fight." He quoted a theater director who exclaimed that boxing "is the most sure-fire mass-fiction formula ever invented! Only it didn't have to be invented. It's automatic. Each man has a story. The two stories come together with a smack and make a third story."[22]

Gaspar Ortega was an easy fighter to remember. For one thing, he was one of the only Mexicans on prime-time television. For another, he had a great backstory. When he fought on TV, announcer Don Dunphy often retold elements of Gaspar's life, explaining how he was "once a cowboy, aspired to be a bullfighter" or that he was a "Lieutenant in the Mexican Reserve Army." Dunphy also emphasized Gaspar's origins linguistically (as in a 1959 fight with Benny Paret): "*La cocina* [the kitchen] is in the belly and that's where Ortega is hitting the Cuban." TV announcer Jimmy Powers would tell the audience, "Ortega is a Mexican Indian. Zapoteco [*sic*] Indian."

Gaspar's persona as "The Mexican redskin" reflected a character he had been cultivating since his youth in Tijuana. He once told a reporter the secret behind his unique, slippery style. "I got my speedy legs, my agile footwork, fighting bulls. Because at 14, when I took up bull-fighting, I was little myself." Manager Nick Corby thought Gaspar needed to play up the shtick. He told him to wear serapes and sombreros into the ring. Corby had Gaspar pose in an enormous feathered headdress for publicity shots. They were big, outlandish things, made in Tijuana with lots of feathers. After some Madison Square Garden victories, the audience got into it, hurling Mexican flags and sombreros into the ring at him.[23]

By 1959 Gaspar was used as evidence of the sport's theatricality. In a montage in the *New York Times* titled "A Punch Is Not Enough—Today's Boxer Must Be a Character," there are three big photos. On the left, a "gay caballero" with a serape and a big sombrero, guitar in hand, is looking wistfully off and apparently singing. In the middle, a "medicine man" wearing an ornamented headdress and feathered cape beats a drum and looks up, "presumably praying for rain." To the right, a typical boxer with hand wraps is posed in a classic form. All three are Gaspar Ortega. Explains the subtitle, "He will fight [a] ten-round main event Friday with Florentino Fernandez, billed as the Ox of Santiago de Cuba. The scene will be the Garden."[24]

Such storytelling illustrates one impact of television on the sport of boxing. Another TV-inspired change was more ominous. Defensive boxing gave way to demands for flashy, hard-hitting fighters unafraid of giving and receiving blows. Charles Einstein recognized it in a 1956 *Harper's Magazine* piece titled "TV Slugs Boxers." He began by noting why the sport made such a good marriage to television: "Compared to boxing, nothing else comes over television so bad so good. In free translation, the good part is that boxing is a superb medium for the television camera, not only for its compact nicety of physical dimension, with all of the action occurring within a twenty-foot square, but for the known concentrate of audience—in this case beer-drinking, cigar-smoking, razor wielding males—so dear to a sponsor's heart." Yet a Faustian bargain had been struck. For starters, television was turning boxing arenas into empty, glorified TV studios. Infinitely worse, it was warping the science of the sport into crude vaudeville. Einstein lamented that "television has decimated boxing as a business and all but ruined it as a sport." What he called "television's boxer rebellion" was reducing the number of boxing promoters, destroying the club circuit in the mad rush to get promising fighters on TV, and turning what clubs remained into television studios for locally broadcast matches.[25]

The mass television audience wanted sluggers, not science, aficionados complained. Boxers who stalked about the ring, carefully looking for openings and opportunities to counterpunch, or who might find a clinch to be a useful tactic, were no longer wanted. TV viewers demanded, in the words of John Lardner, "their fighting rough, wild, and emphatic." Lardner bitterly noted in the *Saturday Evening Post* in 1953 that "the fine old art of fisticuffs is rapidly being replaced by pugilistic soap opera—more blood, more violence, less skill."[26] He mocked Gillette's show as the "regular Friday coaxial bloodbath." A year later Lardner made the same argument in *Newsweek*: "A Mr. Walter Cartier is often knocked out, and just as often he is brought back to the TV arena. Why? Because the producers are mortally sure that Walter will hit, and get hit." Chico Vejar was another example: "Mr. Chico Vejar, whose head has been bounced more times than a poor man's tennis ball, gets plenty of TV spots."[27] A *Newsweek* piece in 1955 lamented that while TV had added millions to the boxing audience, the "one-eyed monster of the living room" could "rightfully claim to have affected the very core of an ancient sport, with fighters and their teachers neglecting defense and the subtleties of boxing technique to give sponsors and their potential customers the free-mixing kind of brawls that can be enjoyed by the most inexperienced of viewers."[28] In 1956 Nat Fleischer, the editor of *Ring* magazine, complained, "We have no men of real ability coming up now. Today's fighter is primarily a slugger. The boxer, the hitter, the combination man—we don't see him. The sponsor wants a man who'll sell his product. Somebody popular, somebody colorful. The sponsor is not looking for ability."[29]

Television was affecting the minds of boxers as well. As Lardner sarcastically put it, boxers "do know what a Barrymore would have done in their places, or what Kirk Douglas would do," but they had no idea what a fighter would do. He complained that skill was out and plain, movie-style brawling and flashiness were in. Things like "blocking, feinting, and footwork" were on their way to the dustbin of boxing history. Making things worse, the home audience did not even know what real boxing was. As Jack Dempsey lamented, "There are millions of people who never saw a fight away from the television set, but they talk about nothing else."[30]

Here Dempsey touched on another aspect of TV boxing. The audience was growing well beyond the original bounds of the small but faithful "fight mob" of the club days. It was becoming almost unrecognizable. Explained *Sports Illustrated* in 1955,

> Five years ago the audience for the average card at Madison Square Garden was eight or nine thousand boxing buffs, and correspondingly less at smaller arenas in smaller cities. Nor were these people, on the whole, our more substantial citizens. But through TV boxing has become a national spectator sport with an audience of millions, many of whom may not know a right cross from a left jab but take an interest—an instinct common to men of all degree—in watching two good men fight it out to see who is better.

In the same article, the author quoted Henry Markson of the IBC as quipping, "In the old days if somebody thought there was something funny with one of our fights, he'd write in and start off, 'You lousy cheating so-and-so crooks.' Nowadays the letters are more likely to start off, 'You reprehensible prevaricators.'"[31]

In the 1955 children's book *Eloise*, there is a scene of the precocious Plaza Hotel–living girl watching TV on a couch with her Nanny. She's holding a parasol and viewing the screen through binoculars while the Nanny leans forward puffing on a cigarette and gripping a glass. The text tells the tale:

> TV is in the Drawing Room
> I always watch it with my parasol in case there's some sort of glare
> And oh my Lord when it's fight night Nanny is absolutely wild and we

have to scamper into our places and get ready and Nanny has to find
her Players and I have to get my binoculars and call Room Service
and order three Pilsner Beers for Nanny and one meringue glacee
for me ELOISE and charge it please
Thank you very much
Here's what I hate
Howdy Doody
Oooooooooooooooooooo I absolutely love TV[32]

The *Saturday Evening Post* ran a parody of the new "rules" of TV boxing.
Here are a few:

7. Between rounds there shall be an interval of at least one minute
   to permit commercials.
8. In one of the later rounds, both fighters should retreat warily from
   each other, striking no blows, and permitting television watchers
   to say good night to their kiddies or let out the cat.[33]

An episode of the prime-time cartoon *The Flintstones* (which originally
aired on ABC between 1960 and 1966) provides perhaps the best chuckle.
Fred and Barney are watching a TV fight involving the caveman "Rocky
Rockciano." The referee explains that there will be "no stopping, except
for occasional commercials."

Television programming lived on commercials, and the businesses that
paid for these commercials inevitably imposed demands that influenced
events onscreen. For instance, if a boxing match ended before every commercial paid for reached the air, a backup plan was required. Recalled
Truman Gibson (a boxing promoter and later president of the IBC), "With
a set amount of time booked on network TV, the show had to go on even
in the event of knockouts, which of course were much desired to arouse
fan enthusiasm. Therefore, a main event pitted two fighters against each
other, with two more boxers waiting in the wings should one of the participants in the main event knock the other one out. That meant we had to
have four fighters ready on fight nights fifty one weeks of the year."[34] This
came out to literally hundreds of boxers, many of lesser quality, scoured
from the numerous boxing clubs and gyms scattered about the country.

Early on, some began to suspect that referees, boxers, and TV producers all conspired to keep some fights going when they should not have.
Especially notorious was the April 1953 Jimmy Carter–Tommy Collins

fight. In this fight, dubbed "The Boston Massacre," the superior Carter knocked the hometown favorite "Irish" Collins to the mat no less than ten times before Collins's corner men stopped it (as the referee counted an again-downed Collins). The four-round debacle was captured live on television. Referee Tommy Rawson defended his decision to allow the bloodbath to go on as long as it did, saying, "It was a championship fight. I thought it my duty to have it end in the most possible decisive fashion."[35] The fight created a media firestorm. Commented *Time*, "televiewers last week finally got more violence than they could stomach. The blood and brutality took place, not on a crime show or a western film, but in the lightweight championship fight." Angry letters poured in to NBC from homes across America. A man from San Francisco wrote that he had to take the drastic step of actually turning off his television because "my wife and kids were crying and I couldn't stand it any longer." A Virginian wired the Boston police department demanding that the referee be charged with "attempted homicide." Sportswriter Jimmy Cannon editorialized that "the fight racket is now television's responsibility. It is no longer an arena sport but a family divertissement. The networks should decide what their cameras gaze at."[36] Significantly, Jimmy Carter was black and Tommy Collins was white. White viewers might have been shocked to watch the spectacle of a black man demolishing an Anglo.

The Carter-Collins debacle seemed to highlight the insidious impact of television on boxing. Noted one writer, "The speed with which fighters like Collins are dropped from television like any TV quiz contestant who muffs the $16,000 question, can be genuinely unfair. A fighter with real talent, rushed to the cathode limelight, can have his career shot with one defeat."[37]

It is clear that TV changed boxing in fundamental ways, from the style preferred by audiences to the quality of contenders to the relentless public interest in boxers' private lives. "Boon or Bane?" asked *Ring* magazine in its 1954 Annual on TV Fights. Sure, the "masses" had been reached, but, argued Jersey Jones, "for the most part these fans are not cash customers."[38] TV made boxing venues into widely watched, glorified television studios, and it emptied them of ticket-buying customers.

While the Garden witnessed empty seats and hollow cash registers, others made a killing from the TV fights. For the monopolistic IBC, boxing meant big revenues—$1.5 million per year from the Wednesday and Friday night shows alone, ventured Jersey Jones. And the mob, it will be seen, did not fare badly, either. But the clubs were clearly suffering. These cradles of boxing were dying out. Lamented Lewis Eskin, "Much like a distorted image on your TV screen, the true evaluation of the picture is blurred. Has the free TV coverage of boxing spoiled the fans to the point where they will not leave TV ringside and turn out to support their local fight clubs?"[39] The answer, for this critic, was, sadly, yes.

But this is not the whole story. Not all of the influence was negative. TV loved boxing, and vice versa. More fighters were probably making a substantial living off of the sport than ever before, and even as boxing clubs lost under the competition with the small screen, boxers (and not just the heavyweights) grasped elusive strands of fame. They became, in the words of the immortal Willy Pep, "Friday's Heroes." Besides, other factors had been draining away the boxing pool before TV ever took hold. World War II, for instance, stopped a whole generation of boxers from training and fighting professionally, and into the void many promoters rushed up kids unprepared for the big time. The postwar expansion of suburbs, part of the reason for the big home audience for Gillette's show in the first place, also had a detrimental effect on the sport. Urban fight clubs were rapidly losing core customers to suburban flight. A general decline in boxers and clubs was already under way by the time *Cavalcade* was a hit. In fact, one might even argue that, initially, television actually reversed the sport's decline.[40]

And television certainly democratized boxing. The audience expanded in ways not even Tex Rickard could have dreamed up. According to Murray Goodman, thanks to new technologies, boxing was now truly the "world's sport." He mused, "The world barriers that can't be reached in politics have been broken down by boxing."[41] Sounds optimistic. But who knows?

Perhaps the best way to understand the effect of television on the sport, to understand how both science and theater played into the persona of the Friday Night Fighter, is to let two boxers stand in for the whole. The first is an exemplar of that group of rugged, quality fighters who made many appearances but whom the history books have let pass unnoticed into the mists of boxing lore. The second was a man almost too perfect for television and wholly unprepared for it.

Kid Gavilan was born Gerardo Gonzalez in 1926 in the village of Palo Seco, outside Camaguey, Cuba. As a young boy he battled other kids on the street, scrapping with urchins for dollars paid by a group of men who gathered to watch. Little eight-year-old Gerardo didn't tell his mom about it. He told her the dollars he gave her each week came from doing odd jobs around town. Eventually, his mom found out about the fighting and beat him soundly before sending him to his room. On his way down the hall, young Gerardo looked back and supposedly told her, "These hands are for becoming a world champion, not for cutting sugarcane."

Gerardo's family moved to Camaguey when he was ten, and there he clandestinely began training at a new boxing gym. When his family found out, they locked him inside the house. So he would sneak up on the roof and rappel down to the street with a rope he had secretly purchased. He started boxing as an amateur in 1938, the year that amateur boxing officially got under way in Camaguey. Gerardo was twelve years old. By this point, his frustrated mother was trying everything to keep her boy out of the ring. "We used to lock him in the house in just his underpants to stop him sneaking out, but he would make himself a sort of loincloth and go to the gym. Or he would sneak out of school and go to the gym, which meant he had to go the whole day without eating." With the help of a local newspaper and some friends, Gerardo made his way to Havana in 1943, where he found a trainer named Manolo Fernandez, and a sponsor as well, a café owner named Fernando Balido. Balido gave him the name "Kid Gavilan," which translates to Kid Hawk. The name was due not to his predatory style but rather to the fact that Balido's café was named El Gavilan and Balido knew something about publicity.[42]

Gavilan made a reputation for himself in Havana, and then in Mexico, before moving on to Manhattan, the Capital of Boxing, with sponsor Balido in tow. There they met a Cuban sportswriter who took them to Stillman's Gym and plugged them into the American boxing circuit. Gavilan won a few matches in New York before going back to Cuba for more fights (and bigger purses from the ravenous Havana fight crowd) and later returning to the States. He mostly won, losing here and there to impressive foes like Sugar Ray Robinson and Ike Williams. In 1951 Sugar Ray decided to go for the middleweight title and got it, relinquishing his welterweight crown and igniting a race that culminated in Gavilan defeating Johnny Bratton for the welterweight belt in May of that year. Bratton left that fight with a broken jaw and a fractured hand.

Kid Gavilan was a member of that elite corps of Friday Night Fighters who appeared on the small screen numerous times and was respected as both a great fighter and a quality entertainer. Another sort of TV fighter was less equipped for the brutal realities of the professional fight game, though often more "entertaining." If Gavilan was the model of the proficient but underpraised, then Chuck Davey represented the appealing but unprepared.

Chuck Davey was born into an Irish family in Detroit in 1925. He learned to box at age twelve, but with his mother's influence he chose the college route, attending Michigan State University and becoming the youngest man ever to win a college boxing title in 1943. His academic career was interrupted by a stint in the Air Force (a war was on, after all), but afterward he resumed his studies and built an impressive boxing record, earning collegiate titles in 1947, 1948, and 1949 and being named captain of the boxing team along the way. Although he continued into graduate studies after getting his bachelor's degree (he wanted to be a teacher), Davey loved fighting and racked up an impressive amateur record. He went pro in 1949 and won or got a draw in his first thirty-nine fights.

Davey's first TV fight was against the experienced but slowing-down Ike Williams in 1952. Davey won after the referee called the fight in the fifth, following a demonstrable beating of Williams against the ropes. By the end of the year, Davey had beaten Chico Vejar, Carmen Basilio, and Rocky Graziano. He'd made himself into a household name and had earned something in the neighborhood of fifty thousand dollars for his efforts.

Davey seemed perfect for TV. He was attractive, well-spoken, blond, and white. And he was a great fighter to watch, too, a rare southpaw who threw machine-gun punches while dancing around the ring. Next thing everyone knew, Davey had a TV shot at the world title.

Close observers saw that something was amiss. For one thing, Davey had gotten his title shot after a mere thirty-nine professional fights. In today's boxing this is not unusual, but in the fifties it was. It was also clear that Davey's management, and perhaps others behind the scenes, were setting up his career for him. Ike Williams, who was managed by mobster Blinky Palermo, would later say that he threw his fight against Davey. (This seems unlikely given the beating Williams took, but one never knows.) In the lead-up to his title fight, Davey's managers pulled him out of a battle with Del Flanagan because, they claimed, the fighters' styles were too similar. This seems like a shady reason to avoid fighting someone most considered to be a strong opponent. Then the fight he had instead, against Fritzie Pruden, was stopped in the third round, and many believed the ref had shut things down prematurely, as if to further coddle the golden-haired one.[43]

For Davey's title fight, he would be facing none other than Kid Gavilan. The difference between the two men was stunning. Gavilan was a dark-skinned Afro-Cuban who had fought over twice as many fights over nearly seven years before he had gotten his first crack at a title. The Davey title fight marked Gavilan's 106th professional outing. The yawning gulf of experience belied all of the media's predictions for an exciting battle. An estimated 30 million home viewers tuned in to watch Gavilan floor Davey once in the first round and three times in the ninth before the referee stopped the lopsided match.[44]

In the fallout of this miserable 1953 bout, TV dropped Davey like a hot potato, and the press had a field day. Gavilan was accused of "carrying" Davey for the TV cameras. One wit called Kid Hawk "the greatest carrier since Typhoid Mary"; another quipped that he was simply "enabling Eloise McElhone . . . to deliver her maiden beer commercial."[45] Although he later lost his title in a fight that seemed not on the level in 1954, Gavilan, Phoenix-like, would continue to make bids for titles until he ended his career in 1958. Davey would quit in 1955 after losing nearly half of the rest of his fights.

Both Gavilan and Davey were classic Friday Night Fighters, but for different reasons. Gavilan was a solid, top-ranked battler. Davey was a bright, entertaining pugilist who unfortunately was not in the same league as Gavilan. TV had a use for both types—skill and theater. And some fighters, like Gaspar "Indio" Ortega, even managed to have both.

PART II

Indio

CHAPTER 4

The Mexamerican

Perhaps the oldest aphorism of boxing is that poverty breeds pugilists. This is certainly the case for Gaspar Indio Ortega, but knowing this is about as useful as reading the opening lines of *Anna Karenina*—"each unhappy family is unhappy in its own way"—and stopping there. Ghettos birth boxers. But why? Under what circumstances do some poor kids choose this dangerous sport? Each case is different. In this one, it begins with a dusty border town.

Tijuana sits perched on the edge of the wealthiest nation in the world. The city features a hungry and diverse chiaroscuro of vendors, beggars, *maquiladora* workers, urban professionals, gamblers, artisans, prostitutes, bankers, street performers, and everything in between. To understand the nature of the patchwork-quilt metropolis, it is best to begin with a central fact: proximity to the Colossus of the North defines the place. Since making the leap from *ranchería* to border town, Tijuana has been profoundly influenced by its imposing neighbor. Ever since the boomtown frontier days of cheap liquor and easy thrills, Americans have seen in Tijuana an opportunity for good times and lucrative investments. Even today, in this "most visited city in the world," shopkeepers and restaurants accept both dollars and pesos as legitimate mediums of exchange. For much of the twentieth century, dollars were actually the preferred mode of exchange here. "Pesos," one long-time resident told me, "were like collectors' items."[1]

From atop the hill above his neighborhood of Colonia Morelos, Tijuana, a young Gaspar Benitez at midcentury could gaze out across the border and over the sprawling farmlands beyond and wonder what life was like in Los Estados Unidos. Bracketed by the mountains and the sea, the agricultural expanse of San Ysidro (a southern attachment of San Diego) looked like a vast and empty green blanket. On Gaspar's side of the border, things didn't look so much different. Farms still made up the bulk of Tijuana in those days. Hard-working rancheros grew wheat, olives, beans, and barley on large patches of the river basin that lends the funnel shape to the city.

Yet things were different on Gaspar's side. Horses and oxen, not tractors, commonly pulled plows through the dark alluvial soil of the Tijuana River Valley. Hand-built houses and improvised lean-to shacks lined dirt paths radiating from the town center. There was no plumbing in Gaspar's neighborhood, no electricity, no street lights, no pavement, and so few telephones that they could be counted on a single hand. Trash might pile up for weeks before it was picked up, though neighbors always took care to bury dead animals before they rotted for too long. Only rarely did an automobile make it up the hill (one neighbor owned a car—a Dodge DeSoto; he would be teased, "Who's *Soto*?"). Every day Gaspar and his siblings trekked down to a natural spring with large plastic buckets strung over shoulder-hoisted wooden poles to retrieve water. They scrubbed their clothes in the river. They cut wood from the hills to fuel their stoves. On weekends, they'd catch fish with nothing but found string tied to cheap hooks. Theirs was a rural, nineteenth-century city that looked on in wonder as American cars and tourists streamed in from across the border to feed a rapidly growing downtown of bars, casinos, and brothels.

As Gaspar matured, his city shifted and stretched under his feet. Yankee dollars poured in and Tijuana expanded from a space covering 400 or 500 acres in the mid-1920s to over 25,000 acres by the 1980s. The city's population tripled in his first decade living there and would grow to over 150,000 persons by 1960. The social transformation wrought by the greenback would influence Gaspar's life from his earliest memories. Eventually, the border itself, for him, would disappear completely. He would traverse countries and cultures as easily as a man might change clothes to complement a new activity.

Before he ever set foot in the United States, Gaspar Benitez had dual citizenship, along with everyone else he knew. He was at once a Mexican and a resident of a place called Mexamerica, an informal name assigned to the region centering on the two-thousand-mile shared border between

Mexico and the United States. Marked by sister cities peering warily at each other across La Línea— El Paso and Ciudad Juárez, Douglas and Agua Prieta, Brownsville and Matamoros, San Diego (or more correctly, San Ysidro) and Tijuana—Mexamerica is less a unified cultural zone than a swirling confluence of cultures, where diverse peoples interact, clash, and sometimes meld. It is the birthplace of Spanglish, Tex-Mex, and Tecate beer. It is also infamous as a place of vice, crime, and illegal crossings. It defies simple definition, while at the same time providing a blank slate upon which multitudes have imposed their own meanings. In *The Long Goodbye*, Raymond Chandler's hard-boiled detective, Philip Marlowe, declares that "Tijuana is not Mexico." It's just another lawless border town, a place where "the kid who sidles over to your car and looks at you with big wistful eyes and says, 'One dime, please, mister,' will try to sell you his sister in the next sentence."[2] Others more correctly note that the vice and crime is less a service to, than a product of, American intrusion. Tijuana, in the words on one analyst, is San Diego's "alter ego." The underground economy that thrives here is driven by U.S. dollars, after all.[3]

Gaspar's family arrived in Tijuana thanks to the Revolution. The first great social upheaval of the twentieth century, the Mexican Revolution ushered in a modern age of nationalist uprisings and internecine bloodbaths. Colorful peasant leaders like Pancho Villa and Emiliano Zapata spoke a strident line of radical egalitarianism and social justice, leaving in their wake the ashes of colonial rule and a fragmented society of Indians, mestizos, and whites of European origin. Following the Magonista uprising of May 1911, when followers of the anarchist Magon brothers overpowered the small garrison of federal soldiers and occupied the city, it was clear to the Mexican government that Tijuana was more than a mere border town; it was a line in the sand. The Mexican Army entered Tijuana on June 22, 1911, and the Magonistas fled across the border, then surrendering to the U.S. Army. As a direct result, the Mexican government decided to create a permanent army garrison in Tijuana. Until the 1960s, soldiers would patrol the streets in force.

One of these occupying soldiers was a man named Aniseto Benitez. He had lived a hard life as a peasant in Oaxaca and had learned not to expect any favors. Among the horrors of his difficult childhood, he had once helped retrieve parts of a child from the gut of an alligator. While Zapata's uplifting message of agrarian reform worked its way through the jungles and plains of the south, Aniseto as a teenager had joined up with federal troops to maintain order. What happened at this point is obscured by alternative versions of family lore, but for certain he did meet up with a fourteen-year-old girl who might have been both selling tortillas to the troops and aiding the Zapatistas. Her name was Sebastiana Ortega. At some point, Sebastiana, accompanied by her mother, decided to follow the young Aniseto and settle down with him. One story has it that he offered her an ultimatum—join up with him or face extermination from the federals.

Aniseto and Sebastiana were not officially married but established a common-law bond familiar to many of the poor at this time. As the children came (there would eventually be fourteen), the two found themselves moving through various parts of Mexico as Aniseto got assigned to various tasks dreamed up by the ever-changing government. During one period in the early 1930s, they lived in a camp in Mexicali while Aniseto worked to construct the road to Tijuana. Here the couple built a one-room, mud-and-wire shack to live in. They cooked outside, over a fire covered with a metal grill that they later replaced with a more solid earthen oven. It was here, in the shack, that Gaspar Benitez was born on October 21, 1935. He came into the world on Saint Hilarion's Day, a day named for a third-century monk who healed barren women and battled demons in the desert. Gaspar himself was named after one of the three kings who visited the baby Jesus in Bethlehem, as well as for an Uncle Gaspar who still lived in Oaxaca, a Zapatista who deserved a namesake.

Aniseto continued work on the road to Tijuana (the city was hardly considered part of Mexico at the time, but rather an isolated frontier post—in fact, it is precisely the most distant place within Mexico from the national capital) until he was permanently stationed there. The Magonistas had taught the revolutionary government the strategic value of the border pueblo.

The other soldiers at the Tijuana garrison in the new neighborhood of Colonia Militar (later renamed Colonia Morelos) helped the Benitez family build their permanent adobe home and dig the outhouse in the back. They worked in the evenings, cutting the red clay into blocks and leaving them in rows to dry in the sun. They put up four walls and a roof, then constructed another partial wall of wood to shelter the fire pit behind the main house. "Homemade" windows were cut into the walls, covered with hinged wooden shutters that could be opened in the cool morning hours and closed in the heat of the afternoon sun. There would be no indoor plumbing in their neighborhood for another fifteen years or so.

Life was a struggle for the Benitez clan. Soldiers were paid next to nothing. One year, heavy rains actually melted their adobe house. They had to build another, stronger structure (this time they used wood). To make ends meet, Sebastiana and the kids sold on the streets food she made at home. She also made frequent trips to the ocean to collect sea salt to grind and sell while Aniseto patrolled the streets. There were other sources of income as well. Sebastiana ironed soldiers' uniforms with a heavy appliance she filled with hot coals. The children worked for neighbors in various capacities. When not working, Aniseto would drink.

Though life was hard, Gaspar, like many children of poverty, did not fully realize his disadvantage. He remembers fishing along the river, scampering about with a slingshot hunting rabbits and doves, and neighbors helping out with food. Everyone knew each other in his Colonia. When the mood took him, Gaspar's dad showed him the best fishing spots and gave him shooting lessons with his 30-30 rifle. At night, Aniseto sometimes cranked an old Victrola record player, playing the emotional *ranchera* and *banda* music that they all loved.

The path to boxing was not preordained for Gaspar, but his family had much to do with his decision to fight. Sebastiana was certainly unafraid of violence. Once, a young Gaspar ran home to report of a fight he had gotten in with an older boy. A little while later, the older boy's irate mother came to the house, hollering at Sebastiana and looking for the boy who had hit her own precious son. Sebastiana, all of four feet nine, hit the woman over the head with a large rock. Fight over. Sebastiana always told Gaspar never to start a fight, but also never to back down when attacked or threatened. Gaspar listened.

Sebastiana is also responsible, indirectly, for Gaspar's ring nickname. She was a full-blooded Zapotec Indian from Juchitán, Oaxaca, a part of Mexico that maintained its own indigenous culture and language despite the onslaught of Mixtec, Aztec, and later Spanish conquerors. She spoke Spanish as a second language with a Zapotec accent, and she wore the traditional clothes of her people. Her children recall the long flowery skirts, the traditional *huipil* blouse, the *rebozo* shawl she wore around her diminutive frame. She cooked delicious Zapotec tamales made with chili and shrimp. She'd prepare tortillas in the old way, using a pot buried in the ground, slapping the thin dough to the walls of the pot. When ready, the steaming tortillas would drop from the sides. She only put on shoes for church. After Mass, she would take them off and carry them home in her hands, so uncomfortable did they make her feet.

The children called her Jefa—Boss—because she ran the house with commanding discipline. They slept without complaint two or three to a

bed, homemade beds constructed from thin logs and cushions laid carefully on the dirt floor. They wore donated clothes. They used newspaper
scraps instead of toilet paper. Sheets hanging from wires provided what
privacy could be had in the single room of the house, the sheets dividing the space into smaller sections. Against one wall, Jefa constructed a
religious shrine to her pantheon of heroes: the Virgin, St. Geronimo (the
patron saint of Oaxaca), and St. Martin de Porres (the saint of charity
and work who was born of Spanish and, possibly, Indian parentage in
seventeenth-century Peru). Every day she lit candles and set aside a cup
of water, and she prayed.

Father was a different story. Aniseto was a soldier, but he was not paid
well and chose to spend his free time drinking and hurling verbal and
occasional physical abuse at his large family. On at least one occasion,
he shoved Jefa hard against the rough adobe wall. Sometimes Jefa would
send the young ones to a neighbor's house when father came home drunk.
Sometimes Jefa and her daughters would put chewed gum in a special
hole in the wall for St. Ramon, the saint of the falsely accused who, in his
mortal life, was silenced by having his lips pierced by a red-hot iron and
sealed with a padlock. They prayed to St. Ramon, pleading that father not
scream at them when he came home. It never worked.

One fateful day, father came home drunk again. On this night, Jefa
decided that the physical violence, at least, would end. Earlier in the day
she had gathered the children and told them all not to worry. She calmly
explained, "Tonight, I'm going to kick his ass." Later, when an inebriated
Aniseto stumbled in and started to pick a new argument, Jefa moved
toward him, fast. She brandished a sharp knife and thrust it at his neck.
Aniseto instinctively reached for a weapon, but he was stunned at his
wife's behavior, and as he scrambled about, some of the younger children
moved in and pinned his arms and legs. Gaspar remembers Jefa wielding
a tortilla rolling pin at one point, beating Aniseto with it savagely. The
older brothers heard the racket and came in, pulling Jefa off before she
killed dad. They managed to get her outside, and things cooled off. After
this, dad left her alone.

Sebastiana proved the stronger role model for Gaspar. He did not want
to be anything like his alcohol-powered dad. His older brother, Sabino,
was most like the old man, and he came to a bad end. Sabino became a
sergeant in the army, and he also drank heavily. When Sabino's wife left
him and moved to Alta California, he disappeared completely into the
bottle. One day he simply went missing. Gaspar and his mother went

looking for him in his barracks, only to find the door locked and the curtains drawn. Gaspar broke in through a window and was the first to discover the body. Sabino had hanged himself.

Searching for an identity took time for young Gaspar. Tijuana in those days (as now) was a dangerous place. He got into trouble in the streets, joining his neighborhood gang, Los Pachucos de la Morelos. He started to get homemade tattoos when he was twelve. They used a sewing needle with string wrapped around it as a grip, then dipped it in pen ink and poked away. The name of his gang symbolized an identity Gaspar shared with many youths growing up in Mexamerica. Though typically associated with Mexican immigrants north of the border, *pachucos* could be seen on both sides of La Línea. In Tijuana, pachuco identity thrived in the cultural hothouse of Yankee influence and Mexican cultural pride. Pachucos symbolized dangerous youth. In the United States, they were a threatening embodiment of nonwhite immigration. Pachucos were hard to miss, defying the conservative suit-and-tie ideal with outlandish "drapes," baggy ensembles replete with exaggerated shoulders and pleated trousers, typically paired with fedoras and long, looping watch chains dangling from the waist.

Gaspar bought his own two zoot suits behind his mother's back and took to the town with his gang, a fresh feather jauntily sticking out of his fedora. He started getting into big street brawls with other gangs. One consistent rival gang was the Cuahuilas, named for another Tijuana neighborhood. Nobody used guns in battles in those days, though knives, brass knuckles, and bludgeons certainly came out. During one street fight with the Cuahuilas, someone stabbed Gaspar in the stomach. He felt the white hot burning of the blade as it entered, though he wasn't sure who had done it. He clutched his groin and got out of there fast, making his way to the hospital where he got stitched up and sent home. Fortunately, the wound was superficial.

Unlike many of his compatriots, Gaspar didn't follow the gang road any further into drugs or more serious crime. He believed his mother when she told him that the ever-present marijuana in Tijuana was a thing of the Devil. Under its influence, Jefa told him, a man could do only evil deeds. The worst Gaspar got was when, inspired after watching a movie about the Revolution with some friends, he bought a bottle of tequila. He held the bottle aloft and exhorted his companions, "Let's be *real* Mexicans!" That night he learned that tequila is a harsh mistress, and he never went back to it.

Perhaps the reason Gaspar didn't drink or take drugs flowed from his ambition. He decided early in life that he could not live forever as a poor, middle child. He wanted to be famous. He wanted to walk down the street and hear people say, "*That's* Gaspar Benitez." But how to get it?

The answer was as clear as the cheering he could hear every Sunday afternoon coming from the stadium down on Boulevard Agua Caliente. Built in 1938, the arena named Toreo de Tijuana attracted the likes of Marilyn Monroe and Eva Gardner, not to perform, but to watch. On Sundays, the crowds could be heard for miles, screaming as bulls lowered their heavy heads and charged the matadors who dared face them. Gaspar idolized these men. He determined to become one of them.

In *The Sun Also Rises* (1926), Ernest Hemingway's Jake Barnes rhapsodizes, "Nobody ever lives their life all the way except bull-fighters."[4] Gaspar had long noticed the myriad ways these heroes stood apart—the way that they dressed, how they wore their hair, how they held themselves. They were demigods on earth, whose lonely stands against violent nature separated them from the anonymous masses who paid to watch them.

At the pinnacle of the bullfighting world is the matador. Cutting a striking figure in his Suit of Lights (purposely designed to accentuate the upside-down triangle figure of a young, virile man), he strides into arenas of adoring fans, facing down the charging monsters that erupt out of the appropriately named Gates of Fear. Matadors, literally meaning "killers" (there is no direct Spanish translation for "bullfighter"), epitomized the definition of masculinity that exalts complete fearlessness and the awesome finality of lethal violence.

Gaspar and his friends were obsessed with *la fiesta brava* (bullfight, literally "the brave festival"). On Sundays they would start by washing car windows in the arena parking lot so as to later ask the owners for money. After the event got under way, the boys used a rope with a hook at the end to rappel up and climb over a cement perimeter wall rimmed with sharp glass. They would then sneak down under the bleachers and watch the performance. One day, a famous Mexican bullfighter named Luis Procuna noticed young Gaspar under the bleachers and asked if he'd like to help. Gaspar couldn't believe his good fortune. He happily agreed to carry water, *muletas* (small semicircular capes used for the final passes), and *banderillas* (decorative spears thrust into the bull's haunches during the charge) for Procuna's crew. The great matador asked Gaspar if he was afraid of the bulls, which could weigh more than seventeen hundred pounds. "No," he responded.

Gaspar learned a lot from his new circumstances. He learned to soak muletas in water and dust them with sand to keep them heavy enough to hang properly in front of the bulls. When Luis made a special signal with his hat, Gaspar would run out into the ring with a bucket of water or other necessaries. He memorized the way Procuna held his feet together when the beast approached, elbow locked to his waist, head up, arm cocked at ninety degrees.

Gaspar told Procuna that he wanted to become a great matador. Luis merely chuckled. The road to matador fame was so impossible that it was not worth encouraging this poor, gangly boy. Not just anyone could slip into the Suit of Lights and stroll into an arena on a Sunday afternoon. This art took time, patience, and a good deal of luck.

The process began with a stint as an amateur, or *novillero*. Local novilleros would fight in the small dusty rodeo in Tijuana first, battling young bulls (called *novillos*) without killing them. These boys were typically untrained, foolish individuals who often learned that even a small bull could exact a tremendous deal of damage. Gaspar got started by practicing caping a charging set of horns rigged to a bicycle wheel pushed by another boy. He then dueled with calves borrowed from the slaughterhouse where he sometimes worked. Gaspar practiced constantly, often alone, remembering what he had seen at the big arena the previous Sunday. He would need to stand very still when the bull approached, an action that went sharply against the natural human instinct to flee. When the bull thrust its horns, he would have to use his muleta to guide the tremendous head closely around his own body. Though the horns might even brush a leg, a monastic, detached calm in a matador was most respected by fans. His feet needed to be locked tightly together, making his center of gravity unstable while at the same time reducing his silhouette as much as possible. He would need to tune out the "olés" and cheers, focusing on setting up the next charge.

Gaspar's first real bullfight took place in 1949, when he was thirteen or fourteen years old. It was held at the rodeo before an audience of perhaps two or three hundred amused spectators, and Gaspar was just one of a group of starry-eyed novilleros trying to make a name for themselves. Gaspar had no money for a bullfighter's outfit, so he wore Levis, cut especially to be tight, a dark shirt, and a borrowed tie. His first bull was a small one, and Gaspar was so nervous that he moved his cape in the wrong direction and stuck out his derrière in fear that a horn might clip him. After a few ungainly passes, he trotted back to the other novilleros. One of them said frankly that his performance was "ugly." Another told him that he had no *huevos* (balls). Shamed, he went out again, this time standing erect and caping the bull properly to the delight of the crowd.

The fights came along easier after that performance. People started to tell him that he was a natural because he showed no fear. By his fourth fight, Gaspar was beginning to feel comfortable, even a little cocky. When the bull came toward him at this show (and it was not a big bull at all), he stood firm and held his muleta in the classic position: feet rooted to the sandy earth, his spindly legs locked, back stiff. The first two passes were perfect. The third pass also looked to be another crowd-pleaser. Yet something went terribly wrong. The bull did not follow the cape as Gaspar swept it around his body. Instead, the animal's forehead plowed directly into his torso. The bull twisted on contact, lifting the stunned novillero high into the air. It then snapped its head in the opposite direction, and the horn penetrated Gaspar's Levis and sank deeply into the back of his right thigh. When the boy met the ground it was at an ungodly angle, neckfirst. Gaspar did not pass out, but he knew that he was badly hurt. He put his hands over his head and lay still as another novillero jumped in and distracted the bull. The stretcher bearers came out.

Bullfighting is a dangerous route to fame, perhaps the most dangerous one of all. One study has shown that by the mid-twentieth century, nearly one-third of the top matadors had been killed in the ring. In recognition of the possibility of onsite emergency surgery, matadors are actually instructed not to eat before a fight. One reporter discovered that the bull's horns were sometimes coated with penicillin. Manolete, the most famous modern bullfighter, was killed in Linares, Spain, shortly after Gaspar saw him perform in Tijuana.

Gaspar's own bullring injuries landed him in the Tijuana public hospital. He had no money, so someone else had to pay for the ambulance at the ring. Once at the hospital, he found himself in a large auditorium filled with beds separated by white sheets draped over long wires. Doctors plugged his wounds with gauze, which quickly became saturated with blood and started to itch and irritate. Screams from other patients kept him awake through the night. Worst of all was the prospect of Jefa's wrath. She had no idea that her son had become a bullfighter. She was going to be really angry.

Gaspar told his brother to tell Jefa that he had fallen off a horse. Upon hearing the news that her favorite son was injured, Jefa ran to the hospital, her bare feet padding through the dusty, trash-strewn streets. Once inside the building, she asked a doctor, in her Zapotec accent, where she might find her child, Gaspar Benitez.

"The bullfighter?"

She looked at him.

The man blithely continued, "Your son will be a wonderful matador some day."

When she found her boy lying wounded in bed, she slapped him hard, again and again. ("She beat my ass," Gaspar wincingly recalls.) Jefa told him that when he got out, he would have to pack his things and get the hell out of her house. No son living under her roof would be stupid enough to fight bulls. Gaspar talked her down as best he could, and she gave him this ultimatum: "The bulls or the house." He promised her no more bulls. He would never participate in a *corrido* again. Almost.

Five decades later, a doctor examined Gaspar's head and neck as part of treatment for throat cancer. In the course of a series of cranial x-rays, the oncologist asked when he had broken his neck. This was news to Gaspar. The healed fracture looked very old, the doctor observed. Considering the years of boxing still in his future, it is a marvel that Gaspar did not suffer irreparable spinal injury at some point.

With the *torero* career over before it properly began, Gaspar felt lost. He had quit his other jobs to concentrate on bullfighting. After he went back to hustling gringos and middle-class Mexicans on Avenida Revolución, a new opportunity availed itself when a shoeshine customer asked him if he did any work in San Ysidro.

"I don't have a passport."

The man laughed. "You're stupid. Just go out to the entrance of the baseball field on Monday morning around seven."

On Monday, Gaspar went to the field, which abutted the border, and a man drove up in a car from the Tijuana side and let off another man next to the wire. Together, Gaspar and a few other prospective workers pushed down the meager barbed wire fence and walked onto U.S. soil.

His first time in America felt no different than walking around in Tijuana. They walked up a country road for about two-thirds of a mile until they arrived at a farm. A white man approached them and asked, in broken Spanish, if they could bring two more friends next time. They nodded. Then he put them to work.

Gaspar crossed over daily to San Ysidro for the next six or seven weeks. It was incredibly difficult work. For thirty-five cents an hour, he had to stoop in the hot sun along the furrows, pulling up heads of lettuce by digging around each plant with a short-handled shovel and hoe and yanking it into one of the wooden crates spaced along the aisles. He pulled up tomatoes and carrots as well; cleared the ground for flower beds; and clipped rosebushes, too. He wore a wide brimmed hat, but he could not afford to buy gloves, and his hands cursed him.

After a few days of work, Gaspar found a metal pipe that they would use to separate out the barbed wires, facilitating an easier trip through the fence. They'd bury the pipe after each use, digging it up for the return trip. He remembers this pipe as "our passport."

Eventually, he quit. This was not a job worth having. Other, longtime farmworkers reinforced his decision, telling him about a life for which he had no desire, about working all day in the fields without a decent bed and experiencing daily derision from Anglos who thought all of these struggling workers were "invaders." Besides, Gaspar had a new career ambition—boxing.

Until he was in his teens, Gaspar had absolutely no interest in boxing. He was an athletic kid, but he preferred soccer and baseball. Boxing, which was wildly popular in Baja California, seemed like it required taking a lot of physical abuse, and he hated to be hit. Bullfighting, he had convinced himself, could be performed with such skill that one could become famous without ever taking serious damage (a notion he was brutally disabused of), but boxing seemed inevitably to demand an exchange of blows. Gaspar explains his logic: "You can fool a bull, but a boxer has two hands, too."

Still, boxing was something he had grown up with, and he knew it intimately. When he was nine or so, his brothers and dad drew a square in the backyard dirt and boxed each other (sister Lalia boxed, too). The backyard boxing later evolved into two heavy bags dangling from metal tubes, a speedbag, and a more permanent ring. By age twelve, Gaspar watched as his backyard filled with amateur boxing fans who congregated to see different locals go at it.

At school, Gaspar had a teacher named Isabella who developed an interesting program for keeping the boys from fighting in the yard. If someone had a beef, he would have to sign up to settle the score with gloves in front of all the other students. The fights were held after school on Fridays, and they required a note of parental consent. Isabella brought the equipment, wrote up "programs," and got her hands on a bell. The Friday fights became a popular sensation. With ten-ounce gloves, the students would wait for Isabella to blow the whistle and then start whaling away for two-minute rounds, tracked on a "big, ugly clock." Isabella would blow her whistle to warn someone for stepping out of the chalk, and she was also the arbiter of victory. Most fights were draws. Gaspar, for whatever reason, got challenged a lot.

Then there was the fire station. One day he discovered that the firefighters kept an impromptu boxing club in the back, and soon he was sparring regularly (many times without the benefit of headgear) and hitting the bags. Gaspar had no formal trainer, but he was a good observer. His older brother, Jesus, called Torito (Little Bull), helped him when he could. Torito was a professional boxer himself, with some fifty-odd professional bouts under his belt and a reputation for charging in and pushing opponents around. Torito taught him some basics of defense and counterpunching and encouraged the habit of sidestepping that Gaspar had acquired from his bullfighting foray. Gaspar proved a quick study, and soon he developed a signature move: a quick step to the side, a push off from the opponent with his right hand, then a sharp left hook. When he eventually arrived in the United States, his impressed trainers told him they had never seen such a move.

Torito encouraged Gaspar to sign up for the Golden Gloves (Guantes de Oro) Tournament of Northern Baja California. Boxing as a flyweight (112 pounds), the tall, lean Gaspar had the advantage of having an exceptionally long reach for his weight class. He wore no headgear and battled with light, eight-ounce gloves.

His first fight was at the Azteca Arena in front of six hundred or so tournament fans. He couldn't afford a robe, so he wore a towel over his shoulders into the ring. His opponent was a student at the Polytechnic College, an older boy of seventeen or so with a good reputation as a scrapper. Gaspar had seen him train and fight in the past and knew he would be a tough opponent. The man was very aggressive, but he was shorter and stockier than Gaspar. Gaspar's strategy was to keep his opponent at a distance, to hit-and-run and avoid taking serious punishment. The plan worked. In the third round, his frustrated opponent knew he was losing and began to get angry. He charged Gaspar, eyes glaring. "So I bullfightered him. When they are like bulls, they don't think straight." He saw his opponent coming and gingerly sidestepped the wild charges. The judges unanimously awarded the fight to Gaspar. Sugar Ray Robinson had taken dancing lessons as a kid, and his boxing showed it. Perhaps Gaspar's future career owed something to the bullring.

His second fight was even easier. Gaspar felt comfortable in the ring now, and his style was such that opponents could not seem to make any hard contact with him. He did receive his first solid hit to the body in the second round of this fight, but he played it off so that his opponent would not know he had done any real damage. Gaspar got the unanimous decision. He won the next two matches in the tournament equally handily and, incredibly, the fifth fight of his life was for the Amateur Flyweight belt of Tijuana.

Gaspar lost the first round, taking a few solid hits to the head and body, but he recovered quickly and came back to win the match. He was awarded the green, white, and red Golden Gloves belt of Tijuana. He was proud of the cheaply made belt, which quickly tarnished into a sad bilious green. It was April 1950. One month later, he turned pro. He was fourteen years old.

Training now took on new purpose. Gaspar's celebrity grew among the local fight mob, and his schoolteacher, Isabella, advised him not to tell anyone who he was on the streets. She said that nobody likes an *echador*, a cocky person. The fact that Gaspar needed to keep his new career choice a secret from Jefa reinforced this restraint.

Gaspar continued to practice at the fire station, but he also trained on his own around his neighborhood. He would hide his boxing gear at friends' houses, and though his siblings and father knew about it, they all agreed it was best to keep Jefa in the dark. His routine became more intense. Each morning, he woke up at 5:30 and ran two to three miles through the hills above Old Town. At the top of the hill behind his neighborhood, Gaspar would shadow box and do sit-ups and leg lifts until he got tired. Then he would go back down the canyon and stop at a flat place where he could look out over the whole city. After this workout, it was back to selling newspapers and shining shoes. In the afternoon, he'd put in another hour and a half of shadowboxing, bagwork, and sparring if a fight was coming up. Always attentive, Gaspar knew that he would need to have a strong chin, so he devised an exercise in which he would lie on his back and, with a towel behind his head, use the back of his skull as a pivot to roll his head from side to side. Bedtime was at nine sharp so he could be up fresh and early the next day.

He picked up tricks as he went. To toughen his face, Gaspar would boil rosemary in water with sea salt, then soak a towel with the liquid and wrap it around his head. Skin toughening techniques like this have a long and dubious history. A young Jack Dempsey, it has been written, soaked his hands in brine and splashed horse urine on his face to make his skin unbreakable.

Gaspar's first professional match was a bantamweight bout against a man named Ramon Garcia. The payment would be one dollar per round, U.S., which was not much even at that time and place, though it was better than the amateur fights, where he had to be satisfied with the coins tossed into the ring by the crowd after each bout. (The two boxers would split the money.) Boxing was a profession that required other sources of income in Tijuana back then. Ramon Garcia happened to be a mailman.

The fight was held at the biggest boxing arena in Tijuana, El Coloseo, with about four thousand seats. Gaspar was on the undercard in a four-round bout. His battle plan consisted of continuous movement to keep the tough but short mailman at a safe distance. Using his reach and speed to his advantage, Gaspar took the decision.

In his corner that night, along with Torito, was a man they called Muletas. Ignacio "Muletas" Gomez was a local boxing fixture, an unusual fellow who helped youngsters train and worked the corner during bouts. He was called Muletas (crutches) for the homemade metal water pipes he converted into crutches for himself. He had been born with one emaciated leg, and he used the pipes to navigate the hard, uneven dirt streets. Muletas had arrived in Gaspar's Colonia around the time Gaspar's family had, but he was about fifteen years older. Muletas's father, like Gaspar's, was a soldier, and his brother was a boxer whom Gaspar admired.

"Crutches" seems an unfair name with which to go through life. In Gaspar's world, nicknames were assigned early and would typically replace a person's given name in informal situations. Gaspar himself fought under the name "Indio." When his brother Torito (thus named for his aggressiveness in and out of the ring) was gravely ill and bedridden many years later, he could not even recognize Gaspar. But when his younger brother said, "It is Indio," Torito's face lit up. Yes, he knew Indio.

Gaspar had acquired his nickname as a child in school. He could not afford shoes, so the kids called him "Indio con Pata Rajada"—the Indian with the Cracked Foot. His mother's dark complexion and "Indian" nose, the other children said, made him look like a native. This he correctly took as an insult. Indians in Mexico have endured a torturous history, and the term *indio* is often employed as a condescending epithet for one who is dark-skinned and poor. Gaspar knew it to mean "no class, no education, nothing." "Indians," he notes, "were supposed to be the stupid ones."

Gaspar himself was a mestizo, and "Indian with the Cracked Foot" was just a nickname, a putdown like many other nicknames. He did not like it at first, but he didn't have much say in the matter. Besides, it could

have been worse. His compatriots typically had unflattering ring nicknames that antedated their boxing careers. Unlike "The Brown Bomber,"
Joe Louis, many of the boxers in Tijuana carried monikers that did not
exactly celebrate their virtues. "Gordo" (fat) Zuniga was overweight. "Ti-
burón" (Shark) Rojas had front teeth that jutted out at an odd angle. "El
Caracol" (shell) Diaz had arrived in Tijuana as a child from deep inland
and had been so amazed when he first saw the ocean that he ran to the
surf and stuffed his pockets with the abundant shells he found, thinking them prizes. The other children noticed this and mocked him for it,
dumping the boy unceremoniously into the waves and baptizing him "El
Caracol" as the shells poured out of his pants. He was introduced as El
Caracol when I met him in 2006.

Indio continued to fight in and around Tijuana for the next two years.
He won every single fight, mostly taking decisions rather than knocking out opponents. He was a volume puncher and a slippery opponent
to catch. No power hitter, he depended on speed as his weapon. As the
money came in, Gaspar started to buy his mother small gifts, such as
flowers in a glass vase for Mother's Day or a beautiful Zapotec cape for
her to wear on special occasions. He was still hiding his new career from
his mom at this point, fighting under the *nom de ring* Ortega rather than
Benitez. When his mom eventually learned about it, he convinced her he
would quit if he started to lose.

Gaspar's first loss was fight number seventeen, against a much older
boxer (probably twenty-four or twenty-five years old) who proved to be
too strong and talented for the young pugilist. Gaspar took the loss well.
Muletas had taught him to respect three things: the referee, the judges,
and the audience. When he lost the decision, Gaspar was humble and
congratulated his opponent.

The first fight officially recorded for Gaspar is on January 1, 1953, against
Miguel Ocana. Due to a lack of textual evidence, the earlier fights live
on only in the memories of Gaspar and a few others and have yet to be
officially substantiated. Gaspar's official boxing record has him down for
176 fights, but in truth it is more likely closer to 200.

Listening to stories from his old Tijuana boxing fraternity, one gets a
sense of a lost age of cartoonish innocence, what one might term Wild
West Boxing. Hot pepper might be mixed with Vaseline and smeared on
gloves. Headlights from a row of cars would be used to light up an outdoor evening bout after the electricity failed. There's the story of a fighter
who once went out to the ring wearing nothing under his robe; in his
nervousness, he had forgotten to get dressed. Another time, a terrified

boxer entered the ring against Gaspar, and when his manager yelled at him to keep his hands up, he actually raised them above his head in a surrender pose. Gaspar knocked him out with one punch.

Gaspar's burgeoning career almost died in December 1951. He had landed a fight at Tijuana's Coloseo, in part because he simply couldn't get any fights outside of Baja due to the provincial nature of Mexican boxing. (Later in his career, on the Mexican TV show *Round Zero*, someone asked the boxing commissioner of Mexico City why the TV stations never broadcast Gaspar's fights, and the man answered that he had never heard of him. This was despite the fact that Gaspar was incredibly popular by this point.) He planned to make a big enough name for himself so that he could no longer be ignored, and the best place to get this kind of attention was at the Coloseo, which brought in both the local fight crowd from Baja and a number of American boxing fans as well.

The fight would never happen. A week before the scheduled match, the Coloseo held a gala benefit for local impoverished children. It was three days before Christmas. Hosted by the Unión de Inquilinos (Tenants Union), the event featured music, dancing, and assorted festivities. Area orphans were invited to share in the joy. A fire started close to midnight, when the electric lights on a Christmas tree short-circuited. The dry tree, the cloth curtains, the wooden furniture, and the decorations all provided terrible fuel for the conflagration, which quickly swept through the crowded dance area upstairs. Black smoke billowed into the night air, and eyewitnesses observed panicked youngsters jumping from the high windows to their deaths to escape the inferno behind them. The fire departments of San Diego and Chula Vista had to come help put out the blaze. A toll of 120 people perished that night, including a number of orphans and a few local celebrities (such as baseball player Angel Camarena Romo and boxer Hector "Super" Tamayo). The next day, U.S. Marines were called in to help clean up the wreckage. Some Tijuanans still recall Marines shoveling up broken, charred human remains amid foul clouds of ash. The Coloseo was closed forever.

Gaspar didn't fight for a good long while after the fire (which he fortunately missed), soon to be dubbed "La Posada Trágica." Boxing left Tijuana entirely for a time, and Gaspar recognized that without a home base, his future was uncertain. He went to work at a shoe factory full time, working nine and ten hour days for eight dollars a week.

Eventually, Gaspar decided to try again in early 1953. Taking to the road with Muletas and Torito, he started fighting up and down the Baja Peninsula, racking up an impressive streak of twenty-one straight wins,

ten by way of knockout. The venues were uniquely Baja: he fought on a
baseball field, near a swimming pool, and in a ring constructed within
in a bullring.

Gaspar fought two to three times a month against an assortment of locals, men called Baby Veloz (Speed), Negrito (Little Black) Desilao, Negro
(Black) Garcia, Roca (Rock) Reyes, and Kid Allegria (Happiness). Baby
Veloz and Baby Franco had youthful appearances. Negro and Negrito
were dark-skinned. Roca Reyes was rocklike: "I hit him so hard, but he
doesn't move at all." As for Kid Allegria, mistakenly called Kid Algeria
in the books, Gaspar remembers shaking his head at his opponent's un-
manly nickname. Insanely, Kid Happiness smiled when he got hit. Gaspar
knocked him out in round six.

Gaspar went undefeated in 1953. He perfected some new tricks, such
as boxing a little in the first round, then looking down at his own feet.
When the opponent looked down to see what got Gaspar's attention, Indio
gave him an overhand right. He managed three consecutive first-round
knockouts doing this. Torito taught him this and other things, preparing
the young fighter for individual opponents by reporting on their weak-
nesses and ring habits. Muletas also helped, assisting Gaspar in defeating
the agile Baby Veloz by saying "don't follow him no more" after Gaspar
chased him around the ring in the first round. He bided his time in the
second, and when Veloz approached, Gaspar connected with a startling
right that floored his opponent. As the referee counted, Gaspar could
see that Veloz was not seriously hurt but rather had chosen to wait it
out on the mat rather than meet with another such punch. In places like
San Luis, Mexicali, and Ensenada, Gaspar soon built up a reputation as
a dangerous, clever boxer.

By this time, Gaspar was making a dollar a round for eight- and ten-
round fights, with one of those dollars going to Muletas ("he was so happy").
This money seemed fine at the time, but later it would seem comical. His
first fight in Manhattan just a year later netted him $150 for four rounds
of work. His first thought would be, "I'm not going back to Mexico."

In 1953 Indio also met a man who would change his life forever. He
had heard that there was an American manager cruising Baja looking for
prospects. Nick Corby (born Nicolas Corby Acevedo) was born in Isla
de Vieques, Puerto Rico, in 1918. His grandparents had emigrated from
Spain to work in the sugar business there, and his mother and sister were
active in island politics. Nick went to school in New York and had boxed
and even managed fighters briefly before moving to San Diego to work

at Convair.[5] He made a decent living at the aeronautical company, but his passion was boxing, and he liked to spend his free time combing the border for talent. He had been told that there was a fighter named Indio who had real potential, so Corby had an appointment set up at a Tijuana boxing gym at noon one day.

Gaspar arrived at 11:15 and waited. A bit after twelve, a man walked up and asked if he knew Gaspar Ortega. Gaspar responded that it was none other than he in the flesh, and the man introduced himself as Nick Corby. Nick was a little on the heavy side, light-skinned, and of average height. He talked nonstop Americanized Puerto Rican Spanish.

Gaspar hadn't brought any gear, so Nick had to scare some up. Then he had Gaspar take off his shirt and get in the ring with a strong sparring partner, a man accustomed to ten-round bouts (whereas Gaspar usually fought four- and six-rounders). Gaspar moved fast, but his opponent had more endurance and wore him out in just a few rounds. Gaspar stopped the session early, explaining that he was too tired to go on.

Incredibly, Nick told him that he liked what he saw, and that with some practice, he would take Gaspar to New York City. Gaspar thought this man was full of it.

"This guy *here* is better than me!" protested Gaspar, as one would explain the obvious to a child. "Why don't you take him?"

"I think you can be the best fighter."

"Why not take me to San Diego, then?" Gaspar countered.

"My connections are in New York."

"How will I get to New York City?" Unlike San Diego, New York would require papers, travel, unforeseen expenses.

"We'll get you a visa."

"I'm underage."

"We'll get permission from your parents."

The guy had an answer to everything.

Within a year, with Nick Corby in his corner, Gaspar had landed his first fight against a real opponent, a nontitle bout against Baja welterweight champion Dave Cervantes. Cervantes was a skilled pugilist, a smart fighter with a hard right and who possessed, in the words of Gaspar, "a beautiful jab." He fought flat-footed, "like a hunter," with no dancing or theatrics, just a steady onslaught. To boot, he was a handsome fellow, popular with the ladies. The odds were so far in Cervantes's favor (18–1, so I've been told) that a fighter on the undercard, a friend of Gaspar's, actually left the arena before the fight began. He just couldn't bear to watch the slaughter. It didn't help that Gaspar had come down with a fever two days earlier and found his energy reserves depleted. The fight, in Baja, was held in an open stadium in Ensenada. The place was packed.

It was the night of Gaspar's biggest payday yet, sixty U.S. dollars. He earned every cent of it, taking such a beating from Cervantes as he had never imagined. He was knocked to the canvas not once (making it the first time in his short career he had been floored) but an astounding seven times.[6] Indio was clearly beaten, yet he would not accept defeat. Cervantes had to take the decision after ten rounds of nonstop work.

In the ride back up to Tijuana in Nick Corby's Jeep, Gaspar did not speak. He knew this was the end. He had come up against the closest thing to world-class competition that existed in Baja and had lost, badly. Corby, as usual, broke the silence.

"You're going to New York."

Gaspar couldn't believe that Nick was saying this. It was almost insulting at this point. He asked, exasperated, "Why me?"

"Because," replied Corby, "after that first knockdown, nobody else would have gotten up."

CHAPTER 5

The Discovery of New York

In the summer of 1954, Nick Corby gave Gaspar a one-way Greyhound bus ticket and five dollars and told him they would meet up in New York City. Gaspar's mom gave her son three quarters and some advice: "If any gringo hits you once, you hit him twice." Indio traveled light, bringing with him three pairs of pants, three shirts, a few pairs of underwear, and one pair of shoes. He said a prayer as he climbed aboard the bus in San Diego. Looking down the aisle he immediately began to relax; he knew these people. They were mostly white sailors from the naval base, the sort from whom he earned his bread working Avenida Revolución. They were heading back home for leave. He found a seat by a window and looked out as the bus pulled away. He would be spending most of the trip like this: watching the scenery unfold.

Ever resourceful, Gaspar managed to avoid spending his own money en route. It was a simple trick that he called "the heads game." He'd find a sailor willing to wager a quarter, using not only his extremely limited English but also the universal language of gambling, and then toss the piece with a blur of the hand and ask which hand the coin had landed in. Practically every time, they guessed wrong. (It's all about speed and a straight face. When Gaspar played the game with me half a century later, I guessed incorrectly, too.) The sailors got frustrated with him—and so another would try to prove that he could do it—but when they saw the Mexican kid put the quarters he had won into vending machines for food at the stops, they couldn't stay angry. The vending machines were a complete mystery to Gaspar. He had never seen one before. He watched what other people did, then approached a machine, put in a quarter, and pressed a random button. He ate whatever the machine gave him. Sometimes he dined on a bag of potato chips. Other times, a cookie or a sandwich might be lunch.

When the bus pulled into a hub in St. Louis and emptied, Gaspar wandered around the station looking for a Spanish speaker. Failing to find anyone, he pulled out a note Corby had written. In English, it said: "I can't speak any English. Can you please point me to the bus to New York City?" A friendly gringo showed him the way, and he was off again.

After three long days and nights, Gaspar arrived in Manhattan. What a sight it was! He'd never seen anything even remotely like it. Long, wide corridors of concrete and glass extended out in every direction, thickly channeled with noisy, car-choked avenues. And beneath this, an endless warren of subway tunnels. At a time when Tijuana had around 100,000 residents (and even this was about 80,000 more than when Gaspar had first arrived there in 1939), Manhattan contained almost 2 million souls. Add in the other boroughs and New York City was over the 7 million mark, a place that featured the nation's busiest port, its largest markets, and the highest concentration of corporate headquarters and factories in the world.

Gaspar got out between Eighth Avenue and Broadway and wandered around the station for thirty minutes, looking for his local contact and new trainer, Hipolito "Happy" (pronounced "Appy") Rodriguez. Neither knew what the other looked like. Happy finally approached a confused-looking, gangly, dark-skinned kid and tapped him on the shoulder. The exchange, in Spanish, went something like this: "Are you Mexican?" "Yes." "Come with me." "I don't know you." "I'm Happy Rodriguez."

They left for Happy's apartment via taxi and then, after a brief introduction to the family (Happy lived with his wife and two teenage children), they went to Central Park. This was another sight Gaspar was unprepared for. In the middle of this great pile of skyscrapers sat a wooded expanse of epic proportions. Happy told the wide-eyed boxer that he could jog here every day, around the reservoir or on the horse trails. Gaspar just stood in silence, unable to wrap his mind around it all. The whole place possessed a scale to which he had no reference. Happy sensed that his provincial charge was in a state of shock and tried to get him to envision the possibilities: "In New York you can do anything you want, anywhere," he explained. "You can box, you can fuck, anything. This isn't Mexico."

Happy then sized up the young boxer and asked him, "How good *are* you?" Gaspar quickly popped down into his stance and let his fists fly, shadowboxing for a good minute and a half. Happy was impressed. The kid was fast, his timing and reflexes natural and sharp. Happy smiled and told him, "You're going to be a great fighter." The next day, Happy took his new charge to Stillman's Gym to start his real education. Here Gaspar received the biggest shock yet. He was already scheduled to fight at what boxing fans called the Center of the Universe. He had a match in Madison Square Garden in just three weeks.

Located just a few blocks away from the Garden in an old, run-down building along the west side of Eighth Avenue between Fifty-Fourth and Fifty-Fifth Streets that looked like "it had been knocked down in the Draft Riots of 1863 and left for dead" (in the inimitable words of A. J. Liebling), Stillman's Gym served a vital purpose. Boxers trained, cultivated their fan base, had their matches arranged, and met who they needed to meet here.

The proprietor, Lou Stillman, lorded over his province like a patriarch of old. He announced the sparring matches, decided who could train on a particular day, and relentlessly harassed everyone within shouting distance. Again Liebling offers the best contemporary description: "He is a gaunt man with a beak that describes an arc like an overhand right, bushy eyebrows, a ruff of hair like a frowsy cockatoo and a decisive, heavily impish manner."[1]

Lou practiced his own sense of humor at the expense of others. Sometimes he would announce the fighters creatively. A *Saturday Evening Post* reporter caught him in fine form one afternoon:

"Now boxing in Ring Number One, Benito Mussolini."

"What's the fighter's real name?" asked the reporter.

"Who cares? Yesterday I introduced him as Herman Goring. What difference does it make?"[2]

The boxer, who spoke no English, didn't seem to mind. As Lou later philosophized, "Big or small, champ or bum, I treated 'em all the same way—bad."[3]

Stillman's Gym played host to a cavalcade of boxing greats and famous followers. Journalist Harold Conrad recalled, "You'd go up there, you'd see everyone from the heavyweight champion to the flyweight champion. You'd see Jack Johnson fooling around—an old man fooling around with guys watching him. It was a fantastic place for fight people. And big audiences all the time. Movie stars, all kinds of people used to go up there."[4]

TV boxing at first was a boon to Stillman's. New boxers were becoming celebrities every week, and so many people wanted to watch the sparring sessions that Lou doubled the admission fee. Fans might come in and see

Rocky Graziano or Sandy Saddler working out, with old time greats like Jack Dempsey or Jack Johnson standing outside the ropes, watching. It was a remarkable time. As a novice boxer later gushed, even "if you were a piece-of-shit fighter, you mingled with the best fighters in the world."[5]

When Gaspar arrived at Stillman's, he encountered a place bustling with activity. Lou would open the steel grille barring the entrance at three in the afternoon, and the crowds would ascend the forty or so steps up the wooden staircase to the second floor. There, they would encounter a turnstile manned by Jack Curley, an infamous curmudgeon who would collect an admission of fifty cents, especially from those he said he did not know. If a well-known boxer was sparring that day, he might charge a buck. The cranky Curley would be remembered as a hard-ass. Recalled one boxer, Curley "wouldn't let Jesus Christ in there without fifty cents."[6]

Inside the gym, two boxing rings sat close together in a surprisingly long space, with rows of metal chairs in the front and a thin gap for boxers and trainers in the back. Stillman himself stood behind an iron railing in the middle, making it so that incomers would have to pass him very closely to move from one place to another. Despite his own sign that forbade spitting, Lou often loudly spat onto the dirty floor.

Above the rings sat a gallery accessible by a spiral staircase, a small space decked out with light and heavy bags and room for skipping rope. The gym also had a small shop that sold candy, sodas, hot dogs, cigars, and the ever-popular raw egg. Some trainers smoked continuously, filling the air with their fumes and leaving stubs all over the unswept floors. Boxers left smelling like ashtrays.

Gaspar's daily routine at Stillman's began with three minutes (one round) of stretching, three or four rounds of shadow boxing, and then several rounds or more each of sparring, bagwork, leg lifts, and neck strengthening. The neck was important; it anchored the chin, which is where knockouts usually happen. Happy looked at Gaspar's unique, slippery style and decided that he should work on body punches more. He explained that while this would not get you a fast knockout, it would wear down well-conditioned fighters and eventually make it easier to score a solid head shot later. Once an opponent started worrying about protecting his body, the head became vulnerable. Gaspar did what Happy said, kept his chin down, and stayed focused on his upcoming fight. After the workouts, he would shower at the gym and be home by six or six-thirty. Lou Stillman was not unkind to Gaspar, but he never spoke with him either. (He would have needed someone to translate his insults, anyway.)

At Stillman's, Gaspar was later introduced to corner man Freddie Brown. Brown was an old pro. Through Brown, Gaspar learned about things like using hand wraps under his gloves for protection, the importance of wearing a mouthpiece, and the trick of smearing Vaseline on the face to give opponents' gloves a surface more difficult to stick to. Brown gave Gaspar boxing tips as well, using body language to help the Mexican understand what he was trying to get him to do. Despite the communication barriers, Gaspar grew close to Brown. He would remember him as "something special." The old man would even take him around the city, just the two of them, window shopping and sightseeing. Brown tried to teach Gaspar a little English, but Gaspar found it too hard. Besides, as a macho Mexican, he felt he had little need for English.

Brown did these things because cultivating a boxer, for him, involved much more than just telling a pug to keep on punching or pinching shut an open gash between rounds. Talking to a reporter in the 1960s, Brown reflected on his dying art. "There are a lot of trainers today who are not teachers. . . . They spend maybe an hour with their fighters in the gym and then knock off for the day."[7] But not Freddie. He would sit down and eat breakfast with them, play cards with them, walk around with them, listen to them.

Gaspar trained religiously for his upcoming Garden premier. He trained with main-event guys when he could, practicing what he had learned. It was easy to stay healthy with a teetotaling father figure like Happy. He stayed away from junk food and cigarettes. He drank no alcohol. And he followed the old boxing superstition of abstaining from sex as the fight approached, since sex apparently drained one's reserves.

His first Garden match would be a four-rounder on the undercard. It was not scheduled for television, but the local fight crowd would be paying close attention nonetheless. New talent was a prized commodity in the Age of Television. After the noon weigh-in, Happy asked the young fighter what he normally ate before fights.

"Chile with tortillas and frijoles."

"How do you fight on *that*?" asked Happy.

"I fight good."

So Happy took the kid down to a Tex-Mex place over on Fifty-Fifth and Eighth where Gaspar ordered *frijoles* (beans) with *carne picada* (spicy beef) and a soda. This would become the prefight meal for all of his Garden battles, except that Happy later cut out the soda.

On fight day, Happy brought Gaspar over to the Garden early, and they got ready in one of its enormous dressing rooms. He told his young charge, "Tonight you debut in the biggest boxing arena in the world." Then he looked the kid in the eye. "Tonight you demonstrate everything you know. Put out your best performance." Gaspar was so nervous already, he really didn't need to hear this. He dressed and prepared in silence and listened to Happy's advice with a serious face. It felt like he was in the middle of a dream.

Once the Mexican had dressed, the two men trotted up the corridor for what seemed to be forever and then entered the largest arena Gaspar had ever seen. The Garden III was a cavernous space, with 18,500 seats in three tiers, each connected by escalators and bedecked with spotlights, stage lights, and public-address speakers. All this was hunched around a brightly lit ring, which became ghostly as the night wore on and cigar and cigarette smoke filled the place. As advertised, it was the only arena in the world built specifically with boxing in mind.

Up the four steps and through the ropes Gaspar went. The announcer introduced him as "Gaspar the Indian Ortego." In the opposite corner bounced another young fighter, a Puerto Rican by way of the Bronx named Iggy Maldonado. This was Iggy's eighth professional fight and his third combat at the Garden. (The earlier two matches had resulted in a win and then a draw.) For Gaspar, this was professional fight number twenty-four.

Maldonado was a little older than Gaspar, and he was a solid puncher. Unfortunately for him, he was also slow. Gaspar played "hit and run" for four rounds, easily taking the decision and putting on a sharp display of speed and finesse. The next day, the *New York Times* printed a small blurb about the fight: "Casper [*sic*] Ortega, 138, Mexico, outpointed Iggy Maldonado, 133, the Bronx."[8] Gaspar, or Casper, as the *Times* would have it, was officially on the radar.

Because of his good performance, a month later Gaspar was back in the Garden, still nervous as hell, this time in another four-rounder, this time against Tommy Barto. Coming out of New Kensington, Pennsylvania, Barto was a strong puncher. He battled Indio to a draw. The *New York Times* reported the next day, "Tommy Barto, 139, Pittsburgh, fought a draw with Caspar [*sic*] Ortega, 141, Mexico."[9] They only got one letter wrong this time.

The fights were coming in faster now. A mere nine days after Barto, Gaspar was in Colonial Heights, Virginia, battling Tony "Butterball" Celano. A squat five-foot-one boxer with tremendous power, Celano bounced

Gaspar off the ropes and onto the mat with a sudden left hook early on in the fight. Gaspar claims that he tripped, but the event is recorded as a knockdown. Though Indio was on his knees by the count of four or five, he watched the referee's fingers (he couldn't understand English yet) and waited for nine so he could be a bit more prepared when he rose. This was an old strategy. He listened to his trainers' advice, and he understood that a few more seconds might give a downed fighter the time he needed to get his head straight.

Gaspar got up and went on to outpoint his tough opponent in ten rounds, mostly by avoiding Celano's sledgehammer left. He scampered gingerly around the ring, sticking and moving and taking advantage of his longer reach. Afterward, one of the judges went into Gaspar's dressing room. He started asking questions, but Gaspar just looked at Happy, who quickly explained that his fighter spoke no English. The judge settled on a single question, which Happy translated.

"How did you get up?"

Apparently, Celano's left hook looked pretty fierce.

"I don't know," answered Gaspar in Spanish. "I just did."

Gaspar's next fight was an eight-rounder at the Garden with Tommy Barto again. This was his first major co-headlining bout, the first of three scheduled eight-rounders in the Garden on a Saturday night. The main event was a match between Jimmy Slade and a nineteen-year-old light heavyweight sensation named Floyd Patterson. The Slade-Patterson fight was an embarrassment. Patterson chased Slade around the ring, flooring him five times and inspiring Robert K. Christenberry, chairman of the New York State Athletic Commission, to withhold Slade's purse pending a hearing. The Barto-Ortega rematch, however, brought the crowd to its feet.

The *New York Times* described Gaspar's match as an epic battle in which the fighters "fought so hard and swung so many punches that in the last minute of the last round both were arm weary."[10] The fight was such an entertaining, all-out spectacle that the crowd actually demanded a *draw*. When the referee lifted Barto's hand, many were upset. Today, Gaspar is fine with that decision. Heck, he feels lucky. "He beat me good," he remembers. Importantly, this time the *Times* spelled his name right.

The trip to New York seemed to be going well. Gaspar was earning more money than he had ever seen, and after each fight he sent half of it home via money order. Nick Corby was ecstatic, dreaming up gimmicks that would make his dynamic boxer stand out in a crowded field. He designed a costume to go with the nickname—an enormous headdress crafted from white feathers back in Tijuana. Gaspar was uncomfortable with this. He didn't want to be a "clown." But he went along, wearing the contraption into the ring a few times and later posing in it for the press, sometimes with a tomahawk. At other times, Corby had him wearing a sombrero, because this Indian was also a Mexican. When Corby tried to get Gaspar to wear a serape (a traditional blanketlike covering), Gaspar drew the line. So Corby ordered a special boxing robe crafted with a serape style, which Gaspar dutifully wore to a number of fights.

Despite the attention and growing media buzz, Gaspar had begun feeling intensely homesick. He wrote letters home nearly every day. He didn't speak the language, and his Puerto Rican neighbors talked so rapidly and used such unfamiliar idioms that it was often hard to follow what they said. He wanted to go home. So he left. He took his first plane trip (a terrifying experience), landing in San Diego and then crossing back over into Mexico.

Once in Tijuana, Gaspar resumed his fighting schedule, defeating a string of local opponents between December 1954 and May 1955, including a satisfying KO victory over his old foe, Dave Cervantes. His time spent training at Stillman's had made him a much more intelligent fighter. The eighth-round knockout of Cervantes felt like retribution. Then, just two months later, Cervantes beat Gaspar again in a battle for the Baja California Norte Welterweight title. Frustrated, he talked to Nick Corby.

"Are you ready to go back to New York City?" Corby asked.

"I've been ready. But I'm afraid I'll get homesick again."

Corby thought about this and suggested that he bring his brother Sapo with him. Sapo was a promising boxer in his own right and was thrilled at the opportunity to train alongside his brother in New York City. Upon their arrival, Sapo seemed even more daunted by the big city than Gaspar had been. He was terrified of the subways ("I wanted to run outside") and was uncomfortable with the fact that it was so hard to see the sky from the street. But he was a tough guy. He put up a brave face and gave American boxing a shot. His persona was matched by his typical Mexican boxing style, static and ferocious. He battled opponents at St. Nick's and the Garden from 1955 through 1957. Unfortunately, his glass jaw and poor eyesight kept him from reaching the top of the sport, and he ended his career with a shaky official record of 7-7-1.

Gaspar and Sapo trained together, jogging three or four miles through Central Park every morning and meeting up at Stillman's Gym in the afternoons after Happy got out of work from his day job at the post office. Gaspar and his brother spoke constantly of building a bigger house for their parents back in Tijuana and of all the other things they would buy once they made it big. They slept in bunk beds in Happy's apartment and grew close to his family. After training ended for the day, they would listen to *ranchera* music on the radio, to the great singers like Pedro Infante, Jorge Negrete, and Amalia Mendoza. Negrete in particular resonated with Gaspar. He was called El Charro Cantor—the Singing Cowboy. He was a dashing man, a former officer whose father, like Gaspar's, had served during the Revolution. Although he died of hepatitis in 1953, his soulful renditions of songs like "Mexico Lindo y Querido" (Beautiful and Beloved Mexico) and "Yo Soy Mexicano" (I Am Mexican) immortalized him, as did the scores of films he starred in. He projected a strong Mexican nationalism that made his countrymen sing proudly in Mexico and tear up in America. Interestingly, Negrete had also started his climb to fame in New York City, where in 1936 he had been contracted by NBC.

Now Gaspar, another Mexican making a go of it in Manhattan, listened to Negrete on the radio and thought about the long way he had come. Back as a kid in Tijuana, he had listened to Negrete on the hand-cranked Victrola his father operated in their adobe shack. He was living his dream.

Gaspar's return to the Garden was a Friday night semifinal match against Frank Bombiani held just before that evening's main event. The other fights had pushed back the start of this bout, and due to the television schedule, it was downgraded from a six- to a four-rounder. Gaspar outpointed his man and won an unremarkable victory, bringing his official record to 32-3-1.[11] It would be the "rugged" Bombiani's last recorded fight.[12]

From here it was out to the War Memorial Auditorium in Syracuse, New York, to battle a Spaniard named Juan Tejada. Then it was on to Cleveland to fight a Latino based out of Orange, New Jersey, named Tony "Tex" Gonzales. Gonzales was a remarkable fighter who in 1951 had won New Jersey's Intercity Golden Gloves championship in the welterweight division. He brought with him a promising record of eighteen wins, three losses, and one draw. He had already fought at the Garden three times, winning twice and drawing once. In their first Cleveland battle, Gonzales outpointed Ortega to take a six-round decision. The fight was so entertaining that a follow-up match was scheduled at the Cleveland Arena on December 7. This time, Gaspar took the unanimous decision. With the series at one and one, the management got the rubber match (meaning the third fight, or tiebreaker, after a one-to-one record) set up for the Garden for February 10, 1957. Gaspar had made it back to the Center of the Universe.

The scheduled six-rounder was more than most folks in the audience had bargained for. The *New York Times* explained:

> In the semi-final Gaspar Ortega of Tia Juana, Mexico punched his way to a decision over Tony (Tex) Gonzalez [sic] of East Orange, N.J. This fight was packed with excitement and the fans yelled encouragement to the fighters without let-up.
>
> Neither fighter displayed much science. They were content to punch away and Ortega happened to land the more wallops.[13]

As with his earlier contest against Barto, Gaspar had upstaged a main event at the Garden. The ten-round fight between Cuban Isaac Logart and Ramon Fuentes of Los Angeles was "brisk enough, except that it followed a semi-final crammed with six rounds of ceaseless action." The difference between the main event and the first battle was so great that referee Ruby Goldstein had to tell the headlining fighters to "pep it up" on several occasions. Logart, a 3–1 favorite, eventually took a split decision victory over his opponent, who tired visibly toward the end. Many in the audience must have wondered why Fuentes and not Ortega was in the ring against Logart that night.[14]

They wouldn't have to wonder long. On Friday, March 16, 1956, Gaspar got not only his first main event fight in America, against Logart, but also his first televised match. That evening he learned about the television schedule, about the necessity of starting the fight the minute the lights went down and the cameras focused in. This was never a problem for the ever-conscientious Indian, who customarily showed up two hours early for a fight. Stepping into the ring against the world's fourth-ranked welterweight filled Gaspar with tension and anxiety. This was it, the first step on the short staircase to the very top.

Gaspar had actually been in the ring with Logart before on numerous occasions. Happy had made arrangements for Gaspar to be Logart's sparring partner for the Fuentes fight, and he had trained with Logart daily at the Cuban's camp in upstate New York. As Gaspar recalls, he gave Logart such a hard time while sparring that a promoter found out about it and sent someone to watch, who reported back that a matchup between the two men would make good TV.

Like Gaspar, Isaac Logart was an outsider. Born in 1933 in Camaguey, Cuba, "Kid" Logart had been boxing professionally since he was sixteen and now entered the ring a fresh-faced twenty-two-year-old sensation. Having climbed up through the ranks the hard way (back in Cuba he had once earned a mere $1.50 for a main-event fight), he had racked up an impressive 41-5-5 record, with eighteen victories by way of knockout. He was well regarded for his ring speed and lightning-fast punches.[15]

Along with fighters such as Kid Gavilan, Luis Manuel Rodriguez, Benny Paret, Florentino Fernandez, and Nino Valdez, Isaac Logart was part of a wave of Cuban boxers storming the American scene in the 1950s. This made sense. American tourists, businessmen, politicians, and mobsters had long kept the island nation tightly within America's sphere of influence. Hotels like the Tropicana, the Hilton, the Riviera, and the Capri were practically bursting with Americans and American dollars. Ferries and airplanes brought in gringos daily, and a U.S.-friendly dictator, Fulgencio Batista, made sure that his country remained more than hospitable to the greenback.

As influenced by America as he was, Batista did not have to convince his fellow Cubans about the lure of American sports. According to *Ring* magazine in 1954, Cuba was "one of the most sports-conscious localities in the Western Hemisphere."[16] The nation had ready access to American sporting events (airplanes flying over the Florida Keys originally serving as relay antennas), and it even provided a hungry market for American baseball cards and magazines. By 1951 Cuba, the first Latin American country to have television, boasted fourteen thousand sets along with nearly one radio per family.[17] The "fight mob" in Cuba and throughout Latin America all had high expectations for Logart. He was a 5–1 favorite to crush Gaspar.

Gaspar lost. An unexpected snow blizzard struck New York that night, and only one thousand diehard fans showed up at the Garden to watch Logart pound away mercilessly at El Indio. According to the papers, the fans were all quite impressed with Gaspar. They were amazed that he did not get knocked unconscious. Logart sent Gaspar reeling about in the sixth and tenth rounds, firing "wicked left hooks to the body and head," sending blood streaming down Indio's nose and making Jackson Pollack designs on the canvas. Yet Gaspar absorbed everything, not once even hitting the deck. Wrote one sportswriter, "the rangy Indian, 20, game as they come, took everything Logart had to offer and kept firing back to win the plaudits of the slim crowd."[18] Indeed, the fans booed the unanimous decision "as a tribute to the underdog's gameness more than anything else."[19]

Gaspar had entered the ring that night with the hopes and expectations of countless family and countrymen. Televisions across Mexamerica had tuned in. In Tijuana, Gaspar's parents had watched it on a friend's TV. Because Nick Corby had told Gaspar that he would be representing Mexico, he had convinced the fighter to stroll into the ring wearing a massive sombrero. Now that pride was poisoned with shame. It had been a great moment, and he had tried to make his country proud, but he had failed. Nevertheless his family told him that they were very proud of him. And at the very least, now he was famous. As an added bonus, Gillette sent him a care package of razors, towels, and shaving cream.

He still to this day uses that razor.

Joe Cortez first saw Gaspar standing around the stoop of the apartment building talking with his brother Sapo, shortly after Gaspar had returned to New York with his brother in tow. The two brothers wore bomber jackets and had their hands stuffed in their pockets. Gaspar's jacket had an enormous Indian chief head on the back, and Sapo had one with a frog and the words "El Sapo." These two mysterious Mexicans looked so out of place that Joe had to see what they were doing here. He asked them what was going on, to which Gaspar quickly replied, "No hablo inglés." So Joe asked them in his Puerto Rican New York Spanish what their names were. They told him. He asked what they did. They explained that they were boxers. Joe was impressed.

Joe intuited that these two could use a friend, and he was right. Soon, Gaspar was bringing Joe along to Stillman's Gym, where Joe got past Curley for free because he was so young. Joe remembers Stillman: "He was always pissed off at everybody . . . mad at the whole world." Joe remembers Happy as a quiet man with an "obvious" black toupee. He recalls Gaspar's hunchbacked co-manager, Jimmy Stinson, as always wearing a long black coat and hat. Nick Corby was a good-looking "ladies' man."

Joe introduced Gaspar and Sapo to his group of friends, and finally Gaspar began to feel more at home in this big, strange city. He began to learn more about the neighborhood. It was nearly all Puerto Rican and African American. Though poor, Spanish Harlem in those days was relatively safe. Go south on Madison Avenue and the neighborhood suddenly became rich and white. Rich and poor might sometimes elbow each other in parts of Tijuana, but the scale of difference was nothing like this.

As time went on, heroin made its way into the neighborhood. Joe remembers guys passed out in hallways with belts tied around their arms. They used boric acid to cook their drug and soda caps for spoons. Addicts would steal stuff right out of your apartment if you left the door open even a crack—things like radios that could be sold on the streets fast for drug money.

Adventure lurked around every corner. For fun, Joe and his buddies would leap from building to building, across the rooftops, along their compact street. They called it "alley jumping." Gaspar told them they were crazy. One time a kid jumped and broke the loose ceramic edge along the next building, winding up dangling high above an alleyway. The others had to go back and pull him back up by the arms.

Joe was like a sidekick or a younger brother to Gaspar. Joe's parents had split up when he was two, and he needed a relationship like this. He actually became quite useful to Gaspar. Joe would translate Gaspar's Spanish to Jimmy Stinson, and sometimes after fights, he would hang out with Stinson, Corby, and Gaspar as they laid stacks of cash out on a hotel mattress to divide up the fight earnings. Joe would interpret for the Indian, and Stinson would give him five bucks for his help.

Gaspar also met someone else during this time. A girl. Her name was Ida, and she lived two blocks down. Every morning she would stop by Gaspar's building and walk to school with Happy's daughter, Vivian. Gaspar just gawked at her, sticking his head out the high window in silence, his brother Sapo poking his face out too. Ida knew that Gaspar stared, it was so obvious, but she dismissed him. She was a city girl and this Mexican was a bumpkin, "so hick-y." He didn't even speak English. Still, she was intrigued. He was a boxer, and he had a quiet, masculine intensity that attracted her. His shyness even made his gawking a little bit cute. He definitely was nothing like the boys she had grown up with.

Iraida "Ida" Ramirez had come into this world in Peñuelas, Puerto Rico, sixteen years earlier. She had drawn a tough lot in life. Her dad was a wandering merchant marine who toiled in the kitchens of large vessels, and her mom, sadly, was not emotionally equipped to care for her. Ida had been born sickly and her mother, Mercedes, had told her grandmother (her father's mother) that the child would not survive. She left her baby in the grandmother's care, perhaps to protect herself from the pain of a dead child or the pain of a failing relationship, or both. Ida's absent parents split soon after, Ida being the only fruit of their union. They may never have been officially married in the first place.

Ida's dad, Miguel, moved to New York City for work shortly thereafter, followed by his sister and a female cousin. Life in Puerto Rico had been hard and the poverty deep, although the grandparents did at least have their own house, which was saying something. When she was four years old, Ida's grandmother Maria took her to New York City. Puerto Rico would become a distant memory.

They moved into a small apartment on Eighty-Fourth Street between Amsterdam Avenue and Broadway, a big building in a mostly Jewish neighborhood. There was only one room (the shared bathroom was down the hall) for all of them—Ida, her grandmother, an aunt, and the cousin. It was sparse. There were two beds for the four of them, so Ida had to share her grandmother's bed. An old radiator put out heat from coal burned down in the building's basement furnace. Ida remembers the big trucks that dumped the black stuff into a street-level chute and down into the bowels of the building. A few years later, her aunt Palmira got married and the cousin moved out. This was good news, because her cousin (who was in her twenties) teased her relentlessly. Yet for the two who remained in the apartment, it was hard to survive financially. They eventually had to move in with Aunt Palmira over on 131st Street. This was an Anglo neighborhood, and young Ida even made a few white friends. Soon, she and her grandmother moved again, this time to a small apartment they could afford in Spanish Harlem. Here she would meet the young boxer from Tijuana.

The new place was the roughest neighborhood yet for Ida. The apartment building's residents were predominantly poor Puerto Ricans, crammed into run-down hovels and living with crime, drugs, and gang violence. In the hot days of summer, the local kids opened the fire hydrants and directed the spray onto passing cars. Sometimes, the occupants would get out of their vehicles and chase after the kids. Ida remembers the young, tough street urchins who would hang out on the street corners, looking for trouble and finding it. Ida also remembers the glassy look some people had as they stumbled about on the sidewalk, appearing to be on the verge of falling, hooked, probably, on heroin. Soon her terrified grandmother refused to let her leave the house.

Still, she had to go to school, and here Ida managed to get into some trouble of her own. It began well. She participated in after-school activities like basketball, and she tried to get good grades, but soon she was playing hooky, smoking Chesterfields and Camels with friends in Central Park, and running with a bad crowd. Her grandmother was forced to concede that her charge was out of control, so she talked with Miguel and sent her to live with her dad and stepmom, Ramonita, over on Ninety-Ninth Street in a different part of Spanish Harlem. In those days, Ninety-Ninth was racially mixed, as Ida remembers it. She recalls kids playing ball in the streets, singing Doo Wop on the corners and on apartment steps. This place was much nicer than her old street. And now, finally, she got her own room in an apartment that even had its very own bathroom.

The new, safer location, coupled with the strict rules her father laid down, reestablished order in Ida's life. Dad drove a taxi, and Ramonita, whom Ida grew very close to, was a seamstress. Ida reapplied herself to her studies, getting on track to graduate. In the mornings, on her way to class, she would meet her school friend, Vivian Rodriguez, in front of her apartment two buildings down. When the girls met up on the street, out of the window came the heads of the two Mexican fighters who were staying with Vivian's family. One day, one of them stopped by Ida's apartment and, in a painfully shy exchange, told her that he was "dedicating" his upcoming TV fight with Isaac Logart to her. Gaspar lost, as we've seen, and afterward withdrew from her. Then the next thing Ida knew, she and Vivian had been invited to watch Indio fight in person against Hardy "Bazooka" Smallwood at St. Nicholas Arena. The young girl was flattered, and she agreed to go.

The night before the match, Gaspar phoned to tell her, once again, that he was dedicating this upcoming fight to her.

Ida remembers: "I don't know how he got my phone number."

CHAPTER 6

Climb

When sixteen-year-old Ida Ramirez showed up to watch Gaspar fight at St. Nicholas Arena, she was impressed. While not quite the Garden, St. Nick's was still a highly respected boxing venue in New York, holding some four thousand seats. The battle was also a TV fight: the Dumont television network had been broadcasting fights from St. Nick's to New York City and a few other localities since 1954 in the Monday night time-slot. So this was Gaspar's first televised Monday Night Fight. Ida could not help but be nervous for Gaspar. She knew that boxing was a rough game. Plus, she might have liked him a little and didn't want to see him get hurt.

Gaspar's opponent this evening was a man named Hardy "Bazooka" Smallwood. Like Gaspar, Smallwood was familiar with long, hard roads. He had been born in the historically Native American community of Indian Woods, North Carolina, in 1933. His parents were black but told him that his great grandma on his dad's side was a Cherokee. He grew up poor. "We were so poor, we were 'po,'" Smallwood laughingly recalls. "Just 'po.'" Hardy's rural world allowed him to learn to hunt as a child, and he still recalls tracking down rabbits with a cord on frosty winter mornings. Winter was best for rabbit hunting, since "rabbits can't run as fast in the snow."

Hardy grew up without shoes or electricity. He was once bitten on the chest by a moccasin, and he cut the wound open with an old nail and poured snuff into it, just as he had been told to do, to stop the poison. "Even today one side [of my chest] is bigger than the other." He once saw a dead body too, a poor black kid from a chain gang that had been flattening out the land for a new highway. Apparently, the young prisoner had panicked upon seeing a snake and a jittery guard had shot him dead. Nothing happened to the guard.

When Hardy was about six or seven years old, his dad moved them off Indian land in order to make his way as a sharecropper in Wilmington, North Carolina. This didn't work out, so they moved again to Eaton, North Carolina, where his dad got a job at a shipyard. After America entered World War II, the family moved once again, this time to the rumored industrial bounty of the North. They got an apartment in Brooklyn, and Hardy's dad got a job as the super for the building, scrubbing floors and repairing pipes throughout the day. Hardy helped out, and then some: "*I* did the work."

After the Korean War broke out, Hardy signed up for the army. He was shipped out overseas and participated as a forward observer with the Eighth Cavalry in the brutal winter campaign in 1951, fighting in Pusan and other places. He saw men shot to pieces and still recalls dying kids "telling me to 'tell my mother.'" He remembers enemy troops (possibly Chinese) wearing white suits in the dead of winter so they couldn't be seen in the snow.

According to Hardy, he was the first black soldier in the Eighth Cavalry. Following President Truman's 1948 Executive Order 9901 integrating the armed forces, Congress passed the Army Reorganization Act in July 1950, and by early 1951, 10 percent of African American soldiers in Korea were serving in integrated units. Hardy recalls the first day he showed up. He heard a white guy asking, "Where's the nigger at?" and so he loudly responded, "Where's he *at*?" The soldiers saw Hardy and started laughing. Someone told him, "You're all right."

In Korea, Hardy had his brush with destiny. He was out on leave one night, "looking for sex," when he got in a scuffle over a girl with the light heavyweight champion of the Army, of all people. The guy threatened to break Hardy's jaw, to which Hardy answered with four or five quick rights. The big guy went down. The next day, a colonel called on him and said he had seen the whole thing from his car. The officer was impressed and asked Hardy if he was a pro. Hardy explained that he wasn't, but that he had done some amateur fighting, mainly "for watches." "You wanna go pro?" asked the colonel. He told Hardy that if he fought like that in the ring and helped lock in a title for the service, "you'll have it made in the

Army." Hardy was intrigued. At first he thought this white colonel must be crazy or even "punch drunk." But he went along. The colonel's name, he soon learned, was William Westmoreland.

Westmoreland put Hardy in the Special Service so he could fight full time. Smallwood soon got set up to fight the marine middleweight champ, and he knocked the guy out, to Colonel Westmoreland's everlasting pride. In 1952 he even managed to get into the Olympic trials, where he lost early to "some white guy." When he finally mustered out of the army in January 1954, Westmoreland was upset to lose his discovery to the civilian world. Hardy would soon get to know Ray Robinson, who told him he would have to build up his record. "You need one hundred fights to get in this business," he explained. I asked Hardy more about Sugar Ray. "He had an attitude."

Thanks to a friend who happened to be connected with the boxing world, Hardy landed a job doing maintenance work at a Bazooka Joe plant down in shipping and receiving. He worked for ninety cents an hour and was allowed to get off early to train in the afternoons at a local boxing gym. He was talked into picking up "Bazooka" as a ring name. When somebody first suggested it, Hardy didn't like it. "But," the other guy explained, "one bazooka can knock a whole tank out." Fine.

Hardy "Bazooka" Smallwood embarked upon his pro career in June 1954 and won seven of his initial eight fights before getting his first undercard shot at the Garden, where he clinched a four-round decision against Dave Cochran. What was it like to fight in the Garden the first time? "*Wooohoo!*"

Gaspar Ortega was fight number twenty-four for Bazooka. Ida watched in horror as Bazooka beat her date soundly for ten rounds, easily getting the unanimous decision, even flooring Indio temporarily in the fourth.[1] Gaspar hid in his bedroom for days afterward, sullenly recovering. ("He fucked me up.") He was so badly hurt and humiliated that he refused calls from Ida. He didn't see her for two weeks.

With two straight main-event losses, Gaspar's prospects for contention grew dimmer. With nothing good on the horizon, he caught a break when he was booked to fight Gene Poirier at St. Nick's Arena for another Monday night TV battle. The man initially slated to fight Poirier, Danny Giovanelli, had sprained an ankle in training and couldn't fight, so Gaspar was called in at the last minute. Later in his career, Gaspar would be called unlucky. But this is not entirely correct. Sometimes, it was just the opposite. He had made it through a broken neck and a bull's horns. He'd been plucked out of obscurity by a fight manager who didn't even live in Mexico. And now, just as the abyss of insignificance seemed to be opening up once again, another shot availed itself.

Poirier was a tough club fighter from Niagara Falls, New York, with a respectable 15-4-3 record. He had fought at St. Nick's many times. But Gaspar had the experience and, unlike his opponent's three losses by knockout, had yet to be stopped. Gaspar came in as a close 6–5 favorite, though some papers had it at even money. Both fighters fought as though they understood that they had reached a moment of transition. For Poirier, wins seemed to be getting harder to come by. In his past five fights, he had lost twice and gotten one draw. Gaspar, who appreciated that this might be his last TV appearance, knew he had to make a good show of it.

From the start, it was clear that both men were fighting to win. They bloodied each other's noses. A nasty bruise inked over Poirier's right eye. In the sixth round, Poirier briefly wobbled on buckled knees. In the seventh, Gaspar appeared to be heading to the canvas himself, but he managed to reverse the fall and keep moving. In the eighth, Gaspar slipped on the spreading wetness beneath him and toppled over briefly onto the floor. At the end of ten grueling rounds, the two judges and referee compared notes. Referee Roy Miller had it 5-3-2 for Gaspar; Judge Joe Eppy had it 6-4 for Gaspar; and Judge Nick Gamboli had it an even 5-5. The Indian had won, but just barely. The Associated Press card, in fact, called it 5-4-1 for Poirier. Pleased with the battle, promoter Teddy Brenner quickly promised to bring them back together soon.[2] Sadly for Poirier, it was not to be. He had just three fights left in his career, all losses by way of knockout, the next two being administered by Danny Giovanelli (the man Gaspar had replaced that evening). Poirier had retired from the ring by the end of the year. For that matter, the Dumont television network retired that year as well. Its last broadcast was in August 1956. It was a boxing match, of course.

After the Poirier win, Gaspar decided to go back to Tijuana to regroup. He needed time to feel at home, to eat his mother's food, and speak in an easy way with friends. Besides, with his fame growing, the Tijuana fight mob wanted to see him engage in a good, redemptive battle. There was money to be made. Hardy Smallwood was talked into coming down south of the border to fight Indio in a rematch.

Smallwood and Gaspar fought in a Tijuana bullring, the same one where a bull had nearly mauled Gaspar to death a few years earlier. Now he was standing on a hastily constructed platform at its center, before seven or eight thousand hysterical fans. Gaspar was shocked. While he was away, television had made him into a star in his hometown. "The crowd was *crazy*," he remembers. He knew this fight would be a chance to prove himself in front of his friends and family. He decided against the sombrero; there would be no gimmicks. Gaspar knew it "was a different game" down here, and he took strength from the friendly ref and the screaming throng, beating Smallwood handily over the course of ten rounds, dropping his opponent in the tenth and watching in stunned respect as Hardy struggled to his feet and finished the fight upright. Gaspar took the decision and the crowd stormed the ring, hoisting him into the air and parading him around the arena three times.

Five days later, Gaspar strolled around Tijuana a new man, not yet famous enough for instant street recognition but warmed by occasional handshakes and praises. Yet he was also daunted by the new sense that he was carrying his beloved city on his back. It was Mexican Independence Day, September 15. At the town park he joined friends and family, happy amid the pushcarts, food, and games. It was a beautiful day, and he was in a beautiful mood until a man bumped into his brother Sapo and then pushed Indio for getting in his way. Gaspar told the guy not to do that to people, especially to his brother. The guy responded, "I'll push him again, and then you too!" A crowd circled. The man charged and Gaspar hit him once, flush on the face with a straight right. Down the man went. Someone in the crowd remarked, "What a *right*!" Nobody in the crowd seemed to recognize Gaspar (especially not the man currently face down on the grass). Gaspar shook his sore hand and left the festival. The next time he visited his city, anonymity would be a thing of the past.

A month later Gaspar was back in the United States, intent on keeping his American career alive, staring across the ring at Isaac Logart once again. The Logart rematch was a nationally televised Wednesday night fight, held at the Mechanics Building in Boston, in front of a studio audience of 906 people. Logart, now rated number three in the world (one step higher than at his previous encounter with Gaspar seven months earlier) and coming off nine straight victories, was a 4–1 favorite. Angling for a shot at the number one welter contender, Boston's Tony DeMarco, Logart and his management must have decided that a crushing victory over Gaspar, who had proved a game (and easily defeatable) challenger in the past, in front of DeMarco's home crowd would be his ticket.[3]

The first round seemed to justify Logart's choice. The Cuban was cool and collected, methodically thumping away at Gaspar's head and making consistent contact. By all accounts, Logart clearly won the round. Then the "dock brawl" started.[4]

This Gaspar was a different fighter from the man Logart had faced the first time around. By 1956 Gaspar had a full retinue of trainers, cut men, and managers, all helping him be better. Freddie Brown offered key advice and would continue to do so for years to come. He had explained to Gaspar (through Happy) that because Logart was a fast, outside boxer, Gaspar needed to modify his approach. Rather than just flick jabs and work the ring, Indio would need to charge in and cut off his opponent's movement. It was a classic "fight the boxer" strategy. So Gaspar crossed his arms to protect himself and went right after his man. In doing so, he made himself an easy target, and the punishment he took was intense. The first round seemed to suggest that this was an unwise strategy. But Logart was not a terribly hard hitter, and after a few rounds the Cuban started showing signs of exhaustion. By the fourth round, a frustrated Logart tried to go inside and beat Gaspar at his own game, but this didn't work, either. Marveled one reporter, "the husky Mexican relished the exchange as he scored repeatedly during the close exchanges."[5] In the sixth, Gaspar had Logart against the ropes and spinning off to the side, and he fired a left and then a solid right that sent his opponent stumbling across the canvas, nearly falling.[6]

Still, Logart proved up to the challenge of Gaspar's new strategy. He kept scoring hits, often slipping Gaspar's wild punches, and went into the last round slightly ahead on points. But those last three minutes! It seemed as though the Indian had just been biding his time, a jungle cat getting ready to pounce. From his days of Tijuana boxing, Gaspar well understood that the finale was more important than the journey. He burst forth, unleashing flurries of body blows and head shots, firing nonstop like a man possessed, sending Logart reeling. The crowd leapt to its feet, stomping and cheering loudly, still roaring for a full minute after the closing bell had ended the match.

The referee and one judge both gave the fight to Gaspar, while the other judge scored it a tie. Sportswriters were positively shocked at the upset. It was reported that "boxing writers had Logart the winner by a 5–1 margin, while several other veteran ring men also figured the Cuban had won."

Logart had style and finesse and was the journalists' favorite. Gaspar was an unranked imposter who had only "apparently landed enough blows against the stylish Logart to gain the necessary votes."[7] In other words, Indio had duped the judges. Journalists even sensed that it was the crowd, and not Gaspar, that had really won the fight for him. Regardless, he had just defeated the world's number three welterweight.

The fight film reveals a couple of other things worth noting. First, it shows just how green a fighter Gaspar still was at this point in his career. In the seventh round, Logart, who seems to be getting battered into a corner, slips partially through the ropes, and Gaspar actually tries to pull him back in. Logart looks to the referee, utterly bewildered. Second, there are the between-round announcements. The person holding up the big cards is not a sexy lady but some guy in a conservative sweater and slacks. Third, one can see a snapshot of the tight connection between advertising and the fight game. When the scores are being tallied at the end, an announcer says, "Well of course right now nobody can be sure how each round will be scored, but we do know exactly what the score is when men go out to buy an aftershave lotion for themselves. It's Mennen Skinbracer two-to-one over any other brand."

So what next? Gaspar had proven himself a dynamic TV presence with a unique, unpredictable style and a definite willingness to get in there and brawl. Plus, as he had proven long ago to Nick Corby, he was not one to get hit hard and go down. His management struck while the iron was hot. He was soon scheduled to fight another main event at the Garden. This time, it would be against Tony DeMarco, a former world champion and the current number one contender in the welterweight division. Indio had gone from being unranked to taking Logart's place for a shot at the top contender. His career was officially entering the stratosphere.

Like a great many boxers, Tony DeMarco was not using his birth name. He was born Lenardo Liotta, after a dead brother of the same name, in Boston, Massachusetts in 1932. ("I was a reincarnation.") He picked up "Tony DeMarco" from a "guy around the corner" back in 1947, when he discovered at age fifteen that he needed to be eighteen in order to fight as an amateur. So he borrowed the guy's name and baptismal records and registered as Tony DeMarco. He went pro a year later at age sixteen (or nineteen, according to "his" birth record). The story actually gets even more interesting—the real Tony DeMarco soon decided that *he* wanted to fight, so he had to borrow someone else's identity (from neighbor Michael

Chimini), who himself then decided that he *too* wanted to box and thus had to borrow yet another identity (from his brother Marco Chimini).[8]

The man who would become known as Tony DeMarco grew up in the rough, Italian American neighborhood of Boston's North End. His dad was a shoemaker who had immigrated from Sicily years before Tony was born and returned once to find a bride to bring back to America. Tony's parents mainly spoke Italian at home, a cramped apartment in an eight-unit building. He grew up running the mean streets with his friends: "I got to be delinquent a little bit." Tony soon discovered the recreational possibilities of the Boys' Clubs and the Parks Department. "We see a pair of gloves, you put them on, start slapping each other." Play fighting with other kids turned into real boxing, and Tony discovered that he was good at it.

After acquiring his new *nom de ring*, Tony knocked out Armetta "Meteor" Jones in the first round of his first fight and earned himself fifty dollars. DeMarco was short (five feet five), stocky, and mean as hell. He had an aggressive street style and won by simply overwhelming his opponents. This made him a good candidate for television. Though most famously known as the "Boston Bomber," DeMarco seemed to attract nicknames like a magnet. His personal favorite is "The Flame and Fury of Fleet Street" (he was born on Fleet Street).

One year before facing Gaspar, Tony DeMarco had defeated Johnny Saxton at Boston Garden for the welterweight title but then lost it two months later in a brutal defeat to Carmen Basilio. He had tried to take back the belt from Basilio later that year in an epic contest voted *Ring* magazine's "Fight of the Year" but once again had lost. Now he was building up steam for another charge at the title. He had defeated four fighters in a row since Basilio, including the very highly regarded Kid Gavilan. Gaspar Ortega would be another feather in his cap, and it seemed like an easy win. The odds for the fight were 4–1 in DeMarco's favor.

A small crowd, about thirty-two hundred fans, showed up to watch the Garden fight (incidentally, this was DeMarco's debut at Madison Square Garden)[9] on November 23, 1956. As in the last Logart fight, Gaspar got roundly pummeled early on in the match. He showed no fear and charged right in, trying to set the pace and control the match. A stunned Jack Cuddy commented, "He showed no fear of the explosive, stocky boxer from Boston." Though Gaspar balanced these charges with movement and jabs that took advantage of his longer reach, what was most impressive, and for DeMarco most unnerving, was the fact that Gaspar did not seem to have a single strategy. One moment he's flicking jabs and hitting-and-running, and the next he's going toe-to-toe with the notorious slugger (even, a journalist noted, "when it appeared he would have been more effective boxing at long range").[10] The overall impression on DeMarco was uncertainty. Gaspar fought as "a very awkward individual. Kinda tall with an awkward style."[11]

DeMarco thought he might have been able to put down his man a few times in the contest. In the fourth round, he pounded Gaspar so fiercely that the Indian looked wobbly enough for referee Al Berl to consider stopping the bout, but Gaspar had gotten out of the line of fire and had recovered enough to keep the match alive. In the fifth, a right to the chin again sent Gaspar stumbling, to the point where his gloves scraped the canvas (Berl ruled it a slip). Again Gaspar came back, closing in to brawl with the hard-hitting North Ender against all logic. By the end of the fight, blood streamed from a high gash on Gaspar's forehead as well as from his nose. DeMarco had sustained a cut above his left eye.

The fight was close by all accounts. The referee and one judge gave the fight to Gaspar, while the other judge gave it to DeMarco. The press this time was less unkind to the Indian. A ringside poll of journalists after the fight had it 8-4-1 for Demarco.[12] One reporter seemed awed by the little-known Mexican's "second shocking upset in six weeks."[13] Later in his dressing room, DeMarco just couldn't figure out what happened. "I was more disappointed in myself than in the decision. . . . It was one of those nights." Gaspar's manager Jimmy Stinson told the press that "it always happens when they make [Gaspar] a big underdog," pointing out that nobody had figured Gaspar would beat Logart, either.[14]

Because the results were so unexpected, Gaspar's defeat of DeMarco did not earn him a shot at the title. Rather, it earned him a rematch with DeMarco. Within days, a second match was set for December 21, 1956. Back home in Tijuana, friends and family could not believe what they had just seen on TV. Even there, people thought that the fight had been a fluke, and that now DeMarco would be really angry and destroy the Tijuana upstart. When Gaspar's mom heard about the upcoming rematch, she had one of her premonitions. Gaspar would not survive. Family members took this vision so seriously that they paid to send Jefa to New York City so she could be with her son. It was her first plane ride. After she touched down at LaGuardia, she looked for a cab driver who spoke Spanish.

"You speak Spanish?" she asked one.

"Yes," he answered in a Puerto Rican inflection.

"I'm looking for my son. He lives in New York."

"You have an address?"

"No. Everyone knows him. He's Gaspar Ortega."

In Tijuana, such instructions would suffice. But Sebastiana Ortega had just arrived in one of the world's largest metropolises. It was an astounding cultural misread. And yet the cabbie was, like many other young men, a boxing fanatic. He knew exactly whom she was talking about and told this tiny woman, "I'll find your son." He picked up her one bag and then went to a pay phone and called Madison Square Garden. They gave him the number of Jimmy Stinson, whom he then called. Jimmy gave the cabbie the address. Stinson then called Happy and told him that Gaspar's mom was on the way over. Happy told Gaspar, who promptly bounded downstairs and waited on the street for a full hour until his beloved mom arrived. When she did, the cabbie smiled at the boxer and told him, "*siete* [seven] dollars." Gaspar gave him fifty.

Sebastiana slept on the couch and worried for her son. She gave him the standard advice: "If he hits you once, hit him back twice." She couldn't help but feel something terrible was going to happen. Gaspar went into his rematch now ranked number four in the world, still behind DeMarco (ranked number one according to the National Boxing Association and number two according to *Ring* magazine) but fully visible in the glaring lights of the highest level of the sport.

Gaspar was finally being taken seriously, having been upgraded from a 4–1 underdog to a 2–1 underdog for this fight. It was shaping up to be "another thriller," one journalist wrote. The theme of the fight was clear: "revenge." DeMarco told reporters, "I'll be heavier this time [he had last fought at 145½ to Gaspar's 147½]. I was too light then. I left my fight in the gymnasium."[15] He also tried retroactively to correct the past. "I don't think he beat me last time. I thought I won, looking lousy. The trouble was that I was a big favorite and everybody expected more." He then turned to another explanation: Gaspar's style was too confusing. "He's an awkward fighter, a hard guy to figure out."[16] With really no basis, Gaspar was now described in the papers as a "the cocky young Indian from Mexicali" out to "prove his previous victory over DeMarco no fluke." If he won, he would be "yelling distance, at least, of the throne room."[17] His past two victories had made him dangerous. If Indio were to win again, it would be time to take him "seriously" as a challenger for the belt.[18]

Both fighters came out slugging—no boxing this time around. Then a shock right at the start: after a fierce round one exchange, Gaspar delivered an uppercut that sent DeMarco hurtling through the ropes and onto the ring skirt. As the referee counted, Gaspar watched as DeMarco struggled up, helped along by hands from the audience pushing the Boston Bomber back in just before the referee would have said "ten." Then proceeded nine rounds of some of the wildest combat seen at the Center of the Universe. A reporter called it "one of the best fights of the year in Madison Square Garden."[19]

At the end, the decision was even closer than the previous one, the fight having to be settled by New York's supplementary points system. The referee and one judge had the fight even on rounds, with Gaspar just ahead on points. The other judge had the fight in favor of DeMarco six rounds to four. As it turned out, what this meant was that Gaspar had won. And this time, for the first time, the ringside poll of sportswriters had the Indian ahead, eight to six (with one calling it a draw).[20] Gaspar had just defeated the world's top-ranked welterweight fighter for the second time in a row. DeMarco thought that he had won the fight. When I told him about Sebastiana's premonition, he chuckled, "I'm glad I lost then."[21]

Now the iron was red hot. Jimmy Stinson told the press that Gaspar had earned his shot at the title. "We want Basilio—or Saxton, if he beats him—and nobody else. We beat the top contender, now we want the champion."[22] This sense of strength was seconded by Harry Markson, the managing director of the International Boxing Club, who said, "Ortega's ready to fight any welterweight in the world now." One sportswriter humorously reported that "a glittery-eyed young Indian from Mexicali, Mexico, war-whooped loudly for a shot at the welterweight bonnet today."[23] As for Sebastiana, she was ready to go back to Mexico. She demanded to return the day after the fight, but Gaspar talked her into staying a few more weeks. Once home, she would never return to the Big Apple. Gaspar himself was on cloud nine and wanted his mother to share the city with him. It was clear that he had finally earned a ticket to the big show. He began to think about how to take down Carmen Basilio. He believed that his speed was the key—Basilio was a hard-hitter, but he was slow.

The throne room was finally in sight.

CHAPTER 7

The Tournament

The Indian had taken the boxing world by storm. Since his first televised fight in March 1956, Gaspar Ortega had ascended from the mass of the unranked to nearly the top of his class. Coming into 1957, Gaspar was the number two–ranked welterweight in the world. He had won five straight matches against top-notch boxers. His odd style had "caught the fancy of fight fans and fistic experts alike," enthused one sportswriter. He was "lithe and graceful" and possessed "dazzling speed." This made for great TV; Don Dunphy would later remark that Gaspar was "never in a dull bout." Another journalist located Indio's appeal in his ring personality: "Many fighters wear an imperturbable mask for a face during combat. Not Ortega. He grimaces and frowns and talks to himself. The fans, watching him, feel themselves being pulled into the ring action almost bodily." He was popular because "he was exciting to watch." So exciting was his recent battle with Tony DeMarco, in fact, that the National Boxing Association (NBA) named Indio boxer of the month in early January 1957.[1]

As Gaspar's fame grew, those around him benefited. Nick Corby finally had a winning boxer on his hands. Manager Jimmy Stinson, now fully out of boxing exile, was pleased to orate his opinions to listening reporters. He was still working at his bank day job, Stinson told them, but he had his reasons. "You can't make a living out of boxing alone today," he explained. "That's why a matchmaker can't even call me at the bank. I don't give anybody my number. I don't want boxing to interfere with the bank. But the minute it hits five o'clock, I'm a manager. I'm at the Garden looking for a match. Or I'm up at the gym to watch the kid work." And Stinson liked what he saw. "This kid," he boasted, "is starting to see punches. He picks them off. . . . With all that height he can outbox anybody." A man of the Old School, Jimmy was pleased to say that Gaspar possessed a defensive capability. He had been paying attention to the changes to the sport wrought by the small screen. Fortunately, Gaspar could counterpunch, block, and move, unlike most of "these television fighters." They come in, Stinson griped, "without knowing anything." They wound up "putting on main events that [look] like two comedians in a I'll-slap-you, you-slap-me act."[2]

Gaspar was optimistic, fully believing that his second defeat of De-Marco was his ticket to the top. Considering that the current number one contender, Johnny Saxton, was set to fight champion Carmen Basilio, it was only logical that Gaspar, ranked number two, should be preparing to fight the winner of that match for the world title. Nick Corby and numerous sportswriters had stated as much in the press after Indio beat DeMarco in December 1956. It seemed strange, then, that instead of preparing for a title shot, Gaspar found himself preparing to battle Tony DeMarco yet again.

Gaspar today feels that his management was "using" him. He had virtually no command of English and was naïve to boot, a fighter who just took the matches that he was given. And this match seemed like a setup for failure. The third straight fight with DeMarco was to be held in the Boston Bomber's home town. It is not entirely clear why this third fight was scheduled. Surely, money was behind it. Perhaps waiting for the Basilio-Saxton fight meant lost opportunities for fast cash, which was to be had if Gaspar went to Boston Garden and battled the down-but-not-quite-out local hero. A day after the Ortega-DeMarco bout was announced, Carmen Basilio said that he would delay his title defense for five weeks due to his hurt hand, so this third DeMarco fight might have happened regardless. Still, there remains the fact that this was a fight where the Indian had everything to lose and nothing to gain. He had already beaten DeMarco twice, had bumped the Bostonian down in the rankings, and had set himself up in the second contender spot. Why risk it with a guy who he had only defeated in close decisions, and why on that man's own turf? It does raise the possibility that something was not on the level. Interestingly, there was a sudden shift in DeMarco's management just before this fight was scheduled. The day before the match was announced, DeMarco got new representation by an IBC-friendly promoter, who replaced his old promoter, Sam Silverman. Silverman raged in the press that the IBC was "trying to put me out of business." DeMarco's longtime advisor, Rip

Valenti, went along with the switch because he knew that the IBC represented the only means of positioning DeMarco for a chance at regaining the title. Valenti agreed to the new promoter because "Tony needs to beat this guy to get in line for the winner of the Basilio and (Johnny) Saxton title fight a week from Friday." It was as if Gaspar was an unfortunate obstacle that needed to be cleared rather than a legitimate contender to the throne. Someone in the IBC, apparently, had decided that DeMarco was to be given yet another chance to redeem himself—in his hometown, in an untelevised match—so that he could move ahead of Gaspar in line.[3]

The third Ortega-DeMarco fight generated considerable frenzy in Bean Town. A huge gate was expected. DeMarco's team recognized that if he lost again, his chances for regaining the title would be distant. As one reporter summarized, DeMarco was "at the crossroads of his fistic career."[4] Another wrote that a third straight loss would "bounce the pride of Boston right out of the welterweight picture." His backers understood the situation, knowing that Tony would be "going for broke" in this one.[5] Nearly ten thousand fans filled the Boston Garden to watch him try. It was a boisterous, partisan crowd; Boston's Garden was located literally down the street from where DeMarco grew up.

In Boston, Gaspar learned what it meant to be hated. The whole town seemed to rise up against him. He got the silent treatment when he worked out at a local gym. On a morning run before the fight, a car slowed down next to him and a man leaned out the window and shouted, "He's going to kill you, you motherfucking Mexican!" Gaspar flipped him off, but he was rattled. On fight night, it got really scary. First there was the deafening roar whenever DeMarco threw a glove, and a deafening silence whenever Gaspar rallied ("when he threw punches the whole place was about to fall down. When I punch it was more quiet than a church"). Sapo, who attended the fight at ringside, found that his presence was not desired, either. As he cheered on his brother, someone actually pressed a knife to his neck and told him to "shut up." He did.

In preparation for the match, DeMarco had thought a lot about Gaspar's style and chose to listen to his corner's advice closely. Rather than simply brawl, as was his wont, he decided to fight a more calculated battle. He would work the body more and defend his own. Additionally, DeMarco planned to switch his style a little bit each round in order to counter the Indian's slippery tactics with some trickery of his own.

The crowd erupted when the first-round bell rang. Both boxers came out fighting, trading blows in what seemed to be an even matchup (though at least one writer believed the early rounds were a bit too cautious and uneventful). As the fight proceeded, however, it looked as though DeMarco finally had Gaspar's number. The Boston Bomber guarded his middle and fired precise shots at the Indian's torso. Gaspar tried to keep DeMarco off balance, but to no avail. DeMarco was connecting much more often—two or three solid blows to Gaspar's one. Several times, Gaspar seemed wobbly, and he clinched his opponent as though he needed support to stay on his feet. In the fourth round the Indian attempted a rally, but DeMarco kept right on coming. In the eighth, Ortega connected solidly with DeMarco's jaw, but this only sent the Bomber into a wild frenzy, which Gaspar cooled off only after much clinching. Though "outclassed," in the words of one reporter, Ortega never went to the mat. Not for a lack of effort on DeMarco's part. He was trying to destroy Gaspar. His performance was epic; he "displayed flashes of his old slugging power."[6]

The referee and both judges awarded the fight to DeMarco by wide margins, as did the United Press. In the locker room, DeMarco told reporters, "This one was a big one and I beat him because I kept my head. I fought the calculated fight that my corner told me to fight, switching my attack during each round. This fight meant either the small time, no money fights, or some more important fights." Gaspar glumly told reporters (through Happy), "I lost because I was nervous, too anxious to knock him out. And the crowd, too, which was all for DeMarco, helped to upset me. I'll fight him again any time—but not in Boston."[7]

DeMarco was right about the fight being his return pass to the big time. He went on to defeat Larry Boardman in front of thirteen thousand screaming fans in Boston in March, and shortly thereafter his new promoter, Johnny Buckley, offered champion Carmen Basilio one hundred thousand dollars to fight his man at Boston Garden.[8] Basilio himself had easily defeated Johnny Saxton in Cleveland in February to retain his welterweight title. The offer to fight DeMarco in Boston must surely have been alluring—especially since the Marine had beaten the Bostonian twice before. However, Basilio made no commitments. He was biding his time, eyeing the even bigger purses in the heavier middleweight division. Besides, Basilio was convinced there were no real challenges left for him in his current weight class. He had already told the press as much: "I don't believe there are any welterweights out there that can lick me." The current middleweight champion of the world was a man named Gene Fullmer, an elder of the Church of Jesus Christ of Latter-day Saints who was anything but saintly in the ring. Fullmer had taken a humiliating 12.5 percent of the gate to Robinson's 50 percent in their January 2 title matchup and had pounded Robinson, the champion, to a pulp over the course of fifteen rounds. Now Basilio wanted a shot at Fullmer's title and was in talks to take on the winner of the upcoming Robinson-Fullmer rematch. The problem, as ever with Robinson, was that Sugar Ray was a wily negotiator and was averse to advance commitments. So Basilio, along with every other welter hopeful, waited.

A week after the DeMarco catastrophe, Gaspar married Ida in a small ceremony at a friend's apartment. Ever since Ida had witnessed Gaspar's beating at the hands of Bazooka Smallwood ten months earlier, the two had steadily been growing closer. There was in fact another suitor, Segundo Perez, who liked Ida, but Gaspar quickly made it known that this was his girl. For Ida's strict Puerto Rican father, of course, there would be no dating of any kind for his daughter. So Gaspar had to meet with Ida clandestinely before and after school, or "bump into her" at a local market at pre-arranged times. Sometimes they would meet on the roof of her apartment building. Since there were no spaces between the buildings on their street, Gaspar would ascend the steps to his roof and head over to Ida's building, then whistle down to her fourth-floor window. She would listen out for him and, when she heard the whistle, would invent some excuse to leave. Sometimes, Gaspar sent notes down on a string. He smiles now thinking about the whole charade. Gaspar aggressively courted Ida, but she was streetwise and easily his match in the wiles department. Sitting at their table in the suburb they currently live in, the old boxer looked over to his wife with a boyish grin as she related their romance: "you always were able to make up a story, find an excuse." Apparently, Ida's father was none the wiser about his daughter's mysterious, sudden "library trips."

Their secret was finally outed by an old woman who lived in Ida's building. In those days, everyone in the building—even in their block of buildings—knew everyone else. It felt like a big, sprawling family. The old woman knew both Happy's family and Ida's dad, and she told Mr. Ramirez that his daughter was seeing a young man named Gaspar who lived down the way. The woman tried to be helpful, telling Mr. Ramirez that Gaspar was a nice boy and that he and Ida should be allowed to date. But Ida's dad was furious. *Who was this guy? What kind of family did he come from?* Father told Ida that she was making a big mistake, that Gaspar was probably already married with all this sneaking around. Then he announced that the relationship was over, period. Gaspar found out and in a panic

wrote a letter to his parents in Tijuana, begging for help. Gaspar's father
Aniseto replied with a letter to Mr. Ramirez, in which he explained that
while Gaspar's family had no money, his boy was not married and was
a worthy son. Apparently, this—and the undoubted pressure put on Mr.
Ramirez from his wife Ramonita, who adored Ida—caused him to relent.
Mr. Ramirez did lay down one important rule for the two lovebirds: "You
say goodnight *inside* the house, not outside."

Freed from secrecy, Gaspar and Ida went out on the town constantly.
Gaspar introduced Ida to his Spanish-speaking Church of Our Lady Guadalupe down on West Fourteenth Street, a place frequented by Mexican
immigrants. He also took her to the Spanish-language movie theater five
blocks away, where Ida discovered the classic films of Jorge Negrete, the
Singing Cowboy. At such places Ida began to learn about Mexican culture, really for the first time in her life. She noted the differences between
her Puerto Rican Spanish and Gaspar's Mexican version of the language.
Vituallas (beans) were *frijoles* in Mexico. A *guagua* (bus) was an *autobus*.
Orita, meaning "later on" for her, meant "now" for Gaspar. At times she
felt like she had to master an entirely new lexicon.

After the DeMarco loss, Gaspar decided that it was time to return to
Mexico yet again to recharge. He knew he loved Ida and struggled with
what to do. He could not leave her. So he asked her dad for her hand in
marriage. Mr. Ramirez assented, and shortly thereafter the two wed. For
the ceremony, they rented everything—her gown, his tux, the presiding
justice of the peace. The very next day the newlyweds got on a plane for
San Diego, where Nick Corby picked them up and drove them south to
the border. There they met the mob.

Ida already knew that her new husband was a well-known boxer, but
she had absolutely no idea that he was a bona fide celebrity in Tijuana.
When Gaspar fought on TV, signs would go up around his home city
advertising it. On fight night, folks would crowd into bars to watch or
gather out on the streets in front of shop windows staring at televisions
placed facing outward. Everyone talked about the man called Indio. Everyone held their breath when his opponents attacked him. You could
hear echoes of "Mexico!" and "Tijuana!" in the streets and bars when
Gaspar swung away on the small screen.

A shiny convertible picked Gaspar and Ida up at the border, and they
paraded down *Revolucíon* with the top down, surrounded by a detail of
Tijuana policemen, slowly coasting through enormous, cheering crowds.
They stayed at the Hotel Caesar (a swank spot where, back in 1930, chef

Caesar Cardini had invented his eponymous salad) on the corner of Fifth and *Revolucíon*. It was absolutely insane. Girls and assorted fans were always trying to sneak past the guards to see Gaspar, and hordes met him and Ida whenever they went out. Gaspar decided to send Ida to stay with his parents at the house. To get himself some peace, Gaspar moved into a small apartment. He needed to focus. He was training for a charity match against Miguel Burciaga, and his family's house was far too crowded.

Staying with Gaspar's family in Tijuana, Ida felt profoundly alone, shocked by the cultural divide she had just crossed. Everyone thought her accent was "hilarious." As a New Yorker, Ida had grown up accustomed to running water and indoor plumbing. Here, she discovered the wonders of outhouses and unpaved streets. She soldiered on for about a month, playing the freshly discovered role of celebrity wife. Gaspar fought Burciaga in a terribly lopsided match in which Burciaga went down in the second round after a sad display of fear and flight. The crowd booed. Gaspar donated his purse to the Red Cross. Burciaga kept his.

The newlyweds shuttled back to New York City for Gaspar's next battle with Isaac Logart set for May 10, 1957. Despite the DeMarco setback, the Logart fight promised to reopen a door to the title. With Carmen Basilio still waiting around for a shot at the middleweight crown (Robinson had beaten Fullmer in a May 1 rematch, but Robinson and Basilio had yet to agree on terms for the division of the payday, with Robinson using the excuse of waiting on the winner of the upcoming Fullmer–Tiger Jones fight as a pressure tactic) and not willing to risk his own title on a top welterweight challenger, the other contenders plotted to position themselves as best they could. Some felt that if Basilio did not vacate his title when he went after the middleweight crown, the winner of the Logart-Ortega fight should get a shot at Basilio. (It went unexplained what would happen to DeMarco in this case.) On the other hand, if Basilio decided instead to vacate the welter title and go up to fight Robinson, then the winner of Logart-Ortega might fight DeMarco for the open title. The nebulous traditions of boxing kept reporters guessing.

Gaspar recalls his management told him that if he won the Logart fight, he would have a shot at the title. Indeed, the press touted the Logart-Ortega fight as a "welterweight elimination bout." Furthermore, as a rubber match, this battle would supposedly decide which of these top-ranked fighters was superior once and for all. Logart was ranked number three and Gaspar number two. The press anticipated an epic contest full of significance, a "12-round elimination match to determine who gets first chance at Carmen Basilio's welterweight crown." Both camps, it was explained, were in the process of preparing to "post a challenge bond with the State Athletic Commission" for Basilio's presumed soon-to-be-vacated title.[9]

For his part, Isaac Logart had not taken his past loss to the Indian well; he was described as being "an angry fighter" ever since. Like others decisioned by the unconventional Mexamerican, Logart believed he had been robbed. As his trainer Mundito Medina explained to reporters, "Logart beat [Gaspar] both times and will prove it once and for all tomorrow night." Gaspar, in turn, was described as a feisty young contender with an exciting back story. His strange past made for great copy. He'd arrived in America "with $5 and a bag of sandwiches" in 1954 and had "picked up ring savvy since he entered the television circuit." According to the *New York Times*, Gaspar had actually learned much of his ring smarts only since his arrival in New York, having "vastly improved" between the first and second Logart fights. (A few years later, the theme of the "mediocre fighter who improved" would be echoed in the Tijuana press to great effect). Although Gaspar was favored to win 7–5 the day before the fight, the odds began to change; Logart was favored 2–1 on fight day.[10]

The fight itself, a nationally televised contest held at the War Memorial Auditorium in Syracuse, drew a disappointing two thousand locals. It was, by all accounts, an exciting battle. In the second round, Gaspar fired three consecutive rights to Logart's jaw that sent him reeling. Logart returned with a low blow that dropped Indio to one knee. Referee Al Berl gave Gasper three or four seconds to recover, and the fierce match resumed. In the eleventh, Gaspar found his second wind and surged ahead on the scorecards, ending the fight with a dramatic, hard-hitting rally. The two judges split over who won. Luckily for Gaspar, tie-breaking referee Berl had Gaspar ahead 7-4-1. The Associated Press scorecard also had Gaspar ahead. The Indian had pulled out an important victory. The *Times* helpfully noted that the fight "increased [Gaspar's] hopes for a title match" with Basilio. Another paper declared even more strongly that the Indian had now finally "earned a shot at the welterweight crown." The New York State Athletic Commission agreed that Gaspar would be considered "most seriously" for a shot at Basilio's belt.[11]

Gaspar was in for disappointment. In early June 1957, Carmen Basilio signed a contract to fight Sugar Ray Robinson for the middleweight title in Yankee Stadium in September. He would not relinquish his title beforehand. While Basilio's earnings would pale in comparison to what Robinson would receive (he got 20 percent to Robinson's 45 percent), he still stood to earn north of one million dollars for the fight. Only when he won would his welterweight title be vacant; only then would some sort of tournament get underway. During the wait, a dispirited Gaspar took two consecutive fights in Miami Beach and lost both. ("I always lose in Florida.") The first was to a nobody named Larry Baker. The second was to a fierce Cuban named Kid Gavilan, the same fighter who had annihilated Chuck Davey on TV back in 1953. Gavilan was famous for his "bolo punch," in which he would wind his arm dramatically and swing his fist upwards. The "Keed," as the press insisted on referring to him, claimed that he had adapted this unique punch from his youthful experiences cutting sugarcane in the fields. So famous was the bolo punch that sportswriters debated its power. Did it really pack more force than a regular punch? Did it merely fool one's opponent? Was it just showboating? Whatever it did, the infamous bolo sure occupied Gaspar's thoughts. He trained specifically to avoid it. Though he managed to dodge Gavilan's windmill windups in Miami Beach, he still lost.

In September 1957, Carmen Basilio defeated Sugar Ray Robinson in front of thirty-eight thousand fans at Yankee Stadium to clinch the middleweight title. After the fifteen-round bloodbath, NBC radio announcer Winn Elliott explained that Basilio "is a throwback to the caveman. I don't mean that in a disparaging sense."[12] As per the rules, the welterweight title was now open.

The boxing world was abuzz with the vacancy. The top welters and their promoters began jockeying to position themselves for a title shot. West Coast matchmaker Jackie Leonard ambitiously tried to create his own tournament for the belt. He set up a new bout between Gaspar and Kid Gavilan to be held at Los Angeles's Wrigley Field in October. Then he offered both Tony DeMarco and Vince Martinez forty thousand dollars, or 30 percent of the gate, to fight the winner for the title. Martinez's camp accepted. DeMarco did not go for it. Leonard knew why: "It's doubtful DeMarco will accept this offer, however, because he seldom fights out of his home town of Boston."[13]

Since the Miami debacle, Gaspar had returned to Tijuana. He took his now-pregnant wife to live in a new house he had purchased for his parents in Colonia Morelos. Once there, he started to pick up some fights for fast cash. He battled his old Baja nemesis Dave Cervantes in Juarez and beat him. Cervantes wisely avoided putting his Baja California title on the line now.

Gaspar and Ida's first baby was due around the time of the scheduled Wrigley Field elimination match, so-called, with Gavilan. Gavilan got sick and the fight was moved from October 15 to the twenty-second. As with many first babies, Ida's child decided to arrive late. As Gaspar prepared for Gavilan and his dreaded bolo punch, the couple decided that she would come up from Tijuana to Los Angeles to watch him fight. Ida felt good; no labor pains yet.

Promoter Jackie Leonard expected a big showing at Wrigley Field, considering that Los Angeles was just up the road from Gaspar's hometown. Born Leonard Blakely, Jackie Leonard (a name he acquired in his boxing days) was a fast-talking hustler who was using this fight as part of his personal campaign to get access to TV's river of money. He had talked himself into being the IBC's West Coast promoter and got named president of the newly created Hollywood Boxing and Wrestling Club. In exchange, Leonard went into debt with the IBC for twenty-eight thousand dollars. Capitalizing on the uncertainty of the vacant title, Leonard sold the Ortega-Gavilan fight as an elimination match for the welterweight belt. He now claimed another tournament match would be held in early February 1958, after which the winner would battle Vince Martinez for the crown.[14]

Leonard had a lot riding on this fight. Wrigley Field was a big venue to rent out for a nontitle affair. Built in 1925 for the Los Angeles Angels baseball team of the Pacific Coast League by chewing gum tycoon William K. Wrigley, the South Central L.A. stadium held about twenty-two thousand people in its stands.[15] The question was whether or not this fight could put bodies in the seats. Beside the fact that it was not entirely clear whether this fight was really an elimination match, some thought that Gavilan was over the hill and unable to put on a show worth paying for. To counter this, sportswriters took pains to note that Gavilan looked as "sharp now as in 1951 when he held the title." Besides, Gavilan had "far too many guns for the Tijuana upstart, who bolted into the limelight just one year ago." Another reporter tackled the age question directly: "Gavilan too old? Over the hill? The Kid grins and in broken English replies: 'I always fight. No old. Look at Archie Moore. Sugar Ray Robinson. Both older than Gavilan.'" Gaspar himself was dismissed as a "nobody" who had "zoomed overnight into title contention."[16]

Unfortunately for the overleveraged Leonard (who was also indebted to mobster Frankie Carbo), the Gavilan-Ortega fight did not draw well.

Wrigley Field was about 75 percent empty that night. Nor was the fight destined to be an elimination for anything. Still, it was a close, exciting battle. Gaspar and his opponent drove briskly at each other. Gaspar effectively neutralized the bolo punch and controlled Gavilan's damaging left hook. When the split decision was announced in Gaspar's favor, many in the crowd booed, and a flurry of ringside reporters cried "robbery." Gavilan, who had lost six of his last seven fights in "hairline decisions" (his one win being his prior victory over Gaspar in Miami), now seemed destined for the fistic dustbin. One reporter who agreed with the decision called Kid Gavilan "way over the hill" and "washed up." The Kid would fight only four more times in his life, losing half of them. As for Gaspar, another "scalp" had been added to his "war belt."[17]

Minutes after the decision was announced, Nick Corby pulled Gaspar aside and said, "You're the *jefe*, you're the father!" "Of who?" "Of Kid Gavilan! . . . and a baby boy!" Gaspar was thrilled. "He was born in the seventh," Corby told him. The night before, Ida had had labor pains and gone to the hospital, where she remained for the day of the fight. Gaspar had been checking in on her intermittently ever since. After the weigh-in, he had hung around the hospital until Ida ordered him to report to the arena: "You can't help me here. You'd better go back." Someone had found Nick during the fight and told him the good news, but he had kept it from Gaspar until the end of the bout to keep his fighter focused.

The two men ran back to the dressing room and got changed, and then Nick drove Gaspar to the hospital. The admitting nurse looked at the bruised young man and mistook him for a new patient. Corby quickly explained why they were here, and soon Gaspar was whisked back to see his new son. The baby had a thick shock of black hair that stuck straight up. The next morning, Gaspar returned to the hospital to visit his wife and child. He told the nurse that he was called Gaspar Ortega but that his real last name was Benitez. The RN went to the nursery and came back with a baby. Who was black. "That's not my kid!" exclaimed Gaspar. They checked the wristband: "M. Benito." The nurse went back and returned with the right baby.

On November 1, 1957, Julius Helfand, chairman of the World Championship Committee and New York State Athletic Commission, announced the six contenders for the upcoming "official" welterweight tournament. He named George Barnes (British Empire champion from Australia), Virgil Akins, Isaac Logart, Vince Martinez, Gil Turner, and Gaspar Ortega. Tony DeMarco was supposed to be on that list, being ranked number three in the world by *Ring* magazine, but just days before he had been knocked out by Virgil Akins in Boston. By the time Akins finished DeMarco off in the fourteenth round, the Boston Bomber had visited the canvas a staggering six times. The fight boosted Akins from sixth to second place in the rankings and blasted DeMarco right off the tournament list. This was too bad for DeMarco, who had put up a game effort (he even put Akins down on the mat once). The peculiar issue now was that Akins was contracted for a DeMarco rematch in January 1958; so while DeMarco was technically out of the running, something of a side door to the belt still appeared to be open for him.

The tournament was to begin as soon as possible, Helfand declared. He gave the contenders until November 11 to sign on. The fighters, if they signed, were to face off in bouts of not less than twelve rounds. Helfand also stipulated that there had to be more than one cycle of fights and that the title must to go to the winner of a fifteen-round battle between the top two finalists. He hoped that the crown would be awarded by March 15, 1958.[18] All of the boxers accepted—Ortega first—though a few grumbled about the setup. Virgil Akins's manager, Eddie Yawitz, who believed his man should have an immediate shot at the title, called the tournament "a joke." He claimed to have been told by National Boxing Association higher-ups that the DeMarco victory had put his man "at the top of the heap."[19] DeMarco, after all, had been the number one contender when they had fought. Akins sent Helfand an indignant telegram, reprinted in the papers: "I am the champion of the welterweight division and I will fight any contender you or any other commission designates me to defend my title against. Thank you very much." The commission did not agree (though the state of Massachusetts recognized him as welterweight champ), and he reluctantly got on board.[20] Isaac Logart's manager, Eddie Mafuz, asked that his boxer get a bye for the first round because he was currently officially ranked number one by the National Boxing Association and *Ring* magazine. This, too, was declined. Eddie Yawitz then tried to get Akins out of the DeMarco rematch set for late January, explaining, "DeMarco can wait. We've already beaten him."[21] Indeed, Helfand recognized Akins's dilemma. He openly pondered that Akins wouldn't have time to fight consecutively a tournament opponent, then DeMarco again, and then another tournament opponent. The question lingered on unresolved. DeMarco's camp wasn't anywhere near ready to let go of their man's title hopes.[22]

Plans for matchups were soon in the works. Gaspar was assigned to fight his old nemesis, Isaac Logart; Vince Martinez got set to battle Gil

Turner; and Virgil Akins, unfortunately, had to first wade through De-Marco again before joining the tournament. British Empire champion George Barnes had not agreed to fight anyone yet, balking that there was not enough money in it for him. On January 23, 1958, the papers reported that the Australian had withdrawn from the tournament entirely.[23]

The Ortega-Logart fight kicked things off in December 1957. The battle took place at the Cleveland Arena and was another nationally televised Friday Night Fight on NBC. Having beaten Logart two times in a row, Gaspar still found himself a slight underdog, likely due to his being behind Logart in the rankings.[24] Happy Rodriguez told the press that his fighter was not worried. "We're never bothered by ratings, and that's why Logart doesn't worry us. Ratings are just opinions."[25]

A total of 6,314 fans showed up on a cold December night in Cleveland hoping to watch an exciting battle. They were in for a disappointment. At various times, both fighters accused the other of low blows. In the third round, Gaspar collapsed to his knees, complaining of a low blow, which caused one of the judges to dock Logart a point. In the intermission between the third and fourth, the referee warned Logart's handlers that *they* were complaining too much about Gaspar hitting below the belt. In the seventh, the ref gave Gaspar a formal warning about hitting low. Gaspar believes the real problem in that fight was the fact that Logart stayed flat-footed and "never attacked." It was just plain frustrating. In the ninth round, Logart found an opening and sent Gaspar cascading into the ropes and down, but the referee did not begin a count. Despite some flurries of actual combat toward the end that brought the crowd to its feet, the fight was largely unremarkable. The unanimous decision went to Logart. Gaspar was out of the tournament.[26]

On January 15, 1958, Vince Martinez beat Gil Turner in Turner's hometown of Philadelphia in a split decision (ringside reporters felt his win was completely obvious, which is why Turner lost the decision in that mob-controlled town). The field narrowed to four men. The next fight was the Boston rematch between Akins and DeMarco, which technically was not part of the tournament. As far as the state of Massachusetts was concerned, this match was a title fight—Akins was already the "world champion." The NBA disagreed, and Massachusetts withdrew in protest from the association. Few outside of Massachusetts sympathized; the fact that DeMarco was from the Bay State made the whole thing a bit dubious.

The Akins and DeMarco rematch went down on January 21, 1958, at a very packed Boston Garden. Reporters licked their chops anticipating a repeat of "their terrific slugfest" less than three months prior. Akins, whom the press played up as the "good" one, he being a former church deacon, claimed that while "Tony is a tough fighter with a lot of guts . . . I should have an easier time." He really pissed off DeMarco with that one. The Bostonian replied, "I'm going to knock him out." It was the first time DeMarco had ever made such a prediction in the press.[27]

Akins knew he would have to best DeMarco convincingly to win on the latter's home turf. He certainly did, flooring the Boston Bomber in the eighth round with a huge uppercut followed crisply by two vicious lefts. DeMarco climbed back onto his feet by the count of seven. In the tenth, Akins delivered such a beating that the fact DeMarco remained vertical seemed a miracle. In the eleventh, the second of two Akins hooks put DeMarco back down on the mat. He got up. A body blow returned him to the floor. He got up again. Like a zombie in a horror flick, DeMarco lurched on towards his prey. In the twelfth round, Akins pummeled away at will on an increasingly undead-looking Bomber. The referee called the fight at 1:53 of that round. Afterward, four ringside doctors pleaded with DeMarco to go to the emergency room. He declined.[28]

Tony DeMarco's big comeback was over. Rip Valenti declared that his man was "through." Valenti told the press, "Even if he wants to fight again . . . I'm the guy who holds the contract and I'm going to decide this time." Tough words indeed. DeMarco ignored them, along with everyone else who recommended that he hang up the gloves. Boxing was his life. How could he just give it up after a loss or two? So he kept fighting, sparsely, for a few more years. But he would never get another shot at the title. His career officially ended in 1962, after five straight fights at his beloved Boston Garden.

So three boxers remained in contention for the welterweight belt: Logart, Martinez, and Akins. To decide who got the bye, Nat Fleischer, editor of the hugely influential *Ring* magazine, pulled two names out of a hat as Julius Helfand looked on. The first name was Akins. The second was Logart. The "handsome" Martinez got the bye.[29]

On Friday, March 21, 1958, Virgil Akins met a heavily favored Isaac Logart under the glaring lights of Madison Square Garden. Logart came at Akins with a dazzle of speed and finesse. Round after round, Akins appeared outmatched. Going into the sixth, the officials had it four rounds to one in the Cuban's favor. Then something happened. Akins seemed to suddenly figure out his opponent, to catch up with him. He connected with a right to the jaw and Logart staggered. Another right, then another, and Logart went down for what he would claim to be the first time in his career. The crowd was stunned. Logart was up at the count of three, but the ref continued on for a standing eight. Akins attacked his apparently dazed opponent savagely, and with another fierce right put him down into the ropes. Logart sat back on the lowest rung, not falling, just sitting there. Referee Harry Kessler ruled it a knockdown and gave him another eight count. Logart got up and Akins went after him for the kill. The "bible reading" church deacon unleashed an attack that sent Logart back once again against the ropes. Blood spurted from an opening above the Cuban's right eye. More blood poured from his mouth. He seemed to be on his way back down to the canvas when the referee intervened and stopped it with only seven seconds left in the round. Akins had won; he now had a ticket to a championship battle against Vince Martinez. A final fifteen-round fight was set for June 6, 1958, in Akins's home town of St. Louis.[30]

The shocking conclusion to the Akins-Logart match caught the fight crowd totally unawares. Or did it? Strange things had happened before the fight that day. Everyone thought Logart would win easily; the last time he had fought Akins, he'd taken a unanimous decision, and he was widely considered to be the better boxer. Then a rumor started to circulate. "The smart money," some now said, was for an Akins upset. Then came the suddenness of the sixth round gore fest. The papers the next day gave boxing fans food for thought with this headline: "Grand Jury Summons Akins, Logart." Apparently, wiretapped conversations of folks involved with the two fighters gave prosecutors reason to believe that a fix was in. After the fight, officers served subpoenas to both boxers. Akins got his handed to him literally in his own dressing room as he chatted with NYSAC commissioner Helfand. Helfand seemed shocked. Wrote one reporter, "The commissioner looked as if he'd been hit in the face with an overripe herring." An inquest was set for April 7.[31]

The indictment matter would go mysteriously quiet until after the tournament finally came to its inglorious end in front of a crowd of 9,777 fans at the St. Louis Arena. The big question of the night was: would Vince Martinez be riding the bicycle? Martinez was known as a "back peddler," a man who did not charge right in but rather backed around the ring, letting his opponents come after him while he looked for his opening. Not very impressive, as far as the TV audience was concerned. Before the fight, Martinez admitted to the press, "I've done too much back peddling." He let it be known he would be fighting with a "new" aggressive style this time around. "This is the big one," Martinez said somberly. Akins's trainer was not convinced: "He's always fought on a bicycle and he'll do the same against Virgil, wait and see."[32]

Fight night came, and Martinez, so it appeared, decided to ditch the bicycle. To his absolute peril. He hit the deck no less than five times in the first round, three from punches, two from pushes. He barely made it through the first three minutes, his face a bloody mess, his legs wobbly. His corner man had to help him find his stool. In the second round, Martinez seemed to realize the error of his new strategy. He started to pedal. He made it through the rest of the second round upright. By the third round Martinez was sticking and moving, the old peddler in him apparently trying to pull something out of the wreckage. Akins was unamused. He caught Martinez solidly as he pedaled back, and the "handsome stylist from New Jersey" took a three count on the mat while the crowd booed. Martinez got up, clearly the worse for wear, and the pummeling recommenced. By the end of the third round, Akins was delivering blow after blow directly to Martinez's face, ten in a row by one count. Martinez wasn't answering with anything. His mouthpiece flew out after one fierce jab. He lurched back against the ropes. The bell rang.

Determined to finish Martinez, Virgil Akins came out in the fourth round with guns ablaze, chasing Martinez until he connected solidly enough to put him down for a nine count. Akins skidded on a pool of wetness at the center of the ring and had to get back up to continue the punishment. A final left to the jaw put Martinez back down on the canvas. Referee Harry Kessler didn't even bother to count, waving and saying "that's all" even before Martinez actually hit the floor. The fight was ruled a technical knockout. Heading back to the corner, Referee Kessler told folks at the ringside, "I could have counted 30."[33] A debate actually ensued as to how many times Martinez, who claimed before the fight that he'd never been floored, had hit the mat. Akins himself wasn't sure. "I don't know how many times he went down. Could be 7, 8, 9, or 10. I was surprised at how he kept gettin' up." Vince himself would remember only one knockdown: "the first."[34]

Gaspar found himself sliding back down in the ranks after his exit from the tournament. In February 1958, he went up against an up-and-coming lightweight from the Big Easy named Ralph Dupas, the same man whose questionable whiteness had imperiled his career in earlier days. Before the fight, Gaspar told reporters "in one of his rare English statements" that he felt he was in "verra good shape."[35] Dupas won the fight in a split decision in front of a crowd of 3,195 at the 11th Annual March of Dimes Boxing Carnival at the Norfolk (Virginia) City Arena. The Wednesday Night Fight, televised on ABC, was a real disappointment to Gaspar.[36] Dupas had a frustrating, "slap and run" style that Indio just couldn't master.

Next it was on to Tucson, Arizona, to fight Bob Torrance at the Sports Center. For this Southwest battle, Nick Corby made sure that Gaspar entered the ring with a sombrero. The hat was kind of embarrassing: "I felt funny." Gaspar won this fight on points, but at a terrible cost. In the seventh round, he crashed a straight right against Torrance's "big damn head" and felt something go *pop*. His forearm went numb. He tried to play it off, finishing the fight with lots of lefts and a few painful right-handed slap-punches. He took the split decision and headed to the hospital.

Gaspar learned in the emergency room that he had broken his hand. The doctor put on a cast and told him to be careful. Two weeks later Gaspar took the cast off, but his hand still hurt, so he gripped a piece of wood and wrapped the whole thing in a bandage.

Two months later, Gaspar was back in Madison Square Garden, his hand still not fully healed, facing Mickey Crawford. Crawford was an odd duck. A couple of days before the fight, the *New York Times* ran a piece titled, "Here a Jab, There a Dab and That's Mickey Crawford." The large photo accompanying the article showed Mickey wearing a black jacket and tie, holding a small white canvas. He's painting a portrait of the man sitting opposite, none other than his next opponent, Gaspar Ortega. The article, written by Gay Talese, explains that both fighters were invited to the IBC office for an event known as the "fistic smorgasbord." It was a "pastrami-and-beer-feast" attended by boxers, managers, and others in the fight crowd. We learn in Talese's piece that Mickey Crawford is more than just another contender: he is an aspiring artist. His paintings, mainly of birds, wildlife, and other standards of "calendar art," are displayed about the boxing office, making the place into an impromptu art gallery. The novelty of it all is both jarring and hilarious.

Legally named Harwood Grant Crawford, Mickey had been born and raised in Saginaw, Michigan, a former lumber town plugged into the automotive-industrial nexus of Flint and Detroit hard to its south. Mickey's father, a former featherweight called Patsy, had set up a backyard ring and trained his son to fight at an early age. His brother Pete later reminisced about his father's fierce, unorthodox training approach: "My dad taught (Mickey) to be more of a boxer than a hitter. He always had him moving and hitting. He made a counterpuncher out of him. He was hard to hit and frustrating to fight." But fighting wasn't Mickey's true calling. Painting was. His first manager, Art Greenwald (who owned an art studio in Detroit), fed both of Mickey's interests. He boasted spending a thousand dollars a month on "boxing gear and paint brushes." Greenwald himself was an unusual character with interesting motives. He once told reporters, "I don't want to get into the fight business but I want a champion. And, make no mistake about it, Crawford can paint."[37]

In the IBC office that day Crawford, the champion painter, sat facing a stoic Indio. Gaspar sat there quietly, decked out in a fashionable two-tone collared short-sleeved shirt. Crawford painted him posed in boxing shorts and wearing an Indian headdress. No matter. It was good work. So good, in fact, that "Gaspar said he would pulverize Crawford." A reporter asked Crawford what he thought of Van Gogh. "Isn't he the guy in *Lust for Life*? Actually, I don't know much about art. I just paint." Gaspar himself didn't seem so eager to talk to the reporters either, not least because he spoke virtually no English. When asked if he had any "hobbies on the side," Indio just sat in silence. His "press attaché" (probably Corby) told a reporter that Gaspar indeed was a man of many interests: "Gaspar Ortega is a lover boy. Women chase him all over town. He used to pick cotton, sell papers, and, in Tijuana, was an apprentice bull fighter. But he quit to fight."[38]

The Crawford-Ortega match was more an exercise in hunting than in fighting. Crawford had too tricky a style for Gaspar's taste. "He ran too much," Indio remembers. "Not aggressive, he just used skills." As Crawford dashed about, giving an excellent exhibition of feinting, speed, and finesse, Gaspar managed to land more, and harder, blows than he received. At the end of the fight, Judge Leo Birnbaum had it six rounds to four in Gaspar's favor. Judge Harold Barnes had it eight to two for the Indian. The surprise came with referee Mark Conn's judgment in favor of Crawford, seven rounds to three. Rarely did a fight draw such a startling difference of opinion ringside. The crowd booed at Conn's dissent. Said the referee later, "I saw Crawford the winner because he boxed beautifully and the other guy waited until the last minute of each round to start hitting." For the judges, Ortega's "sometimes wild but always dangerous blows" were convincing, and so Gaspar got the split decision.[39] The promising up-and-coming painter from Saginaw had hit his first big-league snag.

With the Crawford win, Nick Corby pushed hard for a title fight. He told reporters that Gaspar's victory was exciting to watch. He also mentioned that Los Angeles crowds would show up in droves to see him fight

Akins for the title—hinting at an economic motivation for a big West Coast matchup. For reasons that went unexplained in the papers, Corby announced Gaspar could draw a three hundred thousand dollar gate in the City of Angels. The previous Wrigley Field no-show was not brought up, of course. In fact, later, many people would flock from south of the border to see Indio fight in L.A.[40]

The real story of the first Crawford-Ortega fight is the press's treatment of Gaspar. Indio had gone from up-and-coming challenger to high-profile target. *Sports Illustrated* framed the battle as a proving ground for the Saginaw fighter, with Crawford in the role of the "rising star" and Ortega as the wily and aged battler, a man whose "sun seems to be setting."[41] This fight would set a new pattern for Gaspar. Now young boxers like Crawford saw him as their "ticket" to the big time. This new categorization helped Gaspar by establishing him, at last, as a legitimate top-ranked fighter, a man to be taken seriously. At the same time, it subtly shifted him into the category of stepping-stone. Young fighters trying to prove their mettle now saw him as a rung upon which to climb to get to the top. Gaspar was both a contender and a mark. He would get much more of this treatment in the years to come.

Unfortunately, this would be the least of his problems.

CHAPTER 8

The Secret Government

The tournament loss might have sent a lesser fighter into a death spiral. But Gaspar Ortega wasn't nearly ready to give up on his dream. So Gaspar fought his way back into position, and after beating Mickey Crawford, he found himself again ranked the number one contender in the welterweight division. By October 1958, Gaspar was at the doorstep of a title fight, closer in fact than he had ever been. But things would take a turn for the surreal. The Indian would discover the other, hidden side of the world of professional boxing. The underside.

Before the strange events of October sent Gaspar reeling, the aspiring boxer discovered that his celebrity in America was growing. In August 1958, the *New York Times* profiled him before his scheduled ABC *Wednesday Night Fight* rematch with Mickey Crawford. The substantial article included an accompanying close-up photo of Indio as he prepared for battle. The *Times* described him as "a quiet, somewhat moody person with high cheek bones, piercing brown eyes, and close-cropped black hair. In public he always wears a coat and tie, and a small scar on his right cheek is his only mark of ring warfare." The author of the piece, Howard M. Tuckner, rehearsed Gaspar's humble origins of working odd jobs and then bullfighting in Tijuana, along with his Indian heritage (incorrectly identified as Mayan) and his brief stint as lieutenant in the Mexican Army Reserves. Back when he was seventeen, Gaspar had served a mandatory one-year tour in the army. His dad's connections had landed him an officer's berth. When asked what he liked about being in the military,

Gaspar curtly responded (through Happy), "Nothing. What's to like?"[1] His honesty probably did not help him earn any new American fans.

It was clear to the *Times* reporter that Gaspar was a driven man. He was also, by contemporary standards, a rich man. By 1957 Indio was earning $8,000 for a single TV bout. His take from his third battle with DeMarco at the Boston Garden that year netted him more than $11,000. By way of comparison, the mean annual income for an American male who worked fifty weeks in 1957 was $4,700.[2] Of course, Gaspar did not have a money manager, long-term investments, a tax attorney, or any of the typical protections the wealthy cannot live without. After each fight, he would take the check made out to him and go to the bank with Nick Corby, where papers would be signed and a wad of cash handed over. From there it was on to a hotel room someplace, where the dough was divvied out by his management on a bed. The managers got 33 percent (corresponding to the maximum they could take as fixed by law) and the trainers got 10 percent. Then there were the expenses, which left Indio typically with around 40 percent of the total. For a televised match, Gaspar usually received between $6,000 and $9,000 ($4,000 for the TV show plus another $2,000 or more from his percentage of the gate). Of this he might take home around $3,000. From this, Gaspar might wire up to half home to his extended family in Tijuana. Then there were the New York City bills to be paid. He didn't spend much on himself. He didn't have any expensive habits on which to blow his money anyway.

The 1958 Crawford-Ortega rematch ended as a draw, with one judge favoring Gaspar, the other Crawford, and the referee scoring it as a tie. Crawford loudly proclaimed that he had been robbed.[3] Though he didn't lose, Gaspar had not put on an impressive performance for a man who was the number one contender. The *New York Times* wrote the next day that Gaspar "lost a great deal of his high standing last night."[4] Reporters believed that now there would be a rubber match set up to decide who would make a go at Akins's title. But this was not to be. Gaspar's next opponent was a young man named Don Jordan.

Don "Geronimo" Jordan seemed to have come up from nowhere. His pro career started in 1953, when he began waging battles in Southern California and even once in Mexico. In 1954 Jordan had clinched the California state welterweight title, and in 1955 and 1956 he had beaten such worthies as former world lightweight champion Lauro Salas, Garden regular Joe Miceli, and former lightweight champ Paddy DeMarco. When

Jordan defeated Issac Logart at the Hollywood Legion Stadium in July 1958, he entered the big time. Facing off with Gaspar in Portland, Oregon, two months later, Jordan was rolling on a six-fight winning streak. Still, it does seem odd that the still highly ranked Ortega would go up against a man ranked number six.

The press didn't make a fuss over the pairing of Gaspar and the man they called Geronimo. The battle, aired as an ABC *Wednesday Night Fight*, was not a dazzler. Neither man hit the deck over the course of the ten-round match. Gaspar was clearly the more aggressive of the two, but Jordan's precise shots seemed to tilt the fight in Jordan's favor. The new kid from California took the split decision in what was called an "upset victory." After the fight, Jordan said that although Gaspar was a "strong and durable" fighter, "all his punches are wide, looping punches." He had defeated Indio by simply getting his blows in faster.[5]

A rematch was set for a month later. Jordan's victory had blasted him up into the number one rank as rated by *Ring* magazine. (Gaspar was number three now.) The rematch, to be aired again as an ABC *Wednesday Night Fight*, was held under unusual circumstances. It was to be a charity event for the Optimist Boys' Work Fund. A ring was set up in the ballroom of the Lafayette Hotel in Long Beach, California. A picture in the papers showed a benevolent Don Jordan teaching kids at the Optimist Boys' Club home how to box. Two young waifs look up at the boxer as he punches away, one wearing boxing gloves that look like balloons on his tiny hands, with mouth agape in awe of Geronimo's punches. The informal affair (ties required, but no tuxedos necessary) was to be attended by "Sports-minded Long Beach socialites" who would each pay between fifteen and twenty-five dollars for a steak dinner and a four-bout fight card. One local paper boasted of the classiness of it all: "women definitely will be included in the audience." But the Ortega-Jordan rematch was much more than dinner theater. The winner of the October 1958 event, Los Angeles matchmaker George Parnassus announced, would immediately prepare for a title shot with Virgil Akins. Once again, Gaspar seemed to be within reach of the brass ring.[6]

A few days before the fight, Gaspar got a birthday present. It was from Mickey Crawford—the picture he had been sketching of him the day they'd met at the IBC offices before their first match. Crawford's people made sure that the gift was reported in the papers. Included in the subtitle to the previously published photo of Gaspar posing for Crawford was some important information: "Crawford is a commercial artist." In

September 1958, Crawford had been beaten on a technical knockout by Ralph Jones at Chicago Stadium. He would fight only once more in his life. His birthday gift was something of a farewell notice. He wanted to make clear that he was transitioning into a new, less barbaric career now.[7]

Gaspar felt good coming in to the second Jordan fight. He had prepared himself as best he could. He knew that Jordan was a counterpuncher, but he decided he would still bring the fight to him, impressing the judges with his dramatic, late-round flurries. He came in at 145¾ pounds to Jordan's lighter 143¾ pounds at the weigh-in. No news here; Jordan fought as both a lightweight and a welterweight, and he usually came in light when battling in the latter division. After the weigh-in, Gaspar went back to his hotel room for his customary nap. The phone rang. He picked up, but the caller was speaking English, so he handed the phone over to Nick Corby, who was keeping him company. Corby spoke for a short while and then hung up. He told Gaspar that it was a promoter who wanted to set up a lucrative fight in Montana. Apparently, the promoter was down in the hotel restaurant right now. Corby got up and left. A few minutes later there was a knock on the door.

Gaspar went over and turned the knob. The door opened to reveal a young, slick-looking white guy dressed in a sharp dark suit. He smiled, asking Gaspar in accented Spanish, "¿Cómo estás?" How are you doing?

"Magnífico," replied Gaspar, returning the smile. Who was this guy? A fan? In Spanish, Gaspar asked him if he was Mexican. He doubted it.

"No, Italiano," said the mystery man. Then he cut to the chase. "How would you like to make $10,000 on top of what you'll earn? Straight to you. No taxes, and your manager won't even know about it."

Gaspar kept up his light façade. "If I win, you can pay me."

The Italian shook his head. "No. You go down in the fourth."

Gaspar could not believe this crap. He felt a flush of heat to his face, his anger rising. "No," he told the man decisively. "I'm in good shape and I'm going to win."

It never entered Gaspar's mind to be afraid of the mob. He had known about crooked fights in Mexico. There, a rigged match usually meant that the guy taking the dive would be paid by the winner in a deal worked out beforehand. Nothing more organized than that. Besides the fact that the Italiano's formal, third-person bribe was beyond his experience, Gaspar was a proud man. He was not about to bend, not for anyone. The phrase *La Cosa Nostra* meant nothing to him.

That was the end of their little talk. The Italian just shrugged, turned around, and left.

A little while later, Nick Corby returned. There hadn't been anyone waiting for him in the restaurant after all. Gaspar told him about the mysterious Italian.

"Son of a bitch!" hollered Nick. He looked right at Gaspar. "Tonight you must fight the hardest fight of your life. The only way you're losing is if you collapse and die."

The Jordan-Ortega rematch got underway at six P.M., Pacific Standard Time. The twelve-rounder was hyped in the papers as a contest between the top two welterweight contenders, two young men (both twenty-three years old) who had never been knocked out. Getting into the ring that evening, Gaspar caught a sight he couldn't believe. The Italian was standing right there, ringside. Gaspar quickly went over to point him out to Nick Corby. When he turned back, the guy was gone.

According to most fight reporters, it was a close match. Jordan came out with his characteristic speed, delivering solid rights to the head throughout, especially in the later rounds. Gaspar himself fought like a man possessed. After a rocky start in which he couldn't seem to catch his man, Indio opened up a devastating late-fight attack that resulted in a small gash opening above Jordan's left eye. He fought so furiously that Jordan started gripping Gaspar repeatedly in the closing rounds, attempting to stem the onslaught.

At the end of the fight, the decision was announced as split. Referee Frankie Van and Judge Tommy Hart had it 166–114 points for Jordan (in California they used a points system), while Judge Lee Grossman had it 115–113 in favor of Gaspar. The United Press International card had it 119–111 in favor of Jordan. Remarked the *New York Times*, Jordan had "proved too cagey and too fast for his rugged Tajuana [*sic*] (Mexico) opponent."[8]

To this day, Gaspar insists that it was a setup. "They couldn't get me, so they got the judges." Could this be true? Was there a payoff? To get even close to an answer, it's necessary to step outside the squared circle, cross through the ropes, and slide down into the shadows of the ring lights. It's best to begin with a widely known fact: the mob was in the fight business in the 1950s.

In 1952 *Life* magazine featured an article by the chairman of the New York State Athletic Commission (NYSAC), Robert K. Christenberry, titled

"My Rugged Education in Boxing." In the piece, Christenberry detailed his efforts at waging "a true 'battle of the century.'" Boxing was in grave danger, the chairman wrote. James Norris and the IBC were but the veneer, the part "above the surface." "Below the surface," Christenberry explained, "lurks another, more arrogant, infinitely more outrageous influence: the underworld."[9]

Christenberry seemed to be just the right man to clean things up. He was a former Marine who had lost his right hand in a "defective" grenade explosion back in the War to End All Wars. During the Second World War, he had worked for Mayor Fiorello LaGuardia, who had put him in charge of fingerprinting New York City's inhabitants (a project that never happened) and defending Times Square in the event of a German invasion. Christenberry was described as "unbendable" and "tough," a man who got things done in both private and public contexts.[10] He had unassailable moral fiber: not only was he actively involved in the Boy Scouts, but he still managed to find time to teach Sunday school regularly. After being appointed to the chairmanship of the NYSAC by New York governor Thomas E. Dewey in 1951 (his predecessor had retired after one-too-many New York ring deaths), Christenberry set about cleaning up the sport.

He came out guns blazing. The day after he took office, Christenberry watched a Willie Pep–Sandy Saddler fight at the Polo Grounds that seemed so dirty—it was really more of a wrestling match than a boxing contest—that he revoked Pep's license and suspended Saddler indefinitely. A year later, Christenberry watched a Billy Graham–Joey Giardello fight at the Garden that ended with a decision that drew such loud boos that he felt obliged to order the announcer to inform the crowd that the decision was not official until it had been reviewed. The judge's decision would be reversed. In 1952 Governor Dewey signed a bill authorizing the chairman to revoke the licenses of those in boxing found to be involved in organized crime.[11]

Then came the *Life* article. Here Christenberry publicly declared war against the mob. He recounted the story of how Governor Dewey had told him to address "the so-called Iron Curtain" surrounding boxing, a curtain that "most boxers couldn't punch their way through." Christenberry named names, telling a tale of undercover managers, crooked promoters, and fixed fights. He even included (among a gallery of other rogues) a three-way mug shot series of Frankie Carbo, the "overlord of boxing's underworld." Carbo, he explained, really ran the show. Christenberry even shockingly claimed that Carbo and his cronies "influenced the fate" of *two-thirds* of the most important boxers. Carbo would take a cut from managers as payment for getting their man in the ring in big fights. Fixing fights, Christenberry noted, was actually rare, because "the word gets around too easily." The real control was access to the title. For this, Christenberry implied a connection between the IBC's monopoly of boxing (under James Norris) and the mob.[12]

In retaliation for the *Life* article, Norris threatened to move the big fights out of New York. Christenberry seemed to back off. In 1954 *Sports Illustrated* issued the following verdict: Christenberry, "a glad-hander by instinct . . . [has] suddenly lost his zeal for gangster-hunting."[13] Then things went from bad to worse. Writes Jeffrey T. Sammons, "After 1954 Carbo's role in the IBC escalated dramatically."[14] By 1955 Carbo was engineering bouts of the likes of Jake LaMotta, Carmen Basilio, Willie Pep, and Tony DeMarco for IBC matches. At one point, Jake LaMotta would not schedule a key fight without first getting permission from Carbo.

In later congressional hearings, managers would explain that they could not even get a match without Carbo's approval in the 1950s. Many admitted that they feared him. One New Orleans businessman named Blaize D'Antoni would testify that he witnessed Carbo dividing a map of America with his finger, "giving" James Norris the top half and himself the bottom half. In a truly brazen performance, the IBC put Carbo's supposed fiancée, Viola Masters, on the payroll. "She," one of Carbo's pseudonyms, received forty-five thousand dollars over a three-year period. This was at a time when you could buy a stamp for three cents and a new Corvette convertible V-8 for less than three thousand.

So just who *was* Frankie Carbo? Born on New York City's Lower East Side, the man who would be known simply as Mr. Gray[15] started his criminal life when he was but a mere stripling, getting carted off to a Catholic reform school at age twelve. By age twenty, Carbo had landed his first murder rap after shooting a man to death in a pool hall over possession of a stolen taxi cab. He pled guilty to manslaughter and then went on the lam for four years until he was caught following a holdup in Philadelphia. For this he was shipped off to Sing Sing for a year. Upon getting out of jail, Carbo decided to make killing people his full-time career. He joined up with a notorious group called Murder, Inc., and in 1933, a few witnesses saw Carbo gun down two henchmen in front of a fancy hotel in Elizabeth, New Jersey. Nothing came of the charges that followed. In 1939 Carbo was arrested for his involvement in another assassination, this time of a rival mobster called Harry Schachter (who also went by the name Harry "Big Greeney" Greenburg). Carbo was accused of pumping five bullets into Big Greeney, after which gangster Benjamin "Bugsy" Siegel drove him off in the getaway war. The first murder trial ended in a hung jury. A second trial collapsed after the untimely demise of key witness Abe "Kid Twist" Reles, who plummeted five stories from his hotel room in Coney Island. Six police officers were supposedly in his room at the time. In 1947 Siegel, Carbo's sometime partner, famously met his own doom while sitting in his Beverly Hills home relaxing and reading the paper. The grisly photo of a blood-drenched Siegel, tilting over on his floral-print couch with one eye blasted out of his head, made its way into the newspapers. His crime: not paying the mob what he owed on his loan for the extravagant Flamingo hotel in Las Vegas. The triggerman (according to mob snitch Jimmy Frattiano): Frankie Carbo.[16]

As early as 1946, *Life* magazine called Carbo "one of the most feared men in boxing today."[17] In 1947 the *New York Sun* reported that Carbo was "said to be a secret power in the prizefight world and the under-cover manager of several well-known fighters." The *Sun* article covered an investigation involving Carbo's alleged offer of one hundred thousand dollars to Rocky Graziano to throw a championship fight against Tony Zale. This was the same year that Jake LaMotta drew media attention for apparently throwing a fight with Billy Fox at Madison Square Garden, with loud hints of Carbo involvement. As stunned spectators watched, LaMotta had just stood there, hands at sides, as the lesser Billy Fox pummeled away at his head until the referee stopped it. In 1952 Carbo was again in the papers, being called forth to testify in a big racketeering trial involving mob boss Umberto "Albert" Anastasia. Carbo's alleged boxing operations brought him to the stand. He answered every query the same way: "I refuse to answer the question. I rely on my constitutional rights."[18] He even answered this way when asked to state his name for the record. A 1955 article in *Bluebook* summarized the thoughts of many: "Boxing has been a corrupt sport ever since its early days in England. It has always attracted the criminal element. By comparison with Carbo, however, all who came before him were pikers."[19] By 1958, Carbo's "hidden" role in boxing was the worst kept secret in sports.

So what role might have Carbo played in Gaspar's career? Let's take another look at the tournament described in the last chapter. According to Kevin Mitchell, Carbo called a mob meeting in Miami in late 1957, where he explained that Virgil Akins was to be "steered towards the world welterweight title recently given up by Carmen Basilio, a client of his friend Blinky [Palermo], and that to facilitate his smooth progress, he would be 'placed' in various fights that would be judged to his advantage."[20] Of the six contenders for Basilio's vacant crown, two of them, Virgil Akins and Isaac Logart, were directly managed by Carbo "associates." According to later congressional testimony, James Norris paid Carbo between ten thousand and fifteen thousand dollars to "get" the two managers to agree to fight each other in the tournament. Glickman and Yawitz, Akins's managers, further claimed to have paid Carbo ten thousand dollars to have their man in.[21] It is unclear if Gaspar's managers did the same—they never testified, and they never talked about it to Gaspar.

As noted in the previous chapter, the Akins-Logart fight that led to the Akins-Martinez title match and the welterweight belt for Akins was widely viewed as highly suspect. As Nick Tosches describes the fight, "Logart, the odds-on favorite, had dominated until the sixth round, when he seemed to fall under a spell, as did the referee, who began to count him out while he was still standing and stopped the fight at the count of eight, only seven seconds before the bell would have saved him. Logart's cornermen seemed under the spell as well, for there was not even the show of a protest at the fight's outcome."[22] Then came the subpoenas from New York district attorney Frank Hogan. A month later, James Norris, president of the International Boxing Club, resigned his post as heat built around the possibility of corruption and scandal.

And what about the Akins-Martinez title match that ended the tournament? Martinez had himself been on the wrong end of Carbo's influence in the past. He had refused to take a twenty-thousand-dollar dive against Carmine Fiore in 1954 and soon found himself blacklisted by the Boxing Managers' Guild. The Guild was "the brainchild of Carbo" (in the words of boxing writer Thomas Myler), a front for transferring funds from boxers to the mob by way of putting pressure on managers. The treasurer of that organization, "Honest" Bill Daly, had, in fact, once been Vince Martinez's manager. Martinez had dismissed Daly after he discovered that Daly was paying off judges for favorable outcomes. (By at least one account, Daly was also skimming money from Martinez.) Martinez wouldn't get another chance at the big time for nearly four years.[23] Though it appears pretty obvious that Martinez lost the title bout to Akins fair and square, the feds seemed to suspect the worst. A representative of the New York City grand jury inquiry into boxing attended the match. Further, *Sports Illustrated* would later write that Blinky Palermo was picked up that night

with "an assortment of sleeping potions, including Seconal."[24] A drugged
Martinez seems a stretch, but smoke lingers over the tournament. Perhaps
it can never be cleared away; the truth may never be known.

Over the course of Gaspar's career, many of his most illustrious foes—
Isaac Logart, Tony DeMarco, Virgil Akins, Don Jordan, and Kid Gavilan,
among others—were associated with Carbo through their management.
Watching the fight footage, it is clear that Gaspar's battles with these
fighters were not fixed, and only Jordan's fight raises justifiable questions.
What *is* certain is that Mr. Gray influenced the shape of Gaspar's boxing
career. Carbo played critical roles in determining who fought Gaspar and
when. He and his cronies likely played a big part in getting Jordan up
through the ranks in the first place, and his influence might also explain
why Jordan, a number six contender, got a shot at the much higher ranked
Gaspar. Further, DeMarco's management was supposedly mixed up with
Carbo, and this might have influenced the sudden announcement of the
mysterious third fight in a row with the Bostonian. One can't really know.
Tony DeMarco says that the mob had never approached him directly and
that he never threw a fight. But he did meet Carbo once in New Jersey,
informally, around this time. Carbo was just a "nice guy." Like a "politician" or something. Carmen Basilio told me that Carbo was "friendly" to
him when they met. He had the controlled aspect of "a boss," though.[25]

Don Jordan's run-ins with the mob would eventually help spark the final
firestorm that shut down the IBC itself. As Gaspar puts it, "Carbo went
down when Don Jordan started to open his mouth."

It started right after Jordan beat Gaspar for the second time. Jordan's
manager, a used car salesman named Donald Paul Nesseth, had in the
past struggled to get his fighter a shot at the big time. Initially, Nesseth
found that he was unable to break his man into the New York fight scene.
Frustrated, he had West Coast promoter Jackie Leonard contact Truman
Gibson of the IBC. As if by magic, major TV fights followed. Once Jordan
defeated Gaspar the second time in Long Beach, Geronimo prepared for
his long-dreamed-of title match.

This time, IBC president Truman Gibson (who had recently replaced
Norris) met with Leonard and Nesseth at promoter George Parnassus's
Los Angeles office to discuss the fight. Sometime during the meeting,
Gibson got on the phone with somebody, talked a short while, and then
handed the receiver over to Leonard. On the other end of the line was
mobster "Blinky" Palermo. Blinky told Leonard straight out, "we're in for

half." Leonard said he didn't know what Blinky was talking about. "We're in for half of the fighter, or there will be no fight," growled the mobster. After the call, Gibson explained to Leonard, "Look, this is the way the lightweight and welterweight title has worked since Carbo and Blinky got involved." Nesseth objected, but Leonard knew they had to go along, and they did.

Geronimo got Virgil Akins's welterweight title in December 1958 by decision. A month later, Leonard went to Miami, where he met, among others, Blinky Palermo and Frankie Carbo. In a hotel room, Carbo (who at the time was hiding out from the New York authorities stemming from an indictment for undercover matchmaking) pressured Leonard to get Nesseth to set up a battle between Jordan and one of Blinky's fighters, a tough Philly kid named Garnet "Sugar" Hart. As Leonard struggled to deal with the situation (he correctly knew Nesseth would resist), Carbo put on the pressure. After a nontitle fight between Jordan and Alvarro Guttierez in Los Angeles in which the mob didn't get its cut, Carbo called Leonard and told him, "You sonofabitch double-crosser. You're no good. Your fuckin' word is no good. Just because you are two thousand miles away, that is no sign I can't have you taken care of." Later, a gangster named Jack Sica further warned Leonard, "Look, Jackie, you made a choice. It is a question of either you or Don Nesseth is going to get hurt. Wouldn't you rather go grab him by the neck and straighten him out, than for me to go back and tell The Gray?" A terrified Leonard went to Truman Gibson, who lamely explained that he was in no position to change things. Just get Jordan to fight Hart, Truman suggested, and everything will be fine. So Leonard went to the cops. They convinced him to have his phone conversations with Carbo tapped. In May 1959, Leonard swore under oath that Carbo and Palermo were trying to muscle in on Jordan. Though still on the lam, Carbo was in hotter water than ever. And he was furious.

On June 3, 1959, after getting out of his car at his home, Leonard was savagely beaten with a pipe and then kicked repeatedly by two men. He survived with a concussion. The injuries did not stop Jackie Leonard from playing a big part in sending Carbo off to Alcatraz, and his testimony would also play a role in the government's case against the IBC.

Much has been written about the mob's influence on boxing. Given all the testimony, the press reports, and the books written on the subject, it is clear that becoming a Friday Night Fighter involved dealing, typically indirectly, with the mob. In regard to Gaspar in particular, it is hard to discern the true impact of organized crime on his career. It is quite possible that his management paid to get him into position, perhaps on several occasions, for a chance at a title shot over the course of his career. Did they cut Carbo in for his shots at Logart or Gavilan in 1957? Did Carbo play a role in Gaspar's high-profile battles in 1958 or 1959, or even later? (Prison did not end Carbo's reign). There is no "smoking gun." It is impossible to tell at this point. The managers are dead and gone, as are the mobsters. It is also likely that mobsters held back opportunities for Gaspar. The case of the mysterious Italian before the second Jordan fight is an obvious one, but there may have been other times when more "connected" boxers made their way up the ranks ahead of Indio. Every fighter I've spoken to has denied working with the mob, though they also tell me they didn't really know what sorts of deals their managers were making to get them into position. As DeMarco explained, "I imagine they [mobsters] know who to speak to. They size up the situation."[26]

While the stunning popularity of TV boxing gave criminals greater opportunities than ever to cash in on the action, it must also be noted that boxing hardly represented the main thrust of organized crime. The real money was made elsewhere—in "mob taxes" on construction, waste management, waterfront commerce, and basic staples like groceries and clothing. By one estimate, organized crime added eleven cents on the dollar to all goods and services in America in the 1950s. According to the government, by the 1960s, the mob was siphoning off $7 billion in profits each year. "We're bigger than U.S. Steel," a bugged Meyer Lansky told his wife in 1962.[27]

It is also misleading to transform a degree of mob influence and profit taking into mob *control* over televised boxing outcomes. In his later testimony to Congress, IBC president Truman Gibson asserted that fixed fights would have ruined TV boxing. He explained, "If there were fixed fights, we would be out of business, so we try to protect ourselves in every way against the possibility of a fixed fight ... you only need one or two and you have no more boxing."[28] Indeed, fixed fights, by all accounts, were a rarity. As Gibson explained in his autobiography, a fixed fight "would have been death to TV ratings." Fans wanted to see real combat, not something staged. Further, he notes, "the Vegas gambling kingpins would have taken a suspicious fight off the morning line in a heartbeat."[29]

During his later testimony before the Senate and in the press, Gibson took great pains to refute charges of fight fixing. He seemed to consider only fight fixing evidence of mob influence. Because so few fights were fixed, went his reasoning, the mob was tangential to TV boxing. This is not to say Gibson denied the existence of fixes. He didn't. The problem with Gibson's logic is that fight fixing was not the mob's main way of profiting from boxing. The mob was a business, and like any business, it sought steady, reliable streams of income. It didn't have to control what went on inside the ring. That would have jeopardized business in the long run by creating unnecessary risk. It needed a way to get at the cash circulating *around* the ring. It did this by controlling access to the title. And it controlled access by pressuring managers, not boxers.

In the winter of 1958–59, the Secret Government was actually the least of Gaspar's troubles. It began one afternoon as his wife Ida lay in bed in a private Tijuana clinic, recovering from treatment for a benign cyst in her back. A woman came in to speak with her. She said that if anything happened to her, she wanted Ida to take care of her child.

"What are you talking about?" Ida asked.

The girl told Ida that she had a son. His name was Gaspar Jr.

CHAPTER 9

Trouble

Ida was going home. She had been living in Tijuana since tying the knot with Gaspar, but now all bets were off. It was hard enough adjusting to life in the dusty, chaotic streets of Tijuana, fitting in to a culture much different from her own while trying to raise a baby amid a large, bustling family. Now she learned that Gaspar had begat another child, and even worse, that Gaspar's parents and siblings had known about the other woman and had purposely kept it a secret from her.

The other woman's name was Dalila Perez. Dalila had first met Gaspar during the Independence Day celebration in Tijuana on September 15, 1956, the same day he had knocked out the obnoxious fellow who had tried to push him and his brother Sapo around. Dalila herself had come to Tijuana from Colima, a small state on the western shore of central Mexico, back in the 1940s. Her mother was a homemaker, her father an engineer at a sugar processing plant. Unusual for Mexicans in those days, her parents had divorced when Dalila was still a young girl. After the breakup, her mom had picked up everything and moved to Tijuana with the kids, searching for work and a new life. Dalila would see her dad only a handful of times growing up. He stayed in Colima, living with his mother.

Though born into a middle-class family, Dalila found herself cast into poverty and hardship along with her mother and siblings after the divorce. Growing up in Tijuana, she also discovered the cultural wonders of Mexamerica. Dalila started to dress "like *American Graffiti*." She learned to use dollars and to speak some English phrases. She became a fashion-conscious "border girl." She also learned to work for a wage. When she first met Gaspar, she was employed as a servant for a wealthy family. She had liked his looks, so she had approached the young boxer and started a conversation. The two connected instantly.

When Gaspar traveled to Tijuana with Ida at the start of their marriage, Dalila had come into the room he had rented to be away from his wife and parents. According to Gaspar, he tried to tell Dalila that the affair was over now, that he was a married man. Dalila had teared up, told him that they were meant to be together. Gaspar could not make the decision to expel her from his life, or from his room. Nine months later, Gaspar Jr. was born.

Gaspar wore a gold chain in the early days of his courtship with Ida. When Dalila came into Ida's hospital room that fateful day, she was wearing it. Ida saw this and decided that she had had enough. She left the house, left the furniture, left everything in Tijuana. She took her young son, Michael, and got on a plane back to New York, vowing never to return.

Gaspar followed. He begged Ida for forgiveness; he pleaded, he cried. Ida talked to her beloved stepmom for advice. Ramonita didn't tell her what to do, but Ida knew that Ramonita liked Gaspar and sensed that her stepmom did not want her to abandon him. Ida thought it over and decided to take Gaspar back. But she would never live in Tijuana again.

The romance between Dalila and Gaspar continued. Later, Ida saw her once more in Tijuana, during a visit. She told Dalila, "If you think you're the only one in his life, you're in for a surprise. If you want him you can have him. I wash my hands." By this point Ida knew that Gaspar had a wandering eye. She hadn't expected this when marrying. She was so young, so naïve; and Gaspar seemed so quiet and self-reserved. Once, she got up the nerve to scold Gaspar's parents about their role in it all. "I blame you people. You encourage him. You can keep this house *and* him." She felt that Gaspar's mother resented her from the get-go, this Puerto Rican New York girl who had taken her son away from his family. Ida believed that Sebastiana covered for her son, especially in regard to Dalila.

Of the other women in Gaspar's life, at least one was famous. Back when Gaspar was just starting to date Ida, he had been given the opportunity to present a bouquet of roses to the legendary Mexican singer Amalia Mendoza at a special event at the San Juan Theater in the Bronx. The owner of a Mexican restaurant that Gaspar patronized was a boxing fan, and he arranged for the young fighter to give Amalia the flowers as a publicity stunt. The plan was for Gaspar to wait in the wings of the stage, then come out when his name was called. He stood there nervously watching Amalia from a side vantage point. When he heard his name, he counted to three and then walked out with the flowers in hand while the crowd cheered. Amalia, a worldly woman more than a decade his senior, whispered to Gaspar to meet her in her dressing room afterward. When Gaspar got there, Amalia unashamedly began undressing. Gaspar turned away. At this point in his life, he had extremely limited experiences with women. He had gone on his first date when he was sixteen. His first girl-friend, Rosalinda Bojorques, was a religious, serious girl whom he had met at church. She was old-fashioned and unpopular, always wearing long dresses and sporting a traditional hairdo. Her father was very strict, so they dated on the sly, going out to movies and eating ice cream afterward at the small shop across from the movie theater. They'd mainly just held hands. Amalia saw Gaspar's embarrassment and laughed. How could a professional fighter be terrified of a woman? She called him a dummy. The two wound up having a brief affair. Amalia told Gaspar that she had never met a man like him, "so decent, respectful."

Affairs would be ongoing throughout Gaspar's marriage. When Ida found something out, Gaspar would always come to her, crying for for-giveness. He had been raised Catholic, and he knew that adultery was a sin. Yet he constantly faced adoring women who threw themselves at him. They recognized him on the street, smiling like they knew him. He could never seem to turn them away. Though Ida inevitably forgave him his transgressions, she made it clear that if Gaspar ever decided to leave her and the kids for another woman, he would not be welcome back in her house.

The winter of 1958–59 also brought massive changes to the sport of box-ing. On New Year's Day, 1959, President Fulgencio Batista fled the capital of Cuba for Dominica. Seven days later, a young sports enthusiast named Fidel Castro triumphantly stormed Havana "to the sound of church bells and factory and ship sirens," bloodlessly taking command of the island's capital. He then proceeded to round up two thousand collaborators with the Batista dictatorship and have them shot.[1]

Fidel's sudden rise to global importance was stunning. Happening just ninety miles from Florida, Castro's coup had overthrown a CIA-supported ruler whom Vice President Nixon had once toasted as "Cuba's Abraham Lincoln." Although President Eisenhower was immediately wary of Cas-tro, it was unclear to him whether Fidel's leftist politics translated into

Soviet-influenced Communism. Castro himself was a kinetic, unpredictable presence, a man described by the British ambassador to Cuba as "a
mixture of Jose Marti, Robin Hood, Garibaldi, and Jesus Christ."[2] When
Castro came to America that spring (at the invitation of the American
Society of Newspaper Editors), Harvard students saw in him "the hipster
who, in the era of the Organization Man, had joyfully defied the system,
summoned a dozen friends, and overturned a government of wicked old
men."[3] Ike, now taking heat for letting Cuba go "Red," decided to act. In
March 1959, the president ordered the CIA to train Cuban exiles for an
invasion that would hopefully spark a general revolt.

With so many TV boxers currently coming out of Cuba, some wondered what the Revolution portended for the sport. Castro himself was
an athlete. Back in 1944, he had received a prestigious award for being
the nation's best young sportsperson. As a college undergraduate, he had
once challenged the president of the Student Union to a boxing match
over a debate point of order.[4] A (false) rumor would also circulate that
Castro had once tried out for the Washington Senators baseball team.

For Fidel, professional sports represented the ultimate despoliation
of humanity by capitalism. Taking something as pure as sports and pol-
luting it with money debased the participants, tainted them. As Cuban
Olympic boxer Teofilo Stevenson explained to a reporter in 1976, "Our
commander-in-chief Fidel Castro knows all about professionalism. A professional sportsman stops being an athlete."[5] For Cuba's successful fighters,
the new government's ban on professional sports—pro boxing would end
there in 1961—put them in a terrible bind. If they chose to stay in Cuba
with their families and remain loyal to the Revolution, they had to forgo
lucrative careers that had taken them out of the desperate straits of their
early lives. Even if they chose to continue to pursue their boxing dreams
as Cuban nationals, they would never be crowned champions before the
screaming fans of Madison Square Garden. No mansions, no Cadillacs,
no cash. And the other choice was equally stark: defection. One man facing this choice was a promising welterweight named Benny Paret.

Benny "Kid" Paret was born in Santa Clara, Cuba, and grew up earning two dollars a day cutting sugarcane in Cuba's vast fields. Pacing low
through the thick, volcanic soil that made his homeland a world leader
in sugarcane production (a full half of which was shipped to the United
States on the eve of the Revolution), he would chop away at the thick
bases of cane stems with a machete for ten hours a day, the sun beating
relentlessly down. If the cities seemed modern to the Yankee visitor in the

1950s, back in the rural hinterlands, life went on as if locked in another, much older, time. Most agricultural workers lived without electricity, running water, or adequate education in Batista's Cuba.[6]

Like many of the other characters in this story, Benny Paret fought his way out of impossible circumstances in the hopes of breaking through to the other side of a thick class divide. He had no schooling beyond kindergarten, going straight into the fields as soon as he could grip a machete. He got out of the fields with his fists, winning nearly every amateur fight he signed up for, turning pro while still in his teens. Fighting in Havana one night, Paret was spotted by manager Manuel Alfaro, a so-called white Cuban. Alfaro saw potential in the kid and decided to take him to Manhattan for a chance at the big time.[7] He landed a series of fights in the "other" arena, St. Nick's. The initial results were decidedly unspectacular.

Paret lost two and drew one of his first nine American fights. Not great. But luckily for him, the record wasn't what mattered those days. Paret was a dynamic slugger, a man unafraid to exchange head shots and go in frequently for the kill. He had an "iron chin" and seemed utterly unconcerned with defense. Journalists remarked in awe on his ability to take a punch. In other words, he was perfect for TV.

On Friday, August 7, 1959, Kid Paret got his big chance. Opportunity knocked when Florentino Fernandez, a fellow Cuban, had to back out of a TV fight due to illness, and a substitute was needed ASAP. Paret was actually doubly lucky in this case. The original substitute for Fernandez was a boxer named Charley Scott, who withdrew because he couldn't get into shape in time. Paret, who was originally supposed to be on the undercard that night, seized the opportunity. His opponent was a fighter from Tijuana named Gaspar Ortega.

The year 1959 started as a mixed bag for Gaspar's career. His loss to Don Jordan at the end of 1958 had set him back. In early January 1959, he had landed a Madison Square Garden bout against Denny Moyer. Moyer was a nineteen-year-old French-Irish kid from Portland, Oregon. His first fight against Gaspar was designed to provide a ticket to bigger, better things. It was set to be at the Garden and was also Moyer's first match in the *Friday Night Fights* series. Gaspar was favored early on to win, and he thought he had won when the final bell rang. But he hadn't. In this first TV fight of 1959, Moyer managed to get the decision, much to the amazement of many sportswriters at ringside. One of them, Jack Cuddy, reported that sixteen of eighteen reporters had it for Ortega. "The surprise decision,"

Cuddy ominously noted, "followed a late-betting switch that sent 19-year-old Moyer into the ring favored at 6–5."[8]

Nick Corby complained loudly, "we've been robbed," while Gaspar told reporters, "I think I won the fight with ease."[9] Moyer himself admitted that "it was very close" and that Gaspar had been his toughest opponent yet.[10] Within days, the New York State Athletic Commission was investigating the fight. Less than a week later, the commission ruled that there was nothing crooked about the decision. Julius Hefland told reporters, "We have investigated and talked with all officials, managers and others concerned with the bout, and we found not the slightest hint of any wrongdoing."[11]

Not one to linger on a single failure, Gaspar battled his way back up the ranks after his loss. As with the Moyer fight, Indio's next bout showed once again his emerging role as stepping-stone to the top. His opponent was a man named Rudell Stitch, an African American fighting out of Louisville, Kentucky. Stitch had a short but fantastic record—seventeen wins in twenty one fights, nine by way of knockout. He was known as a brawler and a tough fighter, and this would be his first fight at the Garden, as it had been Moyer's. He was favored to beat Gaspar 2–1.[12]

Gaspar remembers Stitch as one of the hardest punchers he had ever faced. "He didn't knock me down, but I could feel the power of his punches." In the first round, a solid right to the chin shook Gaspar visibly. In the second, Gaspar began to return the violence in kind, and the crowd, which already was rooting for the Indian to break his losing streak, began to go wild. In the third round, an unintentional head butt opened a wide gash over Gaspar's left eyebrow. "I remember the pop and felt warm-hot there. Three seconds later, a brown-black hot thing covered my eye and temporarily blinded me." Gaspar seemed shaken by the force of the blow, reeling about unsteadily for a moment. Stitch, strangely, did not take the opportunity to go in for the kill. Rudell later explained to reporters that he did not "believe in taking advantage of an opponent after a head-butt."[13]

This was in perfect accordance with Rudell's personality. Just a year earlier, he had pulled a complete stranger, a white man and Army Corps of Engineers serviceman, out of the swirling Ohio River near the McAlpine Lock dam.[14] For his heroism, Stitch was awarded a bronze medal in a public ceremony from the Carnegie Hero Fund.[15]

Stitch lost the match with Gaspar that day. After the head butt, Gaspar's corner worked feverishly to stanch the blood streaming down Indio's face. A ringside doctor inspected him after the fourth round, determining that he could continue to fight. By the second half of the battle, Gaspar was actually pulling ahead, staggering the Kentuckian in the eighth and pounding away at him solidly in the ninth. Gaspar took the split decision. Afterward, in his dressing room, a reporter asked Gaspar how many stitches he would have to get for that cut. "Don't mention that word 'Stitch' in here," he quipped back.[16]

Once again, Gaspar had halted an apparent slide down the ranks and had proven himself a top-flight contender. He told reporters, "Now that my luck has changed, I want a good-money fight with either Denny Moyer in Oregon or Art Aragon at Los Angeles." The newspaper *El Heraldo* in Tijuana welcomed the fact that "Lady Luck finally came to help" him. At last, noted the *New York Times*, the "sad-visaged Indian from Mexicali . . . had something to smile about." The Indian was yet again "on the boxing warpath." But Gaspar would have to wait to keep climbing. New York State suspended him for thirty days to give his torn brow time to heal.[17]

Gaspar's next battle, a TV Friday Night Fight held at the War Memorial Auditorium in Syracuse, New York, three months later, was a much-anticipated rematch with Rudell Stitch. Stitch had followed up his loss to Gaspar with a knockout victory over Guy Sumlin at a fairground in Louisville and then with a split-decision win over Jimmy Beecham in Miami Beach. Stitch, too, had momentum. He was hungry to battle Indio again, and he got his chance.

In their second battle, Rudell brought his vicious power punches fully to bear. In the first round, he opened a new cut over Gaspar's left eye. Gaspar explains that he usually got cut only from head butts, but Stitch punched in such a way that he could cut with sheer force. In the third round, Stitch connected fiercely to Gaspar's face with a straight right. Indio suddenly felt disoriented and wobbly. His legs went weak, and he slunk back onto the ropes, managing the presence of mind to keep moving to prevent Stitch from finishing him off. "If he hit me one more time, it would have been a knockout." That might have been a good thing, too. The rest of the fight was basically a punching exposition at Gaspar's expense. Reported the *Times*, this fight was "as one-sided as their first encounter was close."[18]

Rudell Stitch continued his climb up the ranks, defeating six of his next eight opponents. By May 1960, he had achieved the number two spot in the welter ranks. He returned to Louisville, Kentucky, and prepared to sign a contract to fight the number one contender, Luis Rodriguez, in July. The winner of that fight was supposed to get a shot at the title. The day before the signing, Stitch decided to relax and go fishing beneath the Clarksville Dam on the Ohio River with his friend, Charles Oliver; his manager, Edgar "Bud" Bruner; and Bruner's nineteen-year-old son, Edgar Jr. After casting his line a while, Rudell headed back, followed by Oliver and Bud. As they re-traversed the rock shelf where they had gone to reach their fishing spot, Oliver began to feel nervous. A sheet of water continuously flowed over their feet as they went. Oliver swayed a bit and Rudell reached back and clasped his hand to steady him. Then Oliver slipped, pulling them both over the shelf and into the fast-moving river. Rudell quickly disappeared beneath the surface for what seemed like a long time. Bud was surprised, because he knew that Rudell was a strong swimmer. Suddenly Rudell's head came up. He had just been trying to take off his water-filled waders. Soon Stitch and his friend were swimming for shore, though Oliver was clearly having a hard time of it. Rudell looked over his shoulder and saw that his friend was falling back, so he returned to help. But by now Rudell was exhausted, the strong currents relentlessly dragging them both downstream. To the horror of Bud and others standing onshore, the two men vanished under the roiling waters. Neither survived. Rudell would posthumously receive a second Carnegie medal of honor for his valiant effort to save his friend. It would be only the third time that a Carnegie medal had been awarded more than once to a single person.[19]

Gaspar had been bumped down to eighth in the rankings after the Stitch rematch. Another big loss might toss him completely off the radar, and he knew it. So his management signed him up for an easy fight in Tijuana in front of a favorable crowd. His opponent was a kid named Ray Terrazas, who himself fought out of New Mexico. Although Terrazas originally hailed from Juarez, Gaspar drew the cheers from the ten thousand in attendance at the Ciudad Juarez bullring. The crowd chanted "Indio! Indio!" as Gaspar beat mercilessly on the outgunned Terrazas. By the tenth round, Terrazas could no longer defend himself and the referee called it. Because attendance was so high, Gaspar's management decided on a rematch. This time the fight was to be held in Tijuana's famous bullring, the Plaza de Toros. In the rematch, Terrazas made it through the whole fight, but Gaspar remained clearly in control and took an easy win before some three thousand fans.[20]

The far-southern strategy worked. By August 1959, Gaspar was back at the Garden, back on television. Standing across from him now was the latest new kid on the block, a twenty-two-year-old Cubano named Benny

"Kid" Paret. Like Crawford, Jordan, Moyer, and Stitch, Paret understood that Indio represented his big chance to step up into the big leagues. Considering this sudden, accidental trip to the small screen by a relative unknown, reporters tried to work up interest by hyping Paret's fighting skills. This, coupled with Gaspar's increasingly shaky record, put the odds even for the fight. The buzz built. Paret, it was explained, was a "lusty" fighter, whose speed and boxing skills were "highly regarded," even at this early stage in his career. By fight night, Paret was favored to win.[21]

Both men had the dramatic, kinetic styles that TV loved. As the fight got underway, the similarities between Gaspar and Paret became clear; both men swung away, toe-to-toe, often trading wide, looping, furious hooks at each other. Paret, who did not seem concerned about taking abuse, inspired announcer Jimmy Powers to marvel how he "can take a punch." Watching the footage, it is clear that he could. Solid head hits did not seem to faze him.

Paret put on a great show that evening, giving as much as he got. "One of the best fights we've had in a while," noted Powers, as the crowd's Spanish chants echoed through television sets into countless American living rooms. "Paray, Paray, Paray," mimicked Powers. They are "trying to lead their boy home." Gaspar got the decision. Before signing off, Powers noted that "all three Cubans on card tonight were defeated." An odd occurrence, considering the domination of this nationality in the sport of boxing in the 1950s. One of those defeated, a former Cuban welterweight champion named Kid Fichique, met his loss at the hands of a young Virgin Islander named Emile Griffith. It would be Griffith's thirteenth straight win of a career total of thirteen fights to that point. He was one to watch.

Gaspar staggered through the rest of 1959 fighting a hard-hitting Cuban named Florentino Fernandez twice and losing both times. Fernandez was a brutal boxer with an undefeated record, having just knocked out sixteen straight opponents. (He still holds the Cuban record for the most consecutive knockouts). In Havana they called him "El Barbaro del Knockout." Ortega remembers Fernandez's eyes. They seemed to communicate, "I'm gonna kill you."

The remarkable thing about the first Ortega-Fernandez TV fight, held in Miami Beach on September 11, 1959, was that Gaspar made it all the way through. In the first round, Fernandez knocked Gaspar down to his knees. "He had a bomb in that hand!" Indio got up at the count of nine. Typically, when a boxer is knocked to the floor, his corner tells him to wait until eight or nine in order to clear his head. That time, explained Gaspar, the delay was not strategy. Gaspar soldiered on, even trading punches with the Cuban killer to the throaty cheers of a generally pro-Fernandez audience (they were fighting in Miami Beach, after all). It was a poor choice of tactics. In the fourth round, after one such exchange, Fernandez reeled off a string of head shots that put Gaspar back down on his hands and knees. When Gaspar stood at nine, the referee pulled his gloves against his shirt to wipe them off, as was typical practice. This time Gaspar leaned into the ref. He was trying, desperately, to squeeze out a precious few additional seconds of peace. He had never done this before, but he'd never faced the likes of Fernandez, either. Gaspar managed to survive the fight upright, breaking Fernandez's knockout streak. But he lost the obvious unanimous decision.[22]

A rematch was immediately set up. Said Garden promoter Teddy Brenner, the winner of the rematch would "definitely" get a shot at Don Jordan's welterweight belt.[23] It was a bit of a Devil's bargain, of course. Fernandez might actually kill him this time. Freddie Brown urged Gaspar to try a different tack, telling him not to trade punches but rather to bob his head more and provide a moving target. The secret to beating El Barbaro, said Freddie, was to "make him crazy." Gaspar couldn't have agreed more. "So I boxed him."

The TV announcer recognized the change. "On the first night it was stand and slug. Tonight Ortega is boxing." The announcer went on to explain the change to the audience: last time, Gaspar had "sort of discounted the Cuban's punching abilities." But now, "the cagey veteran" practiced a more "shifty, elusive" style. Ortega paced himself and remained outside as much as possible, awaiting openings, trying to "invite a lead, waiting to counter with a right." Typically Gaspar was an inside fighter, which he had been criticized for in the press, given his long reach. Fernandez remained as intimidating as ever. Gushed the announcer, the Cuban had the "upper body of a heavyweight . . . he wears a seventeen inch collar." His shoulders were "terrific."

Gaspar tried every trick in the book to stop the Ox's onslaught. He bobbed his head, weaved his body, ducked down low, stuck-and-moved. He even crossed into shadier realms. At one point, Gaspar clearly could be seen raking his glove laces down Fernandez's face. "I was a little dirty that day."

Another interesting note on the second Fernandez fight can be seen between the rounds. A woman pitched the Gillette razor. "Most women

I know," says a sultry female, "rely on Gillette to protect their loveliness." Never was it clearer that Gillette recognized women as a big part of the audience for the *Friday Night Fights.*

Gaspar lost the second Fernandez fight on decision. It was a close one, and Gaspar thought he had a chance when the final bell rang. The crowd booed the decision. Nick Corby would protest so loudly that he almost lost his license.[24] As the fighters milled about the ring after the match, a man in a white suit ran down the aisle and threw a sombrero up into the ring. A corner man picked it up and stuck it on Gaspar's head. A Mexican flag was tied around Gaspar's neck. So ended Gaspar's latest chance at the title.

Florentino Fernandez would also soon discover the ins and outs of the boxing game. Instead of getting a shot at the title as promised, he found himself battling an unknown Filipino named Rocky Kalingo in Caracas, Venezuela. Stunningly, Kalingo knocked out the undefeated Cuban in the very first round. Fernandez found himself bumped out of the top ten just like that, while the previously unranked Kalingo entered at the number ten position. A month later Fernandez returned the favor, knocking Kalingo out at the start of the second round in a Havana battle. This fight might not have been on the level. According to *Ring* magazine, after Kalingo put Fernandez down in the first round of their second fight, "The [Cuban] mob wouldn't have it. Kalingo was threatened to the point at which he was scared into near-paralysis. He was stopped."[25] Fernandez would have to wait until August 1961 to get his one and only title shot. He tried to move up to the middleweight ranks and battle champion Gene Fullmer for bigger money. He lost the fight.

The first year of the new decade was an eventful one, though nobody could have predicted that this was the start of what has retrospectively been called "The Sixties." In the summer of 1960, Rome hosted the Olympics. Once again the Cold War found metaphorical battle in the contest of athletes, and boxing proved an irresistible forum for imaginarily settling questions of geopolitical might. A big star of the summer was an eighteen-year-old light-heavyweight from Louisville, Kentucky, named Cassius Clay. He showed up at the Olympics full of patriotic pride and got himself dubbed "Uncle Sam's unofficial goodwill ambassador" by the press corps. When asked by foreign reporters about the "intolerance" against his race in his homeland, Clay responded, "Oh yeah, we've got some problems. But get this straight—it's still the best country in the world." Cassius Clay went on to beat Zbigniew Pietrzykowski of Poland to win the gold medal for Team USA, thanks to some fancy footwork and a blistering third round assault on his opponent. The *Ring's* Nat Fleischer called it the most "outstanding" display of the Sweet Science of the entire tournament.[26]

In national politics, a freshman senator from Massachusetts ran against Republican vice president Richard Nixon and won, becoming the youngest elected president in history. John Kennedy's vitality, earnestness, and good looks seemed to bring the youth of the country into the sphere of public policy. Plus, he was another military veteran commander-in-chief, a true Cold Warrior. Kennedy loved boxing, seeing in it a clear test of manhood and might. A fan of TV fights, JFK had once invited heavyweight champion Floyd Patterson to the White House to tell him that he had to defeat the insidious, Mafia-associated Sonny Liston. "You've *got* to beat this guy," the President pleaded to the unassuming Patterson. Later, Liston would assert that Kennedy was the only reason that the timid Patterson agreed to fight him. "After all," he explained, "you don't tell the President of the United States that you are going to do something and then don't do it."[27]

The year 1960 was a roller coaster for Gaspar's career. He began by facing off with Stan Harrington at the Garden in January. Announcer Jimmy Powers recognized that Gaspar was "one of the most popular welterweights around." Indeed, Gaspar had been voted the nineteenth most popular TV fighter of 1959, according to a fan poll. He had fought six times on TV that year and earned many new supporters. Notably, Isaac Logart, Virgil Akins, and Carmen Basilio had all been bumped off their positions on the list of favorites in 1959. Jimmy Powers would tell the home audience that the recent loss to Fernandez was an "unpopular decision as far as viewers were concerned."[28]

Gaspar won the Harrington fight by unanimous decision. True to the mystery surrounding most of his matches, reporters noted that the crowd booed the decision for five full minutes, loudly protesting even as Gaspar's handlers hoisted him into the air and paraded him around the ring. Many believed that the closeness and excitement of the scrap would generate an instant rematch. But, as often happened, the powers that be thought otherwise.[29] Gaspar would next fight a man who was on the undercard that night—Emile Griffith. Ominously, Griffith would be exposing himself to the Curse of the Indian. "If Ortega fights true to form," ran one article, "there will be a disputed, split decision after it is all over. When he lost to

Florentino Fernandez, the critics thought he really won. When he got the decision over Honolulu's Stan Harrington Jan. 8, they thought he lost. In the meantime, the sad Indian keeps banking the TV dollars."[30]

Emile Alphonse Griffith had been "discovered" by his boss at a hat factory in Manhattan in 1956. He was working at Howard Albert Millinery, and one hot summer day, Mr. Albert was walking through his factory and saw a shirtless kid through the stockroom door. Griffith looked like a Greek god, sweat glistening over a torso rippling with muscles and potential energy. Howard, called "Howie," had once been a fighter himself but had found hat making a more lucrative field. Now, staring at this muscled kid in the stockroom, Howie asked if he'd ever boxed. "Oh, yes," replied the kid. "Where?" "Right here, Mr. Albert and you should know; I've been doing it for almost one year now. Catherine and Mabel bring the hats in to me and I box them and put them on proper shelves."[31]

Griffith was something of an Eternal Innocent. He had a supremely buoyant, disarming personality. He took life as it came, relaxed and seemingly unfazed by what might have seemed the enormous setbacks of his difficult childhood. He had been born in St. Thomas, Virgin Islands, in 1938. His father was a policeman who left the family to seek his fortunes in New York City when Emile was still a young boy. When Emile was eight, his mom got an opportunity to be the cook for the governor of Puerto Rico. Emile was sent to live with a female cousin named Blanche who abused him physically, leaving his back a latticework of ugly welts. At this point, he began to get in trouble at school. The abuse at home continued, compounded by an incident of sexual molestation at the hands of a mysterious "uncle" in a lonely shack out in the country. Emile finally managed to extricate himself from his situation, pleading himself into a boy's home, where he stayed for nearly four years.[32]

After more twists and turns, Emile Griffith went to live with his father in an apartment in Harlem, where he dropped out of school and went to work full time at the hat factory.[33] Here his boss, Howie, cultivated Emile to be a boxer, first by showing him some technique in a back stockroom and then getting his friend, Gil Clancy, who trained young boxers through the Parks Department, to work more seriously with him. The kid was a natural. Recalled Clancy, "I never had to tell Emile anything twice. He learned at an incredibly fast rate, much faster than any fighter I had ever trained."[34] After three weeks with Clancy, Griffith was entered in the Golden Gloves Tournament and made it to the final round, losing only by decision. He went on to win fifty-one of fifty-three amateur fights, along with various local Golden Gloves titles. Griffith went pro at age twenty, having boxed for only two years. He beat everyone he faced his first year, losing only once by split decision before facing Gaspar Ortega at the Garden.

Facing Gaspar for the first time, Griffith was cast as the Golden Boy facing the Old Timer. It was a hard fight to predict. Wrote one journalist, "Ortega, known as the 'unlucky Indian' because of his many close, questionable losses, became the 'lucky Indian' in his last start on Jan. 8, when he won an unpopular decision over Stan Harrington of Hawaii." Gaspar began the week with a slight advantage in the betting, but by the day of the fight, most of the papers had it at even money. This was a big step for Griffith, and he knew it. His mom knew it, too. She would later recall how everyone told her that "no fighter with only 16 bouts under his belt should be in the same ring with Gaspar Ortega."[35]

The fight itself was not particularly notable. Emile came out cautiously, and Gaspar seemed wary, though less "sleepy" than usual. Almost immediately Indio raised a lump under Griffith's left eye. Griffith didn't seem bothered by it. By the fifth round, Griffith had come fully alive, impressing many at ringside. Jack Cuddy later gushed that his performance "verged on the sensational." Of course not everyone agreed with this. At the final bell, by their own accounts, both fighters believed they had won.[36]

As might have been expected, the decision produced much turmoil. Taking center stage, ring announcer Johnnie Addie declared, "Referee Harry Ebbets and Judge Bill Recht vote 8–1–1 for Griffith. And Judge Artie Audala votes 7–3 for Griffith." Ebbets quickly hurried over to Addie and engaged him in fast discussion. Addie seemed surprised, then took the mike again. "It is my error," he now said. "Referee Ebbets' vote should be 8–1–1 in favor of Ortega." At this point, the crowd of twenty-five hundred let out a collective gasp.[37]

Although he still won the split decision, Griffith was stunned by Ebbets's vote. He knew that this fight was "the first hurdle in his campaign to win wider recognition in the fight game," and he needed a decisive victory over his first ranked foe. With typical jollity, Griffith told a reporter, "Ebbets must'a been over at Ebbets Field [former home of the Dodgers] instead of Madison Square Garden." He was a "mad hatter," quipped some in the press. Indeed, it did seem like a strange vote. Sixteen of seventeen ringside writers scored the fight in Griffith's favor. Wrote one wit, it was "16–1, not for the free coinage of silver, but for Griffith." The United Press scored the battle a decisive 8 rounds to 2 for Griffith. Marveled a reporter, "No doubt Ebbets called it as he saw it, but what fight was he looking at?" Lest some TV viewers think the fight actually was close, an AP dispatch admonished, "It may have looked [close] at home on television, but it didn't at ringside."[38]

It was a huge win for Griffith, and he knew it. In an interview two decades and ninety-one fights later, he would tell Red Smith, "Gaspar Ortega! How could I forget? My first main event."[39] The "bright new face in the welterweight division" milked the win for all it was worth. He soon landed a fight with the well-regarded Denny Moyer, and he beat him, too. Though he lost the Moyer rematch on a split decision, Griffith went on to take five straight victories against the likes of Florentino Fernandez and Luis Manuel Rodriguez. Rodriguez, an undefeated, hard-hitting Cuban known to fans as "El Feo" (the Ugly One), was a particularly frightening opponent. He had already defeated Paret, Logart, Akins, and Chico Vejar. Gaspar, complaining about his loss to Griffith, told a reporter that Griffith would get "licked, maybe knocked out by some of the top ones, such as Luis Rodriguez." Emile would later say that he entered the ring against Rodriguez "trembling and kicking the ground with nerves."[40] But Griffith prevailed, getting a ticket to a title shot as a result.

Griffith's rise was almost too spectacular to believe. After starting boxing relatively late in life and with no apparent interest in the sport, he had won the prestigious Golden Gloves tournament within a year and a half of putting on a pair of gloves and now, in only his twenty-fifth professional fight, was going up against the welterweight champion of the world. His opponent was a man whom Gaspar had already faced twice by this point: Kid Paret.

The fight was intense. The combat was savage and inside, with both fighters focusing more on offense than defense. Coming into his man's corner after the twelfth round, manager Gil Clancy told Griffith that he was losing this fight. Griffith seemed out of it, sinking down placidly onto his stool. He had a habit of not following through and finishing fighters off. So Clancy slapped him hard across the face. "That smack woke me up," he would remember. The bell rang and both fighters charged out into the thirteenth round. Both seemed to abandon what remained of their defensive sense. Fists flew wildly; the crowd roared. Then Griffith caught the Cuban in the jaw with a left hook, followed it with a right as Paret spun from the first blow, and then crushed him with a solid left. Paret went down. One minute eleven seconds into the thirteenth round, Paret had suffered the first knockout of his career and Griffith had his first belt. Onlookers were stunned to see Paret, known for his ability to absorb punishment, go down. "It took several minutes to get Paret in condition to leave the ring," marveled the *New York Times*. A *Times* photo showed the odd image of Paret lying back, propped awkwardly on an elbow, while Griffith appeared to be doing a back flip. The subtitle explained, "Emile Griffith does a headstand after defeating Benny Paret." According to Griffith's biographer, this is in fact untrue. Griffith was heading over to jump on his manager Gil Clancy and mistakenly launched himself at referee Jimmy Peerless. Upon realizing what he was doing, he altered his course in midair and landed on his rear, doing the back flip in the process.[41]

An unlikely boxer, Griffith was an even less likely champion. He was, literally, a choirboy. The Reverend Joseph D. Albert of the St. James Missionary Church in Harlem told reporters, "He is meek, he loves children, he is good to his family. Sometimes he teaches Sunday School classes. He knows the bible well."[42] On top of this, Griffith told reporters that he designed ladies' hats.

About a month before Emile Griffith took the title from Kid Paret, Fidel Castro officially banned professional boxing in Cuba (the last pro fight there taking place in December 1961).[43] Cuban boxers were told that if they chose to continue their careers, they would have to leave the island. Most moved to Miami.[44] Florentino Fernandez chose to live in Miami Beach. Luis Manuel Rodriguez settled in Miami as well and went on to fight professionally until 1972, even picking up the welterweight title briefly in 1963. Jose "Mantequilla" Lopez would settle in Mexico City. Isaac Logart, whose title hopes never revived after the 1958 tournament loss to Akins, stuck around New York City. For decades after the Revolution, Cuban boxers virtually disappeared from the scene of top contenders. Felix Savon and Teofilo Stevenson, both excellent fighters, refused lucrative offers to defect.

Kid Gavilan, who had actually lived much of his life in the United States in the 1950s, bucked the trend and decided to settle down on a farm outside of Havana (though he had already retired from the ring by that point). He liked Castro but would come to regret his decision to stay. Though the Cuban government provided him with a two-hundred-dollar-a-month pension and did not take any of his land, a decision was made to build a freeway right through the center of his property. This insult, plus the paltry amount of his pension, left the retired boxer bitter.

He had supported the Revolution financially and felt affronted by Fidel. He started making plans for a getaway. When he told a reporter how unhappy he was in Cuba in 1963, the government increased his pension to one thousand dollars a month and promised him cars and houses. He was still unhappy, and his dissatisfaction was compounded by old boxing injuries that began reasserting themselves. His back hurt him, his eyesight deteriorated. He would later tell the *Chicago Tribune* that he was even jailed by the government during this time for preaching his Jehovah's Witness beliefs.

Gavilan desperately worked to find *reclamaciones* in the United States. One way off the island was to be "reclaimed" by an American citizen who was also a relative. He found two, but the Cuban government dragged its feet. According to his then-wife Olga, in 1968 the government finally told Gavilan that he could leave but only after he cut sugarcane for six months. His health was shot by this point, and one can only imagine what the morale-shattering implications of a return to the brutal world of his youth must have felt like. Unable to return to the fields, Gavilan continued to beg anyone in the government who would listen, until finally he stood facing an official who asked him to take off the dark glasses he wore for his bad eyes. "My God. You're Kid Gavilan," said the stunned official. "What are you doing in Cuba? I thought you left years ago."

The official remembered an earlier kindness and soon the old pugilist had a ticket in his hands—but not one for his wife or his stepson. Gavilan soon settled in Miami, but complications getting the stepson out kept Olga back in Cuba. The two finally divorced in 1985. Gavilan stayed in Miami for the rest of his life.[45]

Benny "Kid" Paret had already made New York City his home at the time of Castro's decision.[46] He had good reason to stay: in his early days fighting at St. Nick's, the Kid had met a girl. Lucy Hernandez had been born in Puerto Rico but raised in New York. Her mom died when she was young, and after her dad remarried, tensions mounted until her stepmother kicked her out of the house. Broke and homeless, Lucy found work as a dancer at local Latin clubs, paying five dollars a week to share a room in a small apartment with an elderly woman. Lucy first met Kid Paret as an envoy from the Tropicana, where she danced, part of a Kid Paret cheering section. (Paret's manager owned the Tropicana.) Benny took notice of the sixteen-year-old beauty and had sent her flowers after the fight. Lucy felt special: "We were all there, but I got the flowers." Sparks struck brightly, despite the fact that Paret spoke no English and Lucy hardly spoke a word of Spanish. They went out on the town, caught flicks on the big screen, danced the mambo and the rhumba and the cha cha cha at the clubs. Then Lucy got pregnant. With few options, she moved into Benny's Bronx apartment. They named their little boy Benny Jr. A month after the birth, they were married.[47]

Three months after Benny married Lucy, he got his first shot at the world welterweight title against Don Jordan.[48] Paret defeated Jordan in a blistering fifteen-round Las Vegas slugfest that left Jordan's head badly swollen and gushing blood from several places. Interest in the televised fight was high, especially in the Caribbean. Fidel Castro, yet to officially end pro boxing at this point (1960), cut several hours off of one of his interviews because, he told a reporter, "he wanted to let Cubans see Kid Paret win the world's welterweight boxing championship." Castro had been closely following Paret's career for some time. In December 1959, he had even sent a telegram to Paret before a big fight: "I won my revolution. Now it's up to you to win your battle." Fidel also managed to find time to say in the interview that America's latest threats against his nation "are simply words, nothing more."[49]

The National Boxing Association wanted Paret to battle Federico Thompson for his first title defense, but Paret instead faced off against Garnet "Sugar" Hart in a nontitle match at the Garden. Paret's management knew his belt was worth something, and they milked it for all it was worth. The fight was the first main event in ten years from the Madison Square Garden not to be televised. Attendance was getting so low that the Mecca of Boxing thought cutting off TV now and again would fill some seats. The plan seemed to work—the Garden doubled its normal TV fight attendance that night. Paret knocked out Hart in the sixth. The fight marked another sort of transition for the Garden. The next TV fight, scheduled for October 8, was to be the first *Saturday Night Fight of the Week* on ABC.[50]

Paret managed to avoid Thompson again for his next fight, which was another "overweight" (and thus unofficial) Garden matchup, this time a nontelevised Tuesday night bout against Portland's Denny Moyer.[51] Surprisingly, Paret lost in a close decision, though he did not seem too troubled by the outcome. It didn't seem to matter to him. On December 10, 1960, Paret had to face the music, finally putting his belt on the line against Federico Thompson. He managed to beat him once again, this time in a unanimous decision. Once again, Thompson used Paret as a human punching bag. Once again, Paret absorbed it all and returned more than his share.[52]

Two days after Castro banned professional boxing in Cuba, Kid Paret faced off against Gaspar Ortega at the Olympic Auditorium in Los Angeles. Like the Hart and Moyer fights, this was to be another nontitle affair for the current champ, another payday without the threat of dethroning. Paret was favored to win and came in at his heaviest weight ever, 154½ pounds. But the Indian was not to be underestimated. Gaspar scored an upset victory, taking a "surprising" unanimous decision. Reported the *New York Times*, both men came out fighting "as if it were a four-rounder. They slugged toe to toe and head to head throughout most of the fight." The *Times* also made an observation about the arena audience. It clearly belonged to Gaspar. "Ortega had a rooting section going for him. The crowd stamped its feet and hollered 'Ortega, rah, [rah], rah!' and 'Indio! Indio!' Indio is Ortega's Mexican nickname."[53] Gaspar remembers how the members of the wild crowd stormed the ring after he won, bedecked his pate with a sombrero, hoisted him atop their shoulders, and carried him around for upwards of fifteen minutes as mariachis played song after jubilant song. The Olympic Auditorium was not so different from a Tijuana arena.

Though Paret was still champion of the world, the loss "took some of the shine off Paret's scheduled title defense against Emil[e] Griffith on April 1 in Miami," observed the *Times*. For Gaspar, the victory was bittersweet." The magazine *Puños y Llaves* called him "El Campeón sin Corona del peso Welter." Welterweight champion without a crown. This fight, it sighed, was another one of those strange events in the sport where a victor can go uncrowned while the lesser man retains his title. Gaspar was never more the spoiler. He seemed destined not to be champion but rather to cause headaches (*dolores de cabeza*) for the other contenders in his division.[54] For Gaspar, the Paret victory was bittersweet. He had just defeated the current champion of the world. But it didn't count. Was he cursed?

Then again, the win lifted Indio straight into position to demand a crack at the title as soon as an opportunity arose. The fight world went abuzz as Paret prepared to battle Griffith in Miami. Many believed that Gaspar had rightfully earned a shot at the Cuban if Griffith couldn't take the crown, or a shot at Griffith if he could.

And so Griffith knocked out Kid Paret and did the unintentional ring somersault as Paret rolled insensate and the cameras flashed.

Gaspar saw a door swing wide open.

It was, at long last, his time.

CHAPTER 10

The Shot

According to legend, back in the 1920s there was a Greek restaurateur who was fed up. Fed up with all these young pugs bouncing over from the boxing gym across the street and eating his food on credit, running up mountains of unpaid bills. The Greek came up with a solution: in exchange for the meals, the boxers must let him become their manager. Whatever his actual reasons for getting involved in boxing, by the late 1950s George Parnassus had become one of the most powerful figures in boxing, helping to twist the sport from its East Coast moorings and speed it towards the Pacific.[1]

George Parnassus immigrated to Los Angeles from Methone, Greece, in 1915. He had been told by his brother that success was to be had in the States. As it turned out, his brother was not speaking from personal experience. A period of scrambling about for American dollars ensued. Parnassus washed dishes, lifted a pick and shovel for the railroad, checked hats at a club, even hawked watermelons on Venice Pier. Eventually, he and his brother bought a restaurant in Phoenix, Arizona, and there, in a community heavily influenced by migrants from south of the border, Parnassus found a home. He married a manicurist named Rosalie Montez de Ocas and learned to speak Spanish. With Rosalie's help, Parnassus made his restaurant into a booming success by catering to the local Latino population. He fine-tuned his Spanish and also refined his English, skills that would serve him well in the years ahead.

Across the street from the restaurant was a boxing gym, and Parnassus became a manager of some of the local fighters. Eventually, the migrant

Mexican laboring community upon which his business depended began to dry up when the local cotton boom fizzled in the mid-1920s, and Parnassus threw in his lot with boxing rather than with feeding people. He pulled up stakes and moved to Los Angeles, putting Spanish ads in *La Opinion* to recruit the local fight talent. By 1941 he had built up a stable of forty-three fighters. Like his serendipitous move to an eatery facing a boxing gym, his move to Los Angeles turned out to be another smart decision. He came to be known as a specialist in developing Latino talent. In 1957 the Olympic Auditorium's matchmaker, Babe McCoy, lost his license (for fixing fights), and Parnassus, whose reputation by then had garnered him great local respect, was recruited as his replacement.[2]

Part of George Parnassus's success was due to his independence. He saw the International Boxing Club as an insidious force that strangled rather than helped boxing. By the time he was running the Olympic, Parnassus publicly refused to deal with the organization. This would prove to be a remarkably useful move. The Hollywood Legion Stadium, his competition, was connected to the IBC, and it seemed to be going down right along with the Octopus.

Just before the 1958 Floyd Patterson–Roy Harris world heavyweight title fight that took place at L.A.'s Wrigley Field, ring announcer Leonard Jacobsen announced to the fans that Los Angeles was the "boxing capital of the world." Given that he said this three thousand miles from the Center of the Universe, one might think he was just playing to local pride. But this was not the case.[3] According to *Sports Illustrated*, California by then was garnering more fight dollars than any other state, New York included, and Los Angeles was the only remaining city in the country that hosted two major fight clubs which put on weekly shows. Plus, Los Angeles had a major outdoor venue in Wrigley Field that regularly hosted fight events. Placing the shift in context, *Sports Illustrated* noted that the whole world of sports seemed to be sliding westward. In 1958 the Brooklyn Dodgers became the Los Angeles Dodgers and the New York Giants became the San Francisco Giants. In 1960 the American Football League opened up its western division.

The reason why boxing was so big in Southern California was obvious to every local observer: the Mexicans. Philosophized Hollywood Legion manager Jim Ogilvie, "They enjoy that type of entertainment. It's cockiness. It's the nature of the people." Aileen Eaton, who ran the Olympic with her husband, Cal, broke it down in terms of numbers: "There are no Mexican football players and no Mexican baseball players to speak of. There are Mexican jockeys, but who roots for jockeys? Boxing is their sport here because there is no bullfighting or soccer." Others had different explanations. One man said that it was a cost issue. Boxing was cheap entertainment. "For two bucks you can kill a night."[4]

For whatever reason, Mexican fight fans seemed to be the most faithful fans in the world. More than one mystified Anglo would comment on their "heart" and spirit. What helped was the fact that after Mexico City, Los Angeles had the largest population of Mexican-originated persons in the world. Spanish speakers filled the Olympic every week, often packing the steeply situated 10,400 seats, whistling, singing, playing instruments, setting off firecrackers, charging into the ring to attack "unfair" referees between rounds, and occasionally going so far as to take apart the stands and even the retaining walls when calls went against their man. *Sports Illustrated* captured the Olympic fans with no small dose of condescension: "whistling with mucho sentimentalismo and length at the girls, without regard to beauty, whooping at their fighters—'¡Sígalo! ¡Sígalo! (After him!)'—and drinking enormous quantities of beer."[5]

The owners, Cal and Aileen Eaton, couldn't have been happier. "They drink beer, have a ball," smiled Aileen, whose mile-long Cadillac and loud red hair captured the theater of the sport. "And thank goodness for that. I have the concession." Aileen and her husband catered to the audience further by paying a group of youths to play bullfight music between the rounds. The Original Juvenile Band from East L.A. even had its own uniforms (which they rarely wore). Given this massive local audience, it seemed odd that so few local entrepreneurs looked to develop fighters south of the border. Parnassus, reporters conceded, was "miles ahead" of the rest of the game in this respect. An AP piece noted that the Greek had a "simple recipe for success. . . . Using Los Angeles as the bowl, mix one Mexican and one fighter of any other nationality."[6] In the spring of 1961, the Mexican fighter was an easy choice—Gaspar Ortega.

Between his first match with Emile Griffith in 1960 and his second with Benny Paret in early 1961, Gaspar had fought nine times, winning the first six and losing the last three. The Griffith loss had sent him on a self-imposed Mexico recoup mission, and there he defeated a fellow from Juarez named Armando Muniz. He then headed north of the border to battle such unnotables as Germany's Karl Heinz Guder in Fresno and Johnny Gonsalves in Oakland. Gaspar finally made his way back to Madison Square Garden, where he was defeated by the fearsome Federico

Thompson in a decision roundly booed by the fans but hailed as correct by most fight reporters. Nick Corby threw a tantrum in the ring while Gaspar trotted up and cordially shook hands with his opponent. Again, the disagreement between fans and reporters regarding Gaspar's bout result shrouded his performance.

The loss to Federico Thompson seemed to put a hiccup in Gaspar's step. He lost his next two fights. The first was a rematch against Kid Rayo in Long Beach, California; the second, a tough brawl with aging battler Carmen Basilio in his "comeback" at the Garden ("All these big shots want me to quit," Basilio reportedly complained, "but who'll see to it I make the $10,000 to $12,000 a year I need to get by?")[7]. The Kid Rayo fight was a mess. The boxer called "rayo" (which means "lightning" in Spanish), ran circles around Gaspar. "He was 100 percent faster than me. It was terrible." Though Gaspar had beaten the Nicaraguan "Kid" just months before, in this fight he just couldn't seem to catch up with him. As for Basilio, Gaspar believes that he won that one. Basilio disagrees: "I kicked his ass," he told me. He had been told to watch for Gaspar's slippery style and rugged ability to take a punch. "I handled him pretty good," was his conclusion.[8] The fight was an ABC *Saturday Night Fight of the Week*. Both men put up a dramatic performance, which was all the more impressive for Gaspar, who gave up a full ten pounds to his heavier foe. Don Dunphy warned the television home audience that El Indio "always seems to be in split decisions."

A split wasn't coming, but that didn't mean the Basilio decision wasn't close. All three scorers gave Gaspar four rounds out of ten. It was close enough that Don Dunphy recognized, just before the decision was given, that it could go either way. But Gaspar lost. The fight certainly had its moments, though. One of the most memorable had nothing to do with punching. Coming into the tenth round, the two men touched gloves. It is a common and ancient sign of respect, and between these two men of such vast differences in life experience and background, it was moving. Here, the two were equal. As Kipling once mused,

> . . . there is neither East nor West, Border, nor Breed, nor Birth,
> When two strong men stand face to face, though they come from
> the ends of the earth![9]

Carmen himself would only fight two more times, his final battle a losing last-ditch title shot for the middleweight crown against Paul Pender. Gaspar would next fight Benny Paret at the Olympic and score the big upset victory that vaulted him into position to get a title shot against Griffith. But, of course, this was boxing, so nothing ever was certain. Luckily for Gaspar, there was George Parnassus.

Parnassus was looking for the next Latino sensation. He had managed Los Angeles native Art "The Golden Boy" Aragon in the 1950s, had set him up for a losing title fight against Carmen Basilio in 1958, and then watched him get handed down in the ranks. In Gaspar, Parnassus saw a big, popular score. He saw the first Mexican welterweight champion of the world. Working deals was Parnassus's forte, and he would need to work one with Kid Paret (who expected an immediate rematch against Griffith) to make this happen. Parnassus's ace in the hole was money. Paret could score piles of it by doing nothing. All he had to do was sit out one fight and then battle the winner for the title. It was a win-win for the Cuban.

Still, Parnassus found that it wasn't so easy to make it all come together. He colorfully described a New York meeting to reporters: "We all head into a room at the hotel here—managers, lawyers, everyone. Pretty soon, they all start smoking and there is so much smoke, you can hardly see. And me with asthma. I'm half worrying about the fight and half about my asthma." Parnassus tried to get down to business, but language issues arose. "Then Ortega's and Paret's crowd start talking in Spanish. This confuses me even more and I wonder how I can get back at them. Then it hits me. I start talking Greek and no one in the room understands me. So we all go back to English."[10] Humor aside, Parnassus got Paret's management to sit on the sidelines for twenty thousand dollars while convincing Griffith's team that a Los Angeles fight against Indio would net a huge gate. The Olympic would hand over ten thousand dollars to Paret, while Griffith and Ortega would each fork over five thousand dollars. Parnassus guaranteed the Virgin Islander fifty thousand dollars for himself, while Ortega was to receive 20 percent of the gate and the television money. As a further balm to Paret, if Gaspar won, the Kid was promised the first crack at the title instead of an immediate Griffith-Ortega rematch.[11]

Working with owners Cal and Aileen Eaton, Parnassus diligently pumped up the upcoming battle. He predicted a massive one-hundred-thousand-dollar gate, on top of the sixty thousand dollars they'd pull in from television. A 150-mile radius TV blackout would ensure that local fans had no choice but to come to the Olympic. Tijuana would be blacked out. *El Heraldo* predicted that not only would the Olympic be sold out but "the great majority of Mexican residents of the state of California and Baja California" would fully support Gaspar.[12]

An epic battle was promised. Although Gaspar had lost their first match, neither man had ever been knocked out, and the longer, fifteen-round setting lent novel possibilities for a shocking upset. The unstoppable kid dynamo would face the wily old gladiator. The papers pointed out that Gaspar had already defeated two former world champions—Kid Gavilan and Tony DeMarco—along with one who had held it at the time, Kid Paret. Whitey Bimstein and Nick Corby predicted a knockout for their man. When asked to explain Gaspar's "spotty" record, his team lamely pointed out that now he had an "incentive" to win.[13]

Meeting with Parnassus for the first time, Indio was immediately impressed with the Greek-accented, Spanish-speaking gentleman in the sharp business suit. Parnassus put an arm around him and smiled. "You're gonna be the champion." Parnassus knew a champion when he saw one, he said. He also knew how to cuckold the press. His bright gate predictions, his occasional skirmishes with reporters, the colorful quips he tossed out (he had coined the term *bolo punch* decades before Gavilan was associated with it)[14], and a reputation for fairness toward his fighters made him popular in the boxing world. Parnassus made things happen in Los Angeles.

To say that Gaspar was to fight Griffith before a friendly audience would be an understatement. When Indio beat Benny Paret at the Olympic for the nontitle match, the Mexican fans were in full, fine form. Paret actually blamed his loss on confusion caused by the L.A. audience. It was reported that they did more than just yell; they threw beer at him. Paret's manager later complained, "I was very annoyed at the treatment my fighter got from the crowd." He vowed never to let his man fight there again.[15]

On May 7, 1961, the *New York Times* announced that Gaspar had flown into LAX and would be preparing for the match set for the 27th of that month.[16] Gaspar settled into a downtown hotel and immediately started training. He knew that getting a routine established was essential, and as always, he was diligent and highly motivated. Each morning someone picked him up in a car and took him to McArthur Park to go for a run. Afterward, he would be driven to the Main Street Gym in downtown Los Angeles.

At the Main Street Gym, Gaspar got more than he wanted. The place was completely packed, every day, with Mexicans and Mexican Americans offering support and opinions. It was too much. They gave him fighting tips and worried him by constantly telling him how proud they were. "I knew I was going to fight for them," says Gaspar. The fans did not need to say so. Still, Gaspar tried his best to maintain his strict pre-fight rituals—no women, early bedtimes, lots of steak. Then, on May 14, Griffith's team made an announcement. Griffith was sick. The fight would have to be postponed a week.[17] For Gaspar, the delay probably turned into a liability.

About five days before the new date, Gaspar's trainers brought in a new guy to spar with him. His name was Jose Stable. "I have no idea how he got there," explains Gaspar. "He was Latino or black or something." Stable, who was an Afro-Cuban, did not seem to understand the meaning of sparring. He came right after Gaspar, hard and fast. "It was no train-ing session. It was a fight." Stable battled Gaspar fiercely, tiring the title contender out, driving blows into any opening he could find.

Then things got worse. Gaspar began to feel bad in the days leading up to the fight. His body felt more like it did after a fight than before one. He began to get very worried. Was he getting sick? Was it just nerves? Unlike in New York, in Los Angeles the pressure to win was constant and almost overpowering. Everywhere he went he heard people, many of them Mexi-can nationals, telling him what he had to do in the ring. Nick Corby was no moderating force; he seemed beside himself with enthusiasm. "You're the only Mexican fighter who has raised up Tijuana into the clouds," he would say, eyes afire with ambition. "Do NOT let her fall!"

When Gaspar first learned that he was to be in a title fight, he called his brothers in Tijuana. "We already know," they told him. "It's in the papers." Local papers and magazines were giving Tijuana fans regular updates on the fight. In fact, the Baja media was in something of a frenzy. *El Heraldo* gushed that, "skillfully directed by Nick Corby," Gaspar was now finally in position to give the "universal scepter to Mexico." Columns repeatedly praised Corby and Bimstein and Parnassus and exalted Gas-par as the "shining star of the pugilistic firmament." He would win, they predicted, despite what nay-saying oddsmakers thought. An entire issue of the Baja magazine *K.O.* was devoted to him. In an interview printed in *El Heraldo*, Gaspar explained what this fight meant to him. With "his little eyes shining," the journalist wrote, the contender explained that he would be battling for "my wife, my children, my land." It would be a "culmination" of his career. "I will be welterweight champion," Gaspar supposedly predicted.[18]

The usual title fight hype commenced north of the border as well. Papers noted that the fight had triggered a Mexican invasion, as Ortega fans streamed north from Baja to see the battle.[19] Others reported just how important the fight was to a man like Gaspar. "Ortega is one of the most popular of television fighters," wrote Frankie Goodman, "and has had more appearances on the tube than any fighter except Tiger Jones. He realizes that this is his one and only chance to become world champion and intends to make the supreme effort." Other pieces pointed out that Gaspar "hopes to become first native of Mexico to capture a ring title above lightweight division." The last Mexican to try this was Baby Arizmendi, who lost to Henry Armstrong back in 1939. That fight also happened to be at the Olympic Auditorium.

Given the bizarre decision in their previous contest, Ortega-Griffith II was set up to be something of a grudge match. An ABC ad ran in the *Times* on June 3: "TONIGHT'S TELEVISION HIGHLIGHT . . . Emile Griffith wants to keep his welterweight title. Gaspar Ortega wants it."[20] Both sides openly declared that their man had won the previous matchup. Though the odds were 2–1 for Griffith, they had actually narrowed from 12–5. According to insiders, Ortega's "impressive" workouts had given him the slight last-minute boost. Jose Stable, whether by plan or happenstance, had helped shift the odds and likely generated more betting revenue.

The pressure did not seem to faze Griffith. He smiled and joked with reporters and fans. He didn't care who wore what color trunks, he said when asked. "Let Ortega take his pick." Any glove requests? "Any old kind," he smiled. In one bizarre pre-fight interview, Griffith didn't even want to talk about boxing. "The Jackie Kennedy pillbox," he explained, "will remain in vogue . . . But hats will come in a greater variety of shape and materials than ever this year. We're featuring caribou, ostrich, novelty braids, feathers and velours. With the bouffant coiffure still in vogue, look for higher pillboxes." With his bright smile and penchant for tight pants and suede boots and gold jewelry, Griffith seemed outsized for his humble background, a butterfly aflitter on strong drafts. The stink of the ring could not touch him. At one of his training sessions in Santa Monica, over three thousand people came just to watch him move. It was more people, a reporter noted, than you'd see coming to "most fights today." Two days before the fight, an amiable Griffith did a couple of radio and television spots to build up excitement. He told reporters that he was confident that he would defeat Gaspar, though he wouldn't necessarily be trying to knock him out. Gaspar, after all, had never been knocked out. More than one sportswriter retorted that nobody had thought Paret could be knocked out, either.[21]

Saturday, June 3, 1961. A fighter sits atop a massage table and has his hands wrapped with tape.

Gaspar arrived at the Olympic at 5:30 P.M. He entered from the street and walked down to his dressing room, a smallish affair with lockers, heavy wooden chairs, and a one-person shower. Freddie Brown met him and helped him get ready for the show. After wrapping his hands, Brown left Gaspar alone with his thoughts. The others in the dressing room seemed quiet and contemplative. There was Brown and Whitey Bimstein and Nick Corby, and another second, a Filipino guy whose name Gaspar no longer remembers. Happy Rodriguez was long gone by this point. He had stopped training Gaspar back in 1957. The traveling was tough on his job at the Post Office. According to Gaspar, it was not a great loss; he believes that he was always his own best trainer. Bimstein helped some with strategy, but for the most part, Gaspar's style reflected his personal gym observations and the occasional helpful pointer he received. The discipline he imposed on himself was never matched by the insights of others.

Gaspar hopped off the table and started his warm-up routine. He tried to keep loose. He bent and bobbed, shadow boxed and moved. He kept an eye on the clock. But he could not stop thinking about the pressure. He could feel the audience out there, pulsing, alive. The whole auditorium would be packed, just for him. TV sets would be dialed in throughout Mexamerica. Millions would watch this performance.

At ten 'til seven they moved out. First went a security guy, then Corby, and then Gaspar, looking down the whole time. "I felt like I was going to disappoint my people."

Out into the hall, through the doors, and into the roar they went. It was just as Gaspar had feared. The arena screamed with life. Music, cheers, chants, flags, sombreros, whistles. Up the aisle he went, up the final four steps, through the ropes.

In TV land, Don Dunphy welcomes the world to the *Fight of the Week*, a battle for the welterweight crown. According to Dunphy, this is Ortega's thirtieth TV performance. "You're going to hear an awful lot of cheering," he says. He then remarks on the "thousands" of Gaspar's "countrymen from nearby Mexico [who] have come to see if he can wrest the title from Emile Griffith." At this point, Nick Corby can barely contain himself. He's putting his hand on a rope and leaning in, flipping a toe over his foot. Then he lets go of the rope and takes a few steps. Then he walks back over toward Gaspar, who doesn't seem to be paying attention. In the other corner, Griffith has separated himself from his crew. He rolls his head comfortably from side to side.

Announcer Jimmy Lennon welcomes everyone and introduces a couple of current champions, including lightweight sensation Davey Moore. The champions take turns going to each corner and shaking hands with the fighters, looking sharp in their expensive suits. As Jimmy continues, the screen goes fuzzy. The audio still works, but now there's the all-too-common cartoon still shot of a repair man running to a TV, the screen of which shows a man seemingly oozing out. The title reads, "SORRY, WE'VE LOST OUR PICTURE." The picture comes back in time to show referee Tommy Hart being announced. Hart is standing in a neutral corner, and he looks like a fighter himself. He did, in fact, box as a middleweight during the Depression.

Then come the fighters. Lennon: "Tonight in the role of the challenger, the number one contender, out of the black corner, brightly arrayed, wearing black trunks with a white stripe, coming here from Mexicali and Tijuana in Baja California." The crowd begins to let it out now, whistling and hollering. "146 pounds, Gaspar *Eeeeendio Ortegaaa!*" Jimmy holds his arm out while he's saying the name, notes in hand extending the gesture, pointing squarely at Gaspar. The cheering crescendo builds and washes over the ring. Jimmy finishes the introduction by flipping his hand up sharply, like a conductor. Gaspar emerges from his corner, throws a couple half punches, then heads back, studiously avoiding any eye contact with the crowd.

Jimmy begins to announce Griffith, and the boos begin. "Welterweight champion of the world . . ." BOOOOOOO " . . . Emile Griffith!" Griffith gives a patrician bow to Jimmy. Griffith's corner frantically claps, as if to erase the overwhelming negative energy projected onto their man. The boxers come to the center. Tommy Hart tells them that he's already gone over the instructions in the dressing room, so there's "no need to belabor the point." Gaspar has his back to the camera in a tight shot. His glorious, serape-style robe fills a great chunk of the screen. No three mandatory knockdowns will end the fight, says Tommy. Corby rubs Gaspar's back, pulls the white towel off from around his neck. This is a title fight, Tommy needlessly reminds the boxers. "So let's fight like it."

The fighters return to their corners as Dunphy describes the California point system to the home audience. An image appears of a cigar with boxing headgear and boxing gloves (one of which holds—you guessed it—a cigar). The screen shows "ROUND 1" and beneath that "EL PRODUCTO."

The bell rings.

They come right out. Gaspar seems light on his feet. His trademark bobbing begins. Dunphy: "Look for Ortega to press Griffith and fight in flurries." The two begin to trade ginger punches, feeling each other out. There's an awkward clinch. Griffith seems to have one of Gaspar's gloves. Dunphy points out that the boxers look tense. An exchange. "Ortega may look easy to hit but he rolls with a lot of punches, slides away," says Dunphy. Indeed, Gaspar is moving his body rapidly left to right, combining this with the up and down of his head. He's a slippery target. The round wears on and Dunphy notes that none of the punches thrown by either man have met their mark. "They really haven't opened up, they're very tense." Dunphy also reminds us how frustrated Gaspar has been in his ongoing quest for a title shot. "He should be inspired tonight."

Then Gaspar opens up, both arms making wide hooks, left-right-left-right. Griffith joins him. Both men are throwing punches simultaneously, arms in wide right angles, pumping away. "See what I mean about the flurrying?" Dunphy sounds pleased. They break. Now Gaspar appears to be stalking Griffith around the ring. Of course, this does not mean the Virgin Islander is in any trouble. He moves smoothly, avoiding Gaspar's long, wild throws. The round ends.

As round two begins, Dunphy gushes about Gaspar's robe, "a composite of every Mexican sunset that ever was." It is clear that the second round will be much different from the first. The fighters have loosened up. They skirmish, back off, bounce side to side. Gaspar moves his upper body much more, while Griffith, a counterpuncher by nature, waits for his opportunity. Another ugly clinch. Tommy Hart comes in and separates them. More jabs, more flurries. Griffith still seems to be the prey, backing away. His back hits the ropes and Gaspar goes in. Another clinch. They break. Gaspar moves his shoulders, throws some long-range jabs. Griffith counters with a few impressive lefts. Griffith connects a few times, solidly to Gaspar's head, even while moving backwards. The round ends with another clinch.

Between rounds, the camera closes in on Griffith. As Gil Clancy mimes what look to be uppercuts, Emile looks up at him, intent. The shot switches to Gaspar's corner. You can't see him past Bimstein and Corby. What is he thinking? Watching the tape with me, Gaspar explained, "All my energy left me alone." A superimposed cartoon Sharpie executes soldier arms with a gigantic razor at midring. The bell rings. Round three.

Dunphy has just described the first two rounds as "fairly close." Indeed, while Griffith seems more assured, Gaspar is clearly the aggressor, pushing the fight. Now the fighters come in, and Gaspar begins to punch. Then Griffith comes in. Then a long, ugly clinch. The crowd boos. "Now the boys are getting at the stage where they're annoyed at each other." They try to break, but there's lots of infighting, arms twisted. The crowd yells lots of Spanish. You can hear "Andale!" and "Indio!"

It's in the midst of an exchange when it happens. Indio is hitting away at the body when Griffith finds an opening and tags him on the chin with a solid left. Gaspar is still punching at the time, but the impact causes his next shot to fly wide. He steps back, clearly dazed. "Ortega was rocked back with one there." Griffith comes in and Gaspar begins to move his torso in very wide, low arcs. He seems to be moving unconsciously. His body is acting of its own accord, obeying a deep instinct to present a moving target. Gaspar remembers that he had lost all sense of direction after that punch. That punch made his mind go blank.

Dunphy: "And Gaspar may be a little bit hurt."

It was much worse than that. Gaspar had rarely been hit like that, with such clear, sharp contact. But he stays in the fight. He backpedals and shakes his head minutely. He's trying to clear out the fog. He tries to tie up Griffith, who seems frustrated. But Griffith is very good. He doesn't mind infighting, and he finds holes. His punches seem much faster than Gaspar's now. Still, Dunphy sees a fight. "Both have sampled heavy leather in this round. Gaspar Ortega has taken a little more, maybe." After a minute or so, Gaspar does seem to wake up. He starts a real exchange, ends the round strong.

Round four begins with Sharpie spraying a big "4" with a can of shaving cream. Griffith is looking for an opening, waiting. Gaspar seems wary, no longer interested in pushing the fight. If you look at the feet, you can see another difference. Gaspar is fighting flat-footed. Griffith's feet are still dancing. A solid left about halfway through round four visibly shakes Gaspar. With thirty seconds left, Dunphy notes Indio's excessive holding, his slow counters, the apparent openness of his chin. This is not the Indio we are used to seeing. "He's got Ortega in trouble," Dunphy says. The bell rings. Dunphy notes it was a "big round" for the Virgin Islander.

Round five. "The pace has been exhausting and dogged," notes Dunphy. He tells us that Griffith has been doing a good job defending his title. Almost as if he can hear the home broadcast, Gaspar comes alive once more. He comes out of a clinch and goes right after Griffith, pummeling away with a flurry of right and left hooks. The crowd wakes up, cheering loudly. Griffith backs off with Gaspar still swinging wide, looping punches, then comes in fast for another clinch. He appears to be playing defensive again, determined not to take Indio's bait. The two come together, infight, come apart, blasting away. Dunphy can't think of much to say. He tells the audiences, "it's hard-paced—a rough one."

Round six is brought to us by Muriel Cigars. With still nine rounds to go, one wonders how the two can keep up with this pace. Dunphy tells us that Ortega has a cut above the left eye. Referee Tommy Hart tells Griffith to keep his punches up; he's hitting too low. Gaspar's performance now reminds one of a radio coming in and out of frequency. He fades, then comes alive for brief flurries. Griffith waits, countering when opportunities arrive.

Between the sixth and seventh rounds, Dunphy announces that another title fight will be aired next week, a light-heavyweight bout between the "Ageless" Archie Moore and challenger Giulio Rinaldi. Moore is ancient; Dunphy tells us he started boxing when Rinaldi was one-year old. Round seven begins. Again Gaspar is cautious, and Griffith, awaiting his counter, doesn't throw anything right away. He pops a couple of jabs to get Gaspar swinging again.

Dunphy starts to tell us about Griffith's visible improvement over the past year. But he cuts himself off. Gaspar is suddenly falling back. His shoulders move left and right, as if still dodging blows, but he is going down. He catches his fall with his right glove, then wobbles over onto his left glove. He pops up onto his left knee, but he can't get up. He plunges right, stumbling, looking for the ropes. He looks like a baby horse, seconds old. He makes it to the center rope, grips it, and takes a knee. Tommy Hart is already counting. By the time Hart's down in front of Gaspar he's on number four. He holds his fingers up in front of Indio's face. "Five, six, seven." Dunphy is counting along with him. At eight Gaspar starts to rise. Hart wipes Gaspar's gloves on his shirt and dashes them back together. Dunphy reminds us that Ortega has never been knocked out. Griffith starts head-hunting, looking for the final shot to put his opponent down. Gaspar won't let him find a clean opening; he clinches. Dunphy: "Ortega, calling on all his experience to try to stay in there." A hard left to the head again rattles the Indian, but he won't go down. Another cut, over the right eye, pops up on Gaspar's face. Griffith is sending big, chopping hooks down onto Gaspar's crown. They are awkward, killing punches, punches designed to end a fight. Gaspar looks terrible. He is bent over in half, making low U-shapes to make things hard for Griffith. Occasionally, he sends out a weak, futile punch. Griffith throws a hard left and a hard right, and both punches solidly connect, and Gaspar is down on the mat again. This fall looks much worse. Gaspar is lying on his side. He literally crawls over to the ropes. He pays no attention to Tommy Hart counting away as he slowly, slowly uses the ropes to climb his way back up. "Five, six." Indio pauses at seven for a hard second. He's cognizant again. At eight he is back on his feet.

As soon as Tommy brings the two together, Griffith literally hurls himself at Gaspar, flying behind a long, straight right. He almost shoots straight past his quarry. Gaspar smartly clinches, but Emile keeps Indio back enough to maintain some space for hooks and uppercuts. Gaspar is backing up to the corner. Dunphy hollers, "There's the bell, but they didn't hear the bell!" They keep punching away. Griffith continues to throw big, looping downward blows. Then the bell can be heard, but the boxers seem to ignore it. "Hold everything! Hold everything! Hold everything!" screams Dunphy. Tommy Hart pulls the two men apart. The fighters retreat. Gaspar, says Dunphy, "goes back to his corner after the worst beating he has ever taken in a prize ring." It is true. We've just witnessed the most devastating round of his career. It will never leave him, as long as he will live. "He's never been knocked out, but he came mighty close to it."

Between rounds, Dunphy corrects himself. That was just the warning whistle, not the bell, that he had heard. In the corner, Bimstein works Gaspar's cuts while Corby leans through the ropes and talks to him. Gaspar is again blocked, hidden from the camera by Corby. But his arms are limp, gloves leaning against his inner thighs. It is not a good sign. Round eight begins.

Gaspar looks terrible. His punches look like a cat pawing something lazily on a sunny afternoon. Griffith seems to fire ten shots for every one delivered by the Indian. Yet Gaspar keeps on bending, powered by what can only be called "autopilot defense." Griffith is "trying to get that one shot in there" to finish the slaughter. And Gaspar "is just throwing punches." Somehow, he makes it through the whole round without meeting the floor.

Round nine starts and Gaspar shows more life. He's not going to just let Griffith have his way. He brings forth newfound flurries. Dunphy marvels at how the Indian just "tries all the time." Gaspar closes the round impressively, with uppercuts that look well-aimed and backed with power. Round ten, and Gaspar is, incredibly, getting stronger. Dunphy is amazed. "This must be a surprise to all of us who thought Ortega couldn't make it after round seven, but here he is in round ten." Gaspar is finally working Griffith's body to wear him down, a strategy that he usually stuck with against tough opponents. It is a long-range sort of strategy, the kind of thing you might see when a fighter thinks he has some time left to work. The sense of desperation seems to have left Gaspar. The crowd notices. It comes alive. The spectators cheer as he trades punches with the champ. "Indian Ortega still full of fight, holding Griffith against the ropes." More cheers. Now Gaspar is looking for the head. He's actually trying to turn this thing around.

"Arrribba!! Andale!!!"

But it is not to be. Griffith seems to wake up from his defensive posture. After one Gaspar flurry, the Virgin Islander answers even more furiously. He connects repeatedly. Gaspar bends and moves, but still he gets hit. They clinch. They exchange again, and the round ends. Dunphy remarks that the crowd is mainly for Ortega tonight, as if this weren't obvious. "Many thousands came over from Mexico," he tells us.

Between rounds, Dunphy notes that the next day the network will be broadcasting a "complete word and picture show" of President Kennedy's meeting with Khrushchev.

Round eleven begins. Whatever reserve Gaspar drew upon the previous two rounds seems to have dried up. Dunphy still comments on Indio's amazing endurance, though he is also impressed with how "fresh" his rival is. When not tied up in a clinch, Griffith fires off strong, sure jabs. With less than ten seconds to go in the round, Griffith breaks out of another Gaspar-inspired clinch and connects solidly with an uppercut. Then a left hook. Then a right uppercut. Another left. Another right. He's hitting Gaspar's head solidly, at will. Gaspar still bends and moves, but he is locked in nightmare slow motion. Anyone who's seen him fight on TV more than once understands the significance of this beating. It is devastating to see. He's bending low, swerving his body, but it's useless. It is a caricature of the old Indio. Griffith times his punch and catches Gaspar with a solid uppercut. The head snaps back. Another uppercut, the same damn punch, only this time the connection is full and complete. Gaspar looks like a rag doll. Miraculously, the bell rings.

After a commercial, Dunphy tells us that Tommy Hart "took a good look at Ortega" in his corner. Hart seems to think that he can go on. Round twelve opens, Gaspar lurches off of his stool, and Griffith flies across the ring, eager to finish the job. Gaspar wisely ties him up. He's got nothing left. Just the oldest defense there is. Tie the guy up. Lots of fighters these days wouldn't have answered the bell. The ref breaks the two, and, amazingly, Gaspar decides once more to keep on fighting. But his strategy is lowest common denominator at this stage. He traps Griffith's right glove beneath his left armpit and fires close uppercuts to Griffith's chin with his other hand. Griffith returns some of the fire, awkwardly playing along, but he really just wants to get some space. He alternates shots with pushing away at Gaspar's torso. He seems to be communicating, "let me go, let me finish this." Tommy Hart breaks them, staring hard at Gaspar. The lopsided exchange continues. Gaspar is slowly, robotically punching, while Griffith looks for a clean shot. Every tap reels the Indian. Gaspar's knee briefly dips and bounces off the mat. He's back up again, leaning forward like a carpenter's steel square. Now Griffith is firing devastating head shots, one after the other. But Gaspar won't go down.

So Tommy Hart stops it.

Hart wraps his arms around Griffith. It's all over. Gaspar just stands there, dazed. Hart turns to him and leads him to a corner, a guiding arm around his waist. Police officers pop into the ring to keep out the expected stage rush. But there is none. The crowd is muted. They know what they saw. They will leave quietly.

"Nobody was ever gamer than the Mexicali Indian," says Dunphy.

Griffith briefly raises an arm, then goes over and congratulates his opponent. He puts up a glove, touches Gaspar's head. Even with the grainy black and white, you can see Gaspar's expression. He's crying.

PART III

The Hardest Game

"The sickening thump of a fighter near
death made the whole world wonder how
far a man could go to make money."

Life Magazine, April 6, 1962,
following Griffith-Paret III

"A generation grew up seeing boxing for
free, in its living room, without the tangy
smells and spattered gore of ringside. It
demanded national names, and got 20
years of Gaspar Ortega and Tiger Jones.
Then it got bored and turned on more
predictable and colorful violence."

New York Times,
September 21, 1964

CHAPTER 11

Bloodying the Sport

Emile Griffith defeated Gaspar Ortega on a Saturday night. Before regular TV boxing went off the air, a struggling *Friday Night Fights* limped into the Saturday night slot, then back briefly to Friday before vanishing forever. The reasons for the end read like the ingredients for disaster: some greed, some overexposure, some crime, some death, some changes in audience taste. By the time Indio fought Griffith for the title, the writing was on the wall. Before charting the final lurches into the abyss for both TV boxing and Gaspar's career, it's useful to examine some ominous developments.

Back in 1955, the Justice Department filed a civil antitrust suit claiming that the International Boxing Club violated the Sherman Antitrust Act. The Octopus rebutted, arguing that boxing was akin to baseball, which had previously won a Supreme Court decision that effectively exempted it from antitrust law. The suit was dismissed. The government appealed, stating forcefully that boxing uniquely used interstate commerce in a manner that required a different ruling. Federal prosecutors focused especially on the IBC's use of television and radio. This time, the Court ruled that a "cause of action" was warranted. Thus was a door opened for ambitious congressmen to lead public attacks against the IBC.[1]

Next came the Justice Department's operation to take down the "underworld commissioner" of boxing, Mr. Gray himself. The Akins-Logart fight indictments of 1958 had started the ball rolling. Explained the assistant to New York district attorney Frank Hogan, the fight had "unequivocally" established Mr. Gray as "the most powerful figure in boxing. Not only did he assert control over both contenders, but he also determined where and under what terms the match was to take place."[2]

In his book *Boxing Confidential* (2002), Jim Brady argues that in order to truly understand Carbo's downfall, we must first notice certain events that happened in 1957. On May 2, mob boss Frank "the Uncle" Costello was returning from dinner to his Central Park West apartment when a man in a dark fedora approached him and said, "This is for you Frank," before firing a shot at his head. The bullet grazed Costello's forehead and he lived, but so terrified did he become that he relinquished his part of New York's crime racket to rival Vito Genovese, the man behind the hit. Genovese was not finished. Later that same year, Vito ordered two gunmen to walk into a barbershop in the ritzy Park Sheraton Hotel where Albert Anastasia, "the boss of bosses," was sitting in a chair for his daily shave and trim. The hoods pumped five rounds into Anastasia's head and torso, killing him instantly. Lots of people were around, but strangely, nobody saw anything. In the fallout of the murders, Carbo found himself cast adrift. According to the FBI, Carbo had been "protected" by Costello, who had ultimately answered to Anastasia. Now Carbo's protectors were gone. Without the protective influence of these mob bosses on the justice system, Carbo found that the police suddenly seemed eager to get at him, so he went into hiding.[3]

The man ultimately responsible for "taking down" Carbo was a former Columbia College welterweight champion named Jack Bonomi. Striking an imposing figure with his six-foot, 175-pound frame and penchant for twenty-five-cent Havana cigars, Bonomi had served in World War II (he had been aboard a B-24 en route to Okinawa when Japan surrendered) and now worked for the Rackets Bureau in New York City. He had already been tracking a "top guy" behind the mob's fight racket, referred to variously as "the Uncle," "the Ambassador," and even "She." After the Anastasia hit, a wiretap of a discombobulated hood named Hymie "The Mink" Wallman provided Bonomi with evidence that "the Uncle" was indeed Frank Carbo. Bonomi went back over the transcripts and everything fell into place. Carbo's locations correlated with prior references to the activities of the mysterious fight "Ambassador." Bonomi toiled alone for months with minimal help, gathering evidence to bust the fight racket wide open. He might have gotten some assistance from the FBI, but that organization was headed by the only man in America who didn't think that the mob existed—J. Edgar Hoover. Hoover even banned the *use* of the word "Mafia" in FBI reports and internal memos. There is much speculation as to why. According to some scholars, Hoover was concerned that the mob might use its money to corrupt agents and tarnish the Bureau's reputation or that mob cases were sticky and did not lead to the fast convictions that Hoover liked. Another, conspiratorial school of thought has it that the Mafia had incriminating photos of Hoover participating in homosexual acts.[4] Regardless, the FBI had been gathering files against Carbo for years by this point, but chose not to share its wealth with Jack Bonomi.

The fateful moment came one evening in the summer of 1959, just as Bonomi was washing up for dinner. The phone rang and Jack's wife answered, said it was for him. It was an informant. He told Bonomi that Carbo was hiding in Haddon Township, New Jersey. Bonomi quickly sent one of his best detectives, Frank Marrone, on his way, and placed another four on high alert. Then Jack sat down to eat with his family; stakeouts were more marathons than sprints. After a nice dinner, the phone rang again. It was Marrone. No Carbo in sight. But Bonomi knew that his lead was solid. He sent the other four cops down to Jersey and told the detective to get a closer look at the house. Then he returned to the table and finished his coffee. The clock's hands kept spinning, no word from his men. Then, shortly after midnight, Marrone spotted Carbo watching a movie on TV in the house and called his boss. Bonomi told Marrone that he was watching the same thing. Funny. He ordered the cops to move.

Marrone approached the door and rang the bell. He was greeted by mobster "Blinky" Palermo's son-in-law. Deep in the house, Carbo saw who it was and made a break for a rear bedroom, scrambling out a window. But the house was covered. A policeman yelled, "Stop or we'll shoot!" Carbo flung his hands high, and that was that. At the station in the wee hours, Carbo and Bonomi met for the first time. "You're the guy from Columbia, ain't you?" asked Mr. Gray. A bit later, Carbo tried some humor. "Bonomi? Marrone? Whatsa mattuh? The *paisans* ganging up on me?"

"Yeah, it's the Mafia," quipped one of the cops.

The Carbo pinch was part of a broader action. Now the net came down on lots of others linked to the IBC. Truman Gibson, who served as president of the IBC after Norris stepped down in 1958, was arrested at his home in Chicago in September 1959. He told the cops, "You'd think I was John Dillinger or something," as they cuffed him. Jack Sica and another Carbo thug were arrested in Los Angeles. Blinky Palermo was arrested in Philadelphia. The group was charged with racketeering, extortion, and conspiracy. Honest Bill Daly was also named as a conspirator but was never indicted, suggesting that he was turning state's evidence.

Facing Judge John Meuller, Carbo listened to the charges and pled guilty. He received a mere two years at Rikers Island. For this incredibly light sentence, Mr. Gray responded, "Thank you, Judge."[5] But the actions taken by the state of New York were mere sideshows to a much more serious assault on the Octopus underway. Back in 1957, a federal judge named Sylvester J. Ryan had ruled that the IBC and Madison Square Garden Corporation were guilty of violating the nation's antitrust laws and gave Norris and Wirtz five years to divest themselves of the company. Armed with a legion of attorneys, the IBC battled on to prove its innocence. In January 1959, the U.S. Supreme Court officially dissolved the International Boxing Club altogether, declaring that the IBC had willfully disregarded the Sherman Antitrust Act, "which," a judge lectured, "is so important to our free enterprise system."[6] Thanks to some creative legal maneuverings, the IBC, as the cliché goes, was down but not out. It immediately reappeared in the form of a corporation called National Boxing Enterprises, operating out of Chicago.[7] Then came the government's pièce de résistance, a public Senate hearing. Captained by a modest, inconspicuous senator from Tennessee, the Senate Boxing Commission Hearings captured the public's attention and focused a powerful light on the underside of the sport.

Estes Kefauver did not look like a crime fighter. An unassuming politician from Tennessee, the man who launched the largest assault on organized crime yet was a also former math teacher and Yale Law School graduate, a fellow who came across as an academic and even as a bit of a loner. Yet Kefauver was more than he appeared; he was unafraid to champion dangerous positions, supporting unions and civil rights legislation, two unpopular causes in the South. After serving in the House for ten years, the New Deal liberal from a well-heeled southern family successfully survived being labeled a Communist "fellow traveler" by the Memphis political establishment to become a crusading, popular senator, being elected in 1948.

For reasons that perhaps only he knew, Estes Kefauver decided to build his Senate career on going after the mob. Even his own wife admitted, "It's hard to tell what Estes is thinking." Kefauver's initial resolution to investigate organized crime was stonewalled by fellow Democrats who had something to lose from the airing of possible criminal connections. But after a high-profile mob murder in President Harry Truman's home ward and the devastating political setbacks at the hands of the Republicans in the 1950 midterm elections, Truman and Senate Democrats approved of Kefauver's crusade. A few spotlight-grabbing Republicans tried hard to get in on Kefauver's committee but were shunted off in favor of less-threatening GOP members. One of the snubbed men was a junior senator from Wisconsin named Joe McCarthy. He would go on to find another crusade—rooting out the Communist menace.[8]

The first Kefauver Committee, operating in 1950 and 1951, devolved into a road show in which the senator held mob hearings from Miami to Los Angeles. He invited TV cameras to come along, declaring that "television provides the public with a third dimension [newspapers and radio being the other two] which helps in interpreting what actually goes on." Thus ensued "Kefauver fever" as home audiences eagerly watched a parade of colorful hoodlums flash across their home screens. In some places, telecasts ran uninterrupted for sixteen hours at a stretch. As Kefauver went, he began to connect the shady real estate deals, the book-making, the corrupt law enforcement, and the crooked legislators into a national conspiracy. He had discovered, as he described it, "a secret international government-within-a-government." Kefauver called the organization the Mafia, introducing the word to the greater American public for the first time.[9]

Estes Kefauver's road show made him a celebrity. He was the mystery guest on *What's My Line?* He wrote a best-selling book. He was almost the Democratic presidential nominee in 1952. (He lost to Adlai Stevenson but later beat out Senator John Kennedy to became the Democratic vice-presidential nominee in Stevenson's failed 1956 bid.) For two weeks during the New York portion of the 1951 investigation, somewhere in the neighborhood of 20 million viewers remained glued to their sets. Ratings doubled that of the World Series.[10]

As chair of the Senate's Antitrust and Monopoly Subcommittee, Estes Kefauver was the person who had the best shot at crafting some sort of federal regulation for the sport of boxing. Cynics snickered that Kefauver was doing it because he had a tight reelection race with Republican candidate Judge Andrew Taylor. But his past should have quieted such speculation. By the spring of 1960, the boxing world sat in bated breath as the senator, resuming his challenge against the mob that had quieted somewhat in the decade since his 1950–1951 investigation, compiled lists of witnesses and stacks of police records.[11]

The Senate boxing investigation began in earnest on June 14, 1960, with the testimony of former middleweight champion Jake LaMotta.[12] Speaking in his inimitable style, the "Bronx Bull" proved to be shockingly candid. He admitted to "carrying" fighters; to being offered bribes; and, most scandalously, to throwing the 1947 fight against Billy Fox in order to get a mob-assisted shot at the title. The Fox fight had been universally panned by writers as a sham at the time, but until this point, LaMotta had not admitted to any wrongdoing. Now, in a public spectacle, LaMotta admitted not only to throwing the fight but also to paying a Carbo associate twenty thousand dollars for a chance to fight the new champion, a Frenchman named Marcel Cerdan, a year later. After the stunned interviewer summarized, "You had paid for it and you won it?" LaMotta answered, "Yes, sir."[13]

LaMotta's testimony flung any lingering doubt as to the mob's involvement in boxing out the window for good. The shroud of silence in which boxers usually enveloped themselves was pierced.

At one point, counsel Paul Rand Dixon wanted to know if Jake was afraid for his life:

"No, I ain't afraid. I ain't afraid for myself, sir," said Jake.

"What about your family?" Dixon wanted to know.

LaMotta seemed to equivocate for a moment. "No, I am not afraid for— I am just not afraid for myself. I am not afraid of any of them bums."[14]

The man who personally arrested Carbo, detective Frank Marrone, took the stand a bit later. He was asked about the role of betting in the sport. Was betting the main problem? Would the mob's influence diminish if betting were outlawed? "No," the detective answered. "Today there is a bigger incentive, television." Thus began an ongoing discussion of the problem of the tube. Woven throughout all of the testimony, this topic lingered like an open sore. *Television.* How it warped the sport. How it sent waves of unprepared kids into early, shameful retirement. How it provided a national setting for mob influence. How it emptied local clubs and even the larger venues of talent. In his testimony in December 1960, IBC president Truman Gibson placed TV at the center of the maelstrom. "Boxing can live without the Carbos," Gibson asserted. "But it cannot live without television." TV was in fact the reason for this congressional circus in the first place, Gibson argued. It was the "supervening force in all of this." Why? Because television was "where the money is."

Neither Truman Gibson nor television was the main focus of the second round of the Kefauver inquiries in December 1960. The mob was. Senator Wiley of Wisconsin, who wrote a statement that opened the December proceedings, framed the committee's work in the biggest possible way. Through counsel Nicholas Kittrie (Wiley was unable to attend), the senator thundered that this inquiry represented something far grander than merely shaping up a flawed sport. The very future of the country was at stake. Wiley began by plunging back into the mists of time. The ancient Greeks and Romans, he noted, had recognized that sports instilled in the youth "the basic concepts of democracy." He further explained that sports helped to teach children how to become "law-abiding" citizens. Then he put the two together. Mob corruption in sports represented "a threat to democracy and to the moral well-being of this Nation generally." Wiley finished with a medical metaphor. The purpose of the Senate investigation was not to "kill the patient," despite all of the "abolition" talk floating around Congress. The goal was to "to cure the patient."

The patient was definitely in trouble if the spread of the pathogen of organized crime was any indication. The committee heard about folks like Vincent "Vinnie Blue Eyes" Alo and Anthony "Fat the Butch" DiCostanzo and Anthony "Fat Tony" Salerno. They recorded old histories of mob hits and greased palms, of payoffs and swindled pugs. They uncovered the extent of Carbo's reach through his direct or indirect influence upon every major promoter and manager in the country. When Frank Norris was summoned forth, ill and fragile, in a closed session, he seemed utterly defeated. He told the committee that boxing was "the worst thing that ever happened to me." He even explained that he had offered FBI head J. Edgar Hoover one hundred thousand dollars a year for ten years to head the IBC and clean it up. Hoover had turned him down.[15]

A few boxers offered yet more damaging testimony. Former lightweight champion Ike Williams admitted that he had "carried" opponents at the behest of mob-connected managers. Carmen Basilio, when asked if "persons like Frankie Carbo, Gabe Genovese, and 'Blinky' Palermo should be in the fight business at all," answered, in part, that "there are ladies present here and in all respect to them I have to contain my inner feelings." But he did firmly say, "The quicker we get those fellows out, the better it is going to be for the sport." Basilio offered that federal regulation would "probably cure 99 percent of the ills in boxing."[16]

Even with such testimony, it was clear that the specific incidences of corruption revealed in the chamber represented only a fraction of the actual problem. People were just not talking about certain things. Several key witnesses pleaded the Fifth over fifty times. The thoroughly crooked fighter, Sonny Liston, declined to "pass judgment" on anyone, stating, "I haven't been perfect myself." As one senator said in the June 1960 hearings, "some very hard hands and some very long arms have reached right into this committee room and denied this committee information that would be helpful." If there was a Typhoid Mary for the sport, it was Carbo, and to him they turned on the final day of the December 1960 hearings.[17]

Frankie Carbo was pulled from his current residence at Riker's Island to attend. He brought his lawyer and an escort of U.S. marshals with him. Unsurprisingly, Mr. Gray proved to be an uncooperative witness, despite Kefauver's personal guarantee that this was not a "trial." In a manner reminiscent of the unhappy respondents of earlier congressional inquisitions, Carbo answered virtually everything the same way: "I respectfully decline to answer the question on the ground that I cannot be compelled to be a witness against myself." When Kefauver followed one of these responses with the command, "The Chair directs you to answer the question," Mr. Gray just repeated his mantra. Even the question, "Where were you born?" got the Carbo Stonewall. Kefauver's frustration bleeds through the *Congressional Record*:

> **Senator Kefauver:** You look like an intelligent man. Are you understanding the questions I am asking?
> **Mr. Carbo:** I respectfully decline to answer the question on the ground that I cannot be compelled to be a witness against myself.

The frustration surely must have been compounded by Carbo's appearance. He seemed old. With white hair, thick, black horn-rimmed glasses, and talk of his medical ailments, Frankie Carbo hardly appeared to be the Crime Lord that Kefauver so desperately wanted to take down. Worse, Mr. Gray actually seemed to take the whole thing as a joke. Towards the end, he told Kefauver, "There is only one thing I want to say, Mr. Senator."

"Yes?"

"I congratulate you on your reelection."

The audience laughter is recorded in the testimony.

Nobody seemed eager to directly name Carbo as having orchestrated the biggest mob infiltration operation in sports history. Yet Kefauver plugged on. At the close of the December session, the Tennessee senator tipped the public as to his larger objective. He wanted to create a federal body of oversight for the sport of boxing. Kefauver ominously reported that unless legislation was put into place to "restore integrity to the sport," it "might very well pass from the American scene." In the meantime, he proposed a temporary Federal Boxing Commission to remove "the hoodlum element."[18]

Boxing seemed to be heading back into the criminal shadows of the Red Light District. In February 1961, Carbo, "Blinky" Palermo, and Truman

Gibson were all found guilty of extorting Don Jordan's manager and received sentences ranging from fifteen to twenty-five years. A month later, Kefauver introduced a Senate bill that would create an Office of the National Boxing Commissioner. Co-sponsored by California senator and former amateur boxer Clair Engle, the bill placed the commissioner within the Justice Department. Senator Engle used Senator Wiley's earlier reasoning to bolster his own reasons for cleaning up the sport: "The corruption that is dominating the boxing profession," he stated, "is not only a violation of our laws, but a violation of our democratic ideals." In the House, New York representative William Fitz Ryan sponsored an identical bill.[19] Momentum seemed to be building for a federal takeover of boxing. A hearing for the legislation was scheduled for two days in May and June 1961.

At the hearing, Estes Kefauver pulled out all the stops. Every living hero of the sport made an entrance on Capitol Hill. Kicking off the testimony was undefeated former heavyweight champion Rocky Marciano. Kefauver gave Marciano the opportunity to talk up his new TV show, *The Main Event*, before gushing about what good shape the Brockton Bomber looked to be in. To reinforce Marciano's credentials, Kefauver said, "There are few people in the United States who can give us more good advice about what ought to be done to clean up boxing than you." Well buttered, Marciano went on with a prepared statement in which he enthusiastically supported the creation of a federal boxing commission. Marciano even suggested a name for the first federal boxing czar: Jack Bonomi.

The parade of greats continued: Gene Fullmer, Tommy Loughran, Joe Louis, Jack Dempsey, and Gene Tunney came. All of them supported federal legislation, though a few old timers had to be steered back to the subject when they wandered off course. They also offered insightful critiques of the power of television over the sport. Marciano noted that TV both helped fighters gain "recognition" and "hurt" them by pushing them into top competition before they were ready. Tommy Loughran lamented the fact that TV gave "boxing to the people for nothing," draining local clubs of revenue. Said Gene Tunney, "Through radio and television, particularly television, it has gotten worse and worse and worse as time goes on." Jack Dempsey, who at one point seemed unsure if his fights in the 1920s had been televised said, "We all know television has been great," but "it deteriorated the game."[20]

The hearings concluded with the enthusiastic support of a panoply of luminaries. The chairman of Madison Square Garden's Board of Directors, *Ring* magazine's Nat Fleischer, the executive officer of the California

Athletic Commission, and dozens of others all favored federal interven-
tion. All agreed that though this was a drastic step, it was the only way
to save the patient.

The day after the testimony concluded, a photo circulated in the sports
sections of the country's papers. It was an image of three smiling old
men in dark blazers, each holding up a clenched fist for the camera: Jack
Dempsey, Gene Tunney, and Estes Kefauver. Here were two all-time boxing greats and the man who would clean up the sport and preserve its
legacy. Together, they would KO the bad guys.[21]

If the Kefauver Commission signified a full-throated attack on the rotting
core of televised boxing by the federal government, it signified no novel
assault on a beloved institution. Competing with the legislative attack
was an ongoing cultural one.

The history of boxing criticism in America is as old as the sport. Thomas
Jefferson warned that the young man who went to England "learns drinking, horse racing, and boxing."[22] Associated from the outset with the
fringes of society—with southern "battle royals" amongst slaves; with
bloody, muddy bare-knuckle bouts between Irish immigrants in rough
parts of nineteenth-century cities; with organized criminals; with deca-
dent hangers-on called "the fancy"—prize fighting was an easy target of
reformers. The term *prize fighting* itself connotes viciousness in the service
of Mammon.

In the age of TV boxing, critics attacked the sport for all the old reasons: it was harmful to the boxers and to the morals of the audience, it
was crooked, it demeaned American civilization. To this they added some
new ones: it was a monopoly, it hurt the kids. As boxing entered more
and more homes in the 1950s, critics offered increasingly comprehensive
judgments. Not only was boxing a boon to criminals, but it was a boon to
a secret, national criminal empire. Not only was boxing dangerous to the
participants, but there were quantifiable neurological studies that proved
it. Yet boxing seemed invulnerable. It was not until the Kefauver Commission, coupled with a decrease in the ratings, that the critics seemed
to become much more of a threat to the sport.

An obvious angle for the critic was to express concern for the safety
of the fighters. Boxing damaged bodies and, according to research just
beginning to be published in medical journals, the brain. The lethality of
boxing was well-known by the time Senator Kefauver showed up. Ring
deaths had long haunted the sport, and this period certainly saw its share
of calamities. The difference now was television.

One tragedy in particular set the tone for what was later to nearly capsize the sport. On February 22, 1950, a Texan named Lavern Roach stepped into the ring at St. Nick's Arena to battle Georgie Small for a CBS Wednesday Night Fight. He was carried out on a stretcher, unconscious. Fourteen hours later, he was pronounced dead.

Lavern Roach was an ex-Marine, called "the best fighter developed in the service during the war" by the *New York Times* and named Rookie of the Year in 1947 by *Ring* magazine.[23] He seemed to be ready-made for TV: young, tough, white, and a soldier and a father to boot. But Roach was not ready for the upper reaches of competition. After losing to Marcel Cerdan in an "egregious mismatch" in 1948,[24] he started showing the effects of traumatic brain injury. His manager told him to retire. Even Heinie Miller, executive secretary of the National Boxing Association, told Roach, "one marine to another," that "he ought to quit."[25] Roach agreed and moved to Texas, got married, and got a job selling insurance. But he liked to tell people, "I haven't retired. I'm only resting."[26]

Lavern Roach began his comeback in January 1950 and soon landed a televised CBS Wednesday Night Fight at St. Nick's Arena. His fight with Brooklyn's Georgie Small started well. He was ahead on all the cards. But in the eighth round, Small shot out a straight right hand that split Roach's lip and sent blood streaming from his mouth. The punch did not look particularly devastating, but Roach appeared dazed by it. Blood smeared over Small's gloves and covered Roach's body with each subsequent blow. The red fluid gushed down Roach's chin and dribbled over his black trunks. In the tenth round, Small caught Roach with a few more fast blows to the head and down he went. The ex-Marine struggled back to his feet by the count of nine. Some people in the audience started yelling, "Stop it! Stop it!" to the ref. But the fight continued. Then came another head shot and Roach fell flat on his face. The referee called the fight at one minute and fifty-seven seconds into the tenth round. Roach managed to get up and was helped to his stool. He mumbled, "Damn it, my luck is running out."[27] Then he slumped over, lapsing into unconsciousness and dying the next day.[28]

The ring death of Lavern Roach stunned the boxing world. A photo circulated showing Georgie Small wiping tears from his eyes upon learning of Roach's death. It seemed unreal. Roach was a Marine and a father; a clearer icon of postwar manhood could scarcely be found. A Texas paper mourned that Lavern was "the highest type of American manhood." Letters poured in from viewers demanding an investigation into the fight. An assemblyman from Albany, New York, appealed for an exploration into boxing "in all its ramifications." Arthur Daley wrote in the *New York Times* that "the game is faced with a situation where it must do something or die itself."[29]

Although the New York State Athletic Commission soon after released a new, more comprehensive set of medical guidelines for boxers to follow, the press seemed more interested in the medium than in the violence.[30] "Television Sees It," recorded one newspaper with horror.[31] Although only 9 percent of homes had televisions in 1950, lots of people watched the fights in bars or went over to the homes of friends who had TVs. Boxing ratings were on the rise. Luckily for the show, angry letters and yet another TV Wednesday night ring death later in 1950 did nothing to impede electronic transmission of the fights.[32]

Two 1954 ring deaths just days apart sparked another surge of anti-boxing criticism. On December 12, heavyweight (and former Navy champion) Hayes "Big Ed" Sanders collapsed after a series of blows to the head in the eleventh round against Willie James. For Sanders, this was only his ninth professional fight since finishing his term of service during the Korean War. He did not regain consciousness and was pronounced dead eighteen hours later. The same day that the papers reported Sanders's death, a photo made the papers showing referee Wally Moss counting out featherweight Ralph Weiser. Weiser is sitting against the corner, right arm limp on the floor, left glove propped over the lower rope. Moments later he rose to one knee, then keeled forward onto his face, unconscious. He died a few hours later.[33]

Ruminating on Ed Sanders's death, *Time* magazine published a piece titled "The Manly Art of Murder." That's what boxing was, according to the Boston judge who performed the court's inquest on the match. Since 1900, noted the judge, 327 souls had gone to the hereafter as a result of ring beatings. Like every other fight, the Sanders match was really a simple case of legalized battery. "In the absence of a law legalizing boxing matches," explained Judge Elijah Adlow, "an assault entailing such consequence would constitute murder. . . . Both of the medical examiners insisted that the objective of boxers who engage in a contest is to deliver a knockout punch. In their opinion a knockout punch means nothing more than to inflict a brain injury on the contestant." The esteemed, biblically named judge went on to contrast the sport with baseball, which "not only sanctions the use of a protective device for the head but some of the clubs demand it." The worst of it was the boxing crowd. They weren't mere by-standers. They were "parties to the crime." Summarized Adlow, "In the enforcement of the Boxing Commission rules, the claims of humanity and decency are drowned in the roar of the crowd. It is a sad commentary on our sporting world that as Hayes Sanders sank to the floor, there were boos from the crowd."[34]

Boxing destroyed not only lives but also livelihoods. In the 1956 film *The Harder They Fall*, Humphrey Bogart ruminated on how television sold boxers like "soap." "You sell a fighter, you sell soap. What's the difference?" The public was growing accustomed to watching movies that portrayed ex-boxers as broken has-beens. From Marlon Brando's character opining that he "couldda been a contender" in Elia Kazan's *On the Waterfront* (1954) to Anthony Quinn dancing foolishly around the ring dressed as an Indian chief at the close of *Requiem for a Heavyweight* (1962), audiences couldn't help but feel saddened by the way boxing chewed these poor souls up and then spat them out when their usefulness as entertainers had evaporated. The Quinn film was a redo of a 1956 play of the same name by Rod Serling. The *New York Times* had hailed it as an "indictment" of a "so-called sport."[35]

The monopoly aspect of TV boxing was another easy media target. By any definition, the Octopus was a monopoly. In a 1955 *Sports Illustrated* piece, contributor (and Jack Dempsey biographer) Robert Coughlin asked: "What is this organization? Who runs it? How does it operate? These are basic questions in explaining the sorry condition of U.S. boxing." His answer was that it was a monopoly. ("Whether the IBC turns out to be a monopoly in the legal sense, it has long since proved itself to be one in a practical sense.") It was run by crooks and a rich Mafia fellow traveler named Jim Norris. It operated by controlling access to the championship—forty-seven of the last fifty-one title fights, to be precise. Coughlin concluded with some words of wisdom from the sagacious Lou Stillman: "As my old mother, may God rest her, used to say, 'When three people tell you you're drunk, it's time to go to bed.'"[36]

So who defended boxing? One might argue that the millions of loyal TV viewers did. The pope did as well, apparently. When an Italian Jesuit named Afredo Boschi attacked the sport as something that "must be condemned as something gravely illicit in itself," the Vatican responded in its official *Osservatore Romano* by saying, as quoted in *Time* magazine, that while boxing was "not something to be exalted or encouraged by Catholics," it "is not considered immoral and, in consequence, can at least be tolerated." The argument employed was rather lame: "Should boxing matches be gravely immoral, all promoters, boxers, managers and spectators would be in mortal sin. . . . Many boxers, both in Italy and the U.S., cross themselves before entering the ring, which would be sacrilegious if boxing were essentially immoral."[37] In other words, it can't be a sin because if it were, then we would all be sinners for watching. This, by the way, was precisely the conclusion that Judge Adlow had arrived at in his remarks on the death of Ed Sanders. We were all sinners.

Boxers, of course, also defended boxing. In 1957 Mike Wallace conducted a prime-time interview with Carman Basilio. Wallace was blunt, raising tough questions about the violence and alleged mob corruption. When Wallace asked, "Do you like to get into a ring and try to beat another man unconscious?" Basilio shifted in his seat uncomfortably. Finally, the boxer said, "Well, I don't know if I enjoy beating a man into unconsciousness, but, . . . I do enjoy winning. I like to fight. The boxing world has given me everything that I've got." Wallace asked whether "it's the least bit degrading to earn a living by trying to beat another man unconscious or by getting beaten up yourself?" "No," responded Basilio. "I don't think so. I know there's a lot of people that look upon the boxing game with dislike. But, I have met a lot of honorable men in the boxing game, and . . . I don't feel as though that I am dishonorable." Mike Wallace asked if it did not seem to Basilio "the least bit incongruous about asking God to help you beat up another man. A man who is probably just as good, just as religious a person, as you are." Basilio replied, "It's my belief that if you ask God for help, He'll give it to you. That's the way I believe in God."

When Wallace brought up the issue of banning boxing, quoting sportswriter Jimmy Cannon's 1951 *Pageant Magazine* article in which he called boxing "the garbage pile of sports," Basilio countered with a question about football and hockey fatalities. Wallace retorted that unlike those sports, the explicit purpose of boxing was to "disable" and "beat down" one's opponent. "In a sense, it is 'legalized murder' because a good many men have been killed that way." Replied Basilio, "If that's the case, then football is 'legalized murder' too, or any other sport that is rough like that." Wallace noted that boxing was fifty-nine times more deadly than college football. Basilio pointed out the recent guidelines for safety, explaining that now "they have to have this brain examination to pass."

Switching gears, Wallace asked about the mob. "I've never met any of them," said Carmen. "All I've done is, I've read about them, never met them, I just think that, er . . . these people are ghosts because all I ever do is read about them."[38] If not much of a debate, the Mike Wallace interview certainly provided a public airing of what were becoming growing concerns in the press.

By 1960, TV boxing had much more to worry about than a few critics or TV hosts or even Estes Kefauver. The skeleton hand of the television graveyard was reaching out. Ratings were dropping.

The drop was a long and drawn-out affair. Since the peak of its popularity in the early 1950s, Gillette's *Friday Night Fights* had been losing viewers as a percentage of the total population. Whereas 31 percent of the TV audience tuned in to watch boxing in 1952, that share had shrunk considerably, down to around 11 percent by the early 1960s.[39] The cause of the decline of viewership was the topic of much speculation. There were no more heroes left, some believed. After Rocky Marciano retired undefeated in 1956, there was a dearth of superstars. During the Kefauver Committee hearings, the heavyweight champion, generally a powerful masculine figure who anchors broader interest in the sport, was an undynamic Boy Scout in boxing shorts named Floyd Patterson. Patterson's own trainer even lamented that he "lacks the killer instinct. . . . I have a big job on my hands." Once, after whacking an opponent's mouthpiece out, instead of finishing off his distracted enemy, a concerned Floyd Patterson bent down and helped him look for it. After knocking out mortal foe Ingmar Johansson at the Polo Grounds in March 1961, Patterson cradled him.[40]

In the other weight divisions, champion-quality fighters were increasingly foreign imports, which may have detracted from their mainstream appeal. A *Boxing and Wrestling* contributor found the booming economy to blame for the foreign invasion. "There were well-paying jobs available, jobs which would pay far more, and with a great deal more regularity, than a young fighter could make in the ring. As a result, not a single outstanding U.S. fighter has emerged in the last five years. . . . With the dearth of domestic talent, the television promoters began to import fighters from abroad, the latest influx having come from Cuba." Another writer for *Boxing and Wrestling* magazine agreed with the economics angle, noting that "throughout the country the four and six-round boy still makes the same pay he made 15 years ago. In most places $50 is the base for four rounds. Why should a kid take a beating for $50, less expenses, when he can work as a laborer for $3.00 an hour?"[41]

The Easy Money complaint was a common one. As Freddie Brown lamented to A. J. Liebling in 1952, "When the kids didn't have what to eat, they were glad to fight." Whitey Bimstein struck a deep chord when he reflected on the enormous wave of black fighters coming into the ranks. "The only ones who work hard are the colored boys because for them it's still tough outside."[42] Just as "outside" groups of Jews, Irish, and Italians had marched their way across the ring on their way up the social ladder, now many of the outsiders were literally coming from outside the borders. The old adage, "The ghetto is the nursery of professional boxing," reflects a desperate truth of prize fighting.[43] By the late 1950s, the ghettos in question were less likely to be in New York and Chicago and more likely to be in Camagüey or Havana or Buenos Aires.

More interestingly, TV itself was blamed for the decline of TV boxing. One writer quipped, "There's nothing wrong with the sport that the elimination of television wouldn't cure." Television had depleted the clubs, thus diminishing the pool of good fighters and draining the fountain from whence fighters came. As early as 1951, *Ring* magazine editor Nat Fleischer noted that "in 1950 we had well over 6,000 professional boxers. Right now we've got maybe 3,500." TV was "knocking out hundreds of talent-developing shows."[44] *Ring* magazine periodically wrung its hands over the "serious problems created by the new medium—television," though it also had to acknowledge the tremendous new audience for the sport the "new medium" had created. Still, the apparent effect of TV shows on the clubs was undeniable. *Ring* would note that the tube was putting "the small clubs . . . out of business."[45] In 1955 a journalist described the TV effect as simply "catastrophic."[46] Eddie Borden, editor of *Weekly Boxing World*, agreed that TV "has become the most powerful figure in boxing and the supply is depleted too quickly for comfort." Boxers were being thrown into the ring "overmatched and fighting way over their head" after just ten or twenty fights in some cases. In another article, Borden noted, "If the fighter continues to show unsatisfactorily on TV he is given a permanent vacation. It is also difficult for that same performer to find occupation in other centers not controlled by television. . . . Once a fighter makes a poor showing on TV it generally follows him no matter where he travels."[47]

Reporters often felt inclined to comment on the new role of the Garden as a "glorified television studio." New Yorkers apparently saw little reason to leave the comfort of their easy chairs and hop on the subway to go watch fights at the Mecca of the sport. In a 1954 piece, Jersey Jones wrote that back in 1947, the Garden pulled in 375,716 fans and $1,854,568. By 1952 the numbers had been cut by about two-thirds. By the end of the decade, notes historian Kasia Boddy, the Garden's attendance had plummeted since the late 1940s by up to 80 percent as a direct result of television.[48]

The evolution of television technology, in part funded by boxing revenues, ironically helped hasten the decline of the sport, too. New camera technologies were making baseball, America's national pastime, much more viewable on TV. In the early fifties, the small white ball was hard to see. Now, better sets and better cameras made the ball much easier to follow. But baseball was not the biggest sporting threat. Football was. Football seemed custom made for the small screen. Just as viewers in the stands watched a game progress smoothly from side to side across the hash marks of a field, so could TV cameras mimic the experience, capturing the majority of the action in a single frame while commentators supplemented the action. The famous 1958 Baltimore Colts–New York Giants championship game, watched by some 45 million home viewers, decisively put football in play as the next TV phenomenon.

The gridiron offered a different, but very compelling, model of masculinity. Decked out in armor and facing off in "squads" across enemy lines in a battle for precious territory, professional football players manifested a teamwork sort of manhood reminiscent of the military. War experiences influenced what folks saw on screen. Giants head coach Jim Lee Howell was a former Marine drill sergeant. The Giants' defensive coordinator, Tom Landry, piloted a B-17 in World War II. The team's quarterback, Charlie Conerly, had stormed Guam with the Marines. Also beneficial for the sport was the kind of man who played it. Unlike "imported" boxers, football stars seemed to resemble the middling- and working-class white audience that the sponsors were targeting. In fact, because players didn't earn much in those days, most of them had to work second jobs during the off-season. Johnny Unitas, for instance, worked at the massive Bethlehem Steel plant in Dundalk, Maryland.[49]

The greatest portent of doom for TV boxing occurred when NBC allowed its contract with Gillette to expire on July 1, 1960. ABC swooped in and picked up the *Friday Night Fights*, shifting the show to a Saturday night slot. Despite the fact that the program had declining ratings, many observers hailed ABC's decision as a brilliant one. Suddenly ABC, which used to have the weakest advertising budget, now saw some $8 million of Gillette's money flow into its coffers. The amount was more than all of its radio and TV profits combined for the year 1959. Thanks to the sudden infusion, ABC moved to corner the entire TV sports market. It had already bought the *Wednesday Night Fights* from CBS. With Gillette's money, the network set up its own original sports show—the *Wide World of Sports*.[50]

Sports Illustrated saw fit to cover the death of the *Friday Night Fights* in its July 11, 1960, issue. The magazine understood that something of an era was at an end. After all, the Friday show represented the longest-running program in the history of television thus far. Reflected reporter

William Leggett, "At one time the ratings indicated that one out of every five home television sets were tuned in. And there were few bars across the country which didn't automatically turn on the fights for their customers on Friday." But the shine had worn off. Groused one bar patron, "I was getting fed up with the fights anyway. In my opinion, too many were fixed." Grumbled another, "The greatest contribution television can make is not to put on the fights." Former champ Jack Dempsey agreed. "I'm glad the Friday night fights are gone," the old brawler said. "Most of 'em weren't any good anyway, and they were helping to kill the fight game." But there was some mourning, too. Many bar owners knew that this decision meant less revenue. Lamented one, "Many traveling people used to come in on Friday just for the fights. They used to strike up friendships and sit around for a while. Tonight they came in, drank a beer and left. My business fell off at least $40."[51]

On October 8, 1960, the *Friday Night Fights* became the *Saturday Night Fight of the Week*. Declining ratings would not pick up in the new timeslot. A *Television Magazine* reporter thought he knew why. "Friday at 10 had become accepted as the man's hour in front of the TV set." Saturday night, on the other hand, "belonged to the ladies."[52]

A Friday Night Fighter, Gaspar would finally get his shot on a Saturday night. The fight took place the same day that Senator Kefauver's smiling picture with Tunney and Dempsey hit the sports pages.

CHAPTER 12

The Ship Goes Down

Dismantling the Indian placed Emile Griffith firmly in the uppermost reaches of boxing royalty. He made fifty thousand dollars from the match and was named "boxer of the month" by the National Boxing Association. He bought a house on Long Island for himself and his family. He was "perpetually happy," wrote the reporters, and now he had "more money than any 22-year old has a right to expect." But, of course, he had every right to expect big money. He was probably the best pound-for-pound fighter in the world at the time. Plus, Griffith had personality, style, grace. His manager recalls, "He didn't need much additional promoting. His face was on the tube almost as much as Ed Sullivan's." Griffith's handlers started looking for bigger money fights; they decided to get him ready to move up to heavier weights and greater paydays. Garden promoter Teddy Brenner tried to set up a match between him and Sugar Ray Robinson, but it fell through. Griffith did test a middleweight opponent in July at Madison Square Garden, getting the unanimous decision with ease.[1]

For Gaspar, the title battle with Griffith was not just a loss. He had let down his family, his country. While Dunphy and Griffith filled the remaining TV time (it ended early, in the twelfth round) with chatter while firecrackers popped in the balconies, Gaspar crept through the ropes, looking like the Elephant Man with his white towel completely over his head and face. Griffith, meanwhile, was all smiles with Dunphy. "I don't think he hurt you at any time," says Dunphy. Replies Emile, "No he didn't, he really didn't." "But," Griffith quickly adds, "he is a very game fighter." Dunphy agrees. "He's a wonderful fighter. He's a real credit." They go on to banter about Benny Paret, about moving up into a higher weight class, about the possibility of Griffith getting his own TV show with that personality of his.

Tommy Hart would later admit that he almost stopped the fight in the seventh round, when Gaspar was clearly in trouble and hardly able to defend himself properly. He had allowed it to continue as long as it did because, he felt, "Ortega was a dedicated man fighting for his country." An ex-pro, Tommy Hart understood a boxer's heart. He understood that there are worse beatings than mere physical punishment.[2]

Gaspar returned to his dressing room and cried for twenty minutes. He didn't care that reporters were there to watch. They recorded him saying, in Spanish, "Oh, mother, why did you make me lose this fight—when you knew I had to win it?" After translating this, Corby added that by "mother," Gaspar meant not his own mom but "Our Lady of Guadalupe, the patron of Mexico."[3]

Gaspar cried because it was all over. He knew he wouldn't get another shot at the title, not after a beating like that. TV was far too unforgiving. Reporters knew it, too. They were writing him off before he made it back to his dressing room.[4]

The dynamic Griffith was expected to show even more improvement in his second Paret fight. He was favored 3–1; he seemed confident and cocky. Kid Paret had not fought anyone since being laid out by Griffith in the thirteenth round of their last fight. The Cuban had been paid well to sit out the Ortega-Griffith fight, and now Paret stood to clear another twenty-five thousand dollars for his upcoming title rematch. Red Smith quipped that if twenty-five thousand dollars didn't seem like a big payout for a title fight, it would have taken Paret thirty-four years and four months of cutting sugar cane at twenty cents an hour to make the same amount. "By then he would be 59 and highly skilled with a machete." Paret seemed like such a nonthreat that reporters were already talking about Griffith's likely *next* title defense, against Argentina's Jorge Fernandez in Las Vegas in December. The Paret fight was just pro forma, just filling out a previous contract.[5]

But Paret won. Like just about every Paret battle, Griffith-Paret II was a hard-fought bloodbath. The Cuban seemed to take three punches for every one that he threw, and Griffith proved staggeringly accurate. By the thirteenth round, both of Paret's eyes were badly swollen and blood streamed from a cut under his right eye as well as from his mouth, but still he came on. Paret took the split decision, with one judge and the referee putting him over the top. Sportswriters did not agree with the results, but they noted that Paret seemed to have regained his remarkable ability to absorb every punch thrown. Griffith just couldn't put his man down, and Paret managed to connect with a number of solid inside punches.[6]

Perhaps the reason Griffith did not decisively beat his foe had to do with something that had happened earlier in the day. During the weigh-in, Griffith had noticed Paret joking with reporters. He saw Paret flipping his wrist limply and mincing about in a high, mock-girl voice. Paret was talking about him.

Paret and Griffith knew each other from the neighborhood. They'd lived blocks apart in upper Manhattan and had even played basketball together. They weren't exactly friends, but they weren't mortal enemies either. (How could jovial Griffith even *have* a mortal enemy?) Like everyone else in the neighborhood, Paret had heard the rumors about Griffith, and he was not above capitalizing on them. Besides the hat designing and the tight flashy clothes and the choir singing, there was the cohort of young Latino boys that Griffith was always seen hanging around with. One of them seemed to be especially close. Griffith called him "son" and would let him borrow his car. So folks talked. At the weigh-in before the fight, Griffith saw Paret mocking him, and then he heard Paret say a Spanish word that he knew but had not yet heard directly applied to him. *Maricon.* Faggot.

Griffith had a hard time focusing on the fight that evening. He couldn't get his mind off what Paret had done and said in that room full of reporters. Emile thought more about this than anything else. He lost all focus. Still, he believed that he beat Paret. When the announcement was made, Griffith was stunned. Gil Clancy railed, "We were robbed without a gun," to anyone who would listen. Paret's manager, Manual Alfaro, made things even worse by announcing that there would be no Griffith-Paret III. He said he was going to take his fighter to Europe to "make some money" with nontitle fights.[7]

A different Griffith came to the surface after the loss to Paret. He began to fixate on the Cuban. "Benny is a nice boy," he softly told one reporter, "but I would like to kill him."[8]

Nick Corby called Gaspar on the phone one day while he was recovering from the Griffith fight. The loss had been physically ruinous and emotionally devastating. He was pissing blood. Ida had never seen her husband so physically damaged. Now Corby proposed a new game plan: a tour. They would travel throughout Mexamerica, picking up every single fight they could find. "You don't even have to train much," Corby said. Go from town to town, beat the local, take the payday, and move on. It was a cynical bid for cash, yes, but it was also a reasonable plan, considering Gaspar's nosedive off of the television radar. They could try it for a year, a year-and-a-half maybe, and then see if anything new developed. After enough wins, who knows, the Garden might show some interest in him again.

Short on options and with nothing else to fall back on, Gaspar agreed. Corby sent out word and soon calls were flooding in from managers across Mexamerica. And so began a new incarnation of Indio Ortega: The Boxing Gypsy. He started by easily knocking out welterweight journeyman Bobby Brown in a bull ring in Nogales on August 22, 1961. On September 2, he knocked out Reybon Stubbs in a small, packed arena in Cuidad Obregon. Five days later, Gaspar knocked out Negro Veloz in Hermesillo. Three days after that he knocked out Federico Payan. Three days after that, it was Georgie Hart in Guaymas in the state of Sonora, Mexico. A week later Gaspar was in Arizona, annihilating Negro Veloz in a mere four rounds. In less than a month, Gaspar knocked out six fighters. By year's end he would fight another seven times, winning six and losing only once, by decision.

By early January 1962, the *New York Times* had taken notice. William J. Briordy wrote that fight folks called Gaspar "the matchmaker's delight" because "he will fight any one at any time and at any place." He had fought an astonishing sixteen fights in 1961. Briordy reflected with amazement, "The record book shows that no fighter in modern history has fought as much in one year as Ortega."[9] Perhaps most impressively, all but three of these battles had taken place after July, and of these thirteen fights, he had knocked out ten opponents.

But the fights did not simply fly past. Some opponents were easier than others. Gaspar describes Charlie Wright as "a bum they picked up off the street." When Wright fought Gaspar, Wright was on a three-fight losing streak against a string of nobodies. He had never even been in a ten-round fight. Gaspar gave Wright a TKO in the third. Another guy named Roberto Garcia was so intimidated by Indio that when he was knocked down, he just refused to stand back up. Appropriately, Gaspar fought him in circus tent. Other fighters presented a bit more of a problem. Negro Veloz landed an uppercut that pushed one of Gaspar's teeth straight through his lower lip. As blood began to pour down his chin and over his chest, Gaspar attacked with all he had, knowing that the referee would probably stop it soon. He knocked Veloz out in that same round. For Gaspar's next fight three days later, the doctor put a skin tone Band-Aid over the stitches on his lip. The stitches irritated his mouthpiece, so he fought without one. Luckily, he knocked Federico Payan out in the second round.

The tour seemed to be working; Gaspar got himself back in Madison Square Garden for an ABC *Saturday Night Fight of the Week* against Charley Scott of Philadelphia in January 1962. It was, in large part, due to fortunate happenstance. The original fight was supposed to be between Sugar Ray Robinson and Denny Moyer, but Robinson had to reschedule due to a hand injury. Then it was supposed to be top-ranked welter Ralph Dupas against Charley Scott, but Dupas had to back out due to a hip injury. Scrambling, the matchmakers found Gaspar. And so the world's hardest-working boxer got another shot on TV. Indio put on the headdress for publicity shots and joked around with reporters before the fight, saying at one point, "I like clothes, San Diego, and more fights." Gaspar told them that he was planning on becoming a U.S. citizen as well. Corby made sure that the reporters also knew that his man wanted a title shot against Paret. Now that Paret had the belt again, Gaspar would fight as many opponents as necessary to get to the Cuban and relieve him of it. He knew he could do it; he'd already beaten Paret twice.[10]

The Ortega-Scott match did not go well for Gaspar. The Indian came out swinging away in the first round and seemed like his old self. But by the second, he was visibly tiring, and Charley Scott's wicked lefts were making a dent. Despite occasional flurries, this was not one of Indio's better fights. He had let his conditioning lapse. Don Dunphy suggested that Gaspar's blistering fight schedule might be "taking a toll" on him. The fight ended with both men mechanically firing away at each other in the corner, the crowd cheering on the rhythmic movement. Scott got the unanimous decision.[11]

The fight gave Charley Scott another TV appearance and sent Gaspar back to the cow towns and bull arenas of *la frontera*. But first he decided to take a few months off due to a lingering injury in his right hand. A doctor looked at it and informed him that surgery wouldn't do any good. He put the hand in a removable cast that kept the wrist straight and immobile. Gaspar trained without hitting anything. Now he really knew his career was in bad shape. In April, he started the "tour" again, this time in New Mexico. A week after that he was in Sonora.

Benny "Kid" Paret, meanwhile, was milking his newly reclaimed title for all it was worth. His manager got him scheduled to step up to the middleweight division for a shot at Gene Fullmer's title belt, which came in December 1961. Manuel Alfaro, who talked for the Spanish-only-speaking Paret, told reporters that his man would not relinquish his welterweight belt even if he took Fullmer's. Said Alfaro, "Titles are won or lost in the ring. If we beat Fullmer, we will consider we hold both championships." Alfaro also stated that Paret would not be returning to Cuba so long as it was under Communist rule. Paret despised Castro, his manager dutifully reported. Paret planned on becoming an American citizen.[12]

The Fullmer fight, for which ABC paid a whopping one hundred thousand dollars, was an unmitigated disaster for Paret. The muscular Utah brawler won every round, battering Paret about the ring like a mannequin. Coming into the ninth, Paret's corner put a mysterious, chalky substance on his face that gave him a ghoulish aspect. The referee held up the fight until they removed it. Early in the tenth round, Fullmer delivered a blow that sent the Cuban stumbling back a full twelve feet, "looking," a journalist colorfully recorded, "something like a wounded duck fluttering into the marsh." The blow sent Paret into his own corner, where he came to rest seated on the lower rope. After the ref gave him a mandatory eight count (which wasn't supposed to happen in this fight), he came suddenly back to life, charging Fullmer with a flurry of lefts and rights. Fullmer, unimpressed, sent Paret down to the canvas for a two count. Again Paret came back. Then a big Fullmer overhand right connected and put Paret back down on the mat. The Cuban struggled, but he could not rise. He had suffered the second KO of his career.[13]

In his dressing room, Paret spun the loss as not boxing-related but really having to do with Fullmer's bullying style. "It was the pushes that exhausted me, not the punches."[14] The truth was that Fullmer was just too strong for him.

The loss sent Paret back down to earth. He could no longer ignore Griffith, who had beaten three men since their last fight. "[Griffith] was in seclusion much of the time," a relative later said. "He didn't want to hang around too much with anyone. He just wanted to train, train, train." A rubber match was set for March 1962. Leading up to the bout, an uncharacteristically angry Griffith told reporters that he planned on knocking Paret out. He would not make the same mistakes that he had made last time, he said. "This time, I tell you, I won't let up. I'm going after him from the opening bell. If he flurries I'll go right with him. If I get him in trouble, like I did a couple of times in the last fight, I'll knock him out. Then I won't have to worry about any decision."[15]

The odds were set heavily against Paret to retain his title. For one thing, Griffith had a much more consistent record. But also, ominously, the Fullmer beating was reported to have damaged the Kid. Paret tried to dispel the rumors. "Everybody talks about the Fullmer fight," Paret said dismissively. "They seem to think he gave me such a beating that I won't be able to beat Griffith. That's a lot of baloney. I do the fighting. I know I feel as strong as I ever was before I fought Fullmer. I licked Griffith before and I can do it again." His manager agreed. "The odds are crazy," Alfaro told reporters. "Benny will show them."[16]

Six days before the fight, ABC invited Don Dunphy over to its studios. Upon his arrival, Dunphy discovered the he was going to be a part of history. The network would be trying out a new technology for the big upcoming Saturday night fight. Dunphy practiced by narrating a one-round exhibition match while a special video camera recorded the fight. Then, in front of a studio audience, they replayed the video, sometimes in slow motion. It worked perfectly. Griffith-Paret III would see the inaugural use of the slow motion videotape replay.[17]

The day of the fight, Griffith was tense, focused mainly on what Paret might say or do at the weigh-in. He told his manager, "If he says anything to me at the weigh in, I'm going to hit him." At the weigh-in, Emile stripped down to his underwear and socks and got on the scale. Photographers snapped away, reporters scribbled in their note pads. Then Griffith heard his manager say "Watch out" to someone nearby. The next thing Griffith knew, Paret was right behind him, moving against him, grabbing him low and inappropriately. "Hey *maricón*, I'm going to get you *and* your husband." Griffith spun around, spurted that if Paret didn't stop, they would fight right here. Benny just smiled mockingly at him. Clancy stepped between the two, told his fighter to "save it for tonight."[18]

Something deep within Griffith jostled awake. Yes, Griffith did have what today we would call a "boyfriend." But at the time, he did not consider himself gay or straight or anything. He was just Emile. He simply loved whom he wanted. And this was 1962. There were no openly homosexual celebrities or politicians. And a gay *boxer*? Such a thing simply evaded the realm of reason. The Stonewall Riots were still over seven years into the future. Psychiatry still defined homosexuality as an illness. Nearly every state outlawed sodomy. A few years earlier, the flamboyant pianist Liberace had sued *Confidential* magazine for printing the article, "Why Liberace's Theme Song Should be 'Mad About the Boy.'" Liberace won the suit.

Griffith-Paret III went on at the Garden, a live TV fight in front of seventy-six hundred at the venue and millions more at home. Both men came out swinging. Often they seemed not to hear the bell that ended the rounds, continuing until the referee pried them apart. If Griffith was fighting out of anger, Paret was battling out of defiance. Incredibly, in the sixth round Paret caught Griffith with a short, hard left to the chin and dropped him. Just seconds earlier, Griffith had been pummeling the Kid so freely that referee Ruby Goldstein was about to do something about it. Then, suddenly, Griffith was on the mat. "That's the first time I've seen him down," said an amazed Dunphy. "I don't think he knows where he is." Griffith got up, a bewildered expression on his face. They moved back together and the bell rang, possibly saving the Virgin Islander from his first knockout loss. Between rounds, as Griffith cleared his head, Clancy told him to get inside and keep punching until Paret held him or the referee broke them apart.

In the tenth round, Griffith pummeled Paret fiercely with a series of blows that seemed to tire him out as much as they reeled Paret. Paret looked like he would never go down. In the eleventh, Griffith seemed to rest, regaining his composure.

Then came the worst round in the history of TV boxing. Things began to go south about halfway through, just after Dunphy noted that this is "probably the tamest round of the entire fight." Emile caught Paret with a solid right that sent him along the ropes and into a neutral corner. Paret put up his hands, Griffith backed up a step, and then came in hard and fast. Short lefts and rights found home, and Paret seemed dazed, momentarily putting both his gloves down on the ropes. The old Griffith would have hesitated at this point, with such apparently open prey in front of him. But not now. Paret, strangely, seemed to lean forward as Griffith sent hard right uppercuts into his head, one after the other. The camera angle was low, making clear that Griffith determinedly working away, the piston movement of his right arm going up and down. Finally, the force of the blows caused Benny's head to tilt back grotesquely, his body held up only by the ropes, his arms low in a modified Christ pose. With a full, clear field of fire Griffith opened up once more, throwing vicious right-left-right-left combinations, as if angry at a bag at the gym. Paret's head lolled with each blow, while Griffith continued, mouth open, face blank.

Finally, referee Ruby Goldstein intervened and threw his arms around Griffith. But the camera did not follow the winner. It stayed on Paret, his unconscious form sinking down slowly, his right arm still slung up over the rope. A ring doctor and corner men came in and laid Benny out flat on the mat. For some reason, his knees tucked up automatically, his legs looking as though he was sitting back on an invisible chair. Perhaps this was a reaction to a stimulant injected by the doctor. His eyes did not open.

At ringside that night, along with all the reporters and politicians and fat cats and mobsters, sat a famous writer named Norman Mailer. His first novel, a semi-autobiographical tale about a group of soldiers in the Pacific titled *The Naked and the Dead* (1948), had catapulted him to celebrity after World War II. Mailer was a huge boxing fan, and his report of Paret-Griffith III worked its way into an article that he wrote ostensibly about a Sonny Liston–Floyd Patterson fight for *Esquire*. "I had never seen a fight like it," he would write. In the last round, Mailer imagined Griffith "a cat ready to rip the life out of a huge boxed rat."

> He hit him eighteen right hands in a row, an act which took perhaps three or four seconds, Griffith making a pent-up whimpering sound all the while he attacked, the right hand whipping like a piston rod which has broken through the crankcase, or like a baseball bat demolishing a pumpkin. I was sitting in the second row of that corner—they were not ten feet away from me, and like everybody else, I was hypnotized. I had never seen one man hit another so hard and so many times. Over the referee's face came a look of woe as if some spasm had passed its way through him, and then he leaped on Griffith to pull him away. It was the act of a brave man. Griffith was uncontrollable. His trainer leaped into the ring, his manager, his cut man, there were four people holding Griffith, but he was off on an orgy, he had left the Garden, he was back on a hoodlum's street. If he had been able to break loose from his handlers and the referee, he would have jumped Paret to the floor and whaled on him there.

Mailer enjoyed boxing, but not this. This fight, he reported, was infused with hate and murder at the get-go. Mailer had heard that Paret did not like "that kind of guy"—homosexuals—and that the "rage" in Griffith was "extreme." When Griffith finally unleashed all of his anger and frustration on Paret, he seemed to have turned his muscles over to some dark reptilian instinct. When Paret finally went down, the Cuban seemed to become a metaphor for something else, something dying in the sport or in humanity. "He went down more slowly than any fighter had ever gone down, he went down like a large ship which turns on end and slides second by second into its grave. As he went down, the sound of Griffith's punches echoed in the mind like a heavy ax in the distance chopping into a wet log."[19]

Out in TV Land, millions sat transfixed, horrified. In Berkeley, Bob Hink watched with his dad and grandparents. "I can still see [Paret] getting the hell beat out of him. I can see him in the corner." In New Haven, John O'Connor watched with his amateur-boxer dad. His dad told him, "Don't worry, Paret will get off the ropes." Dad knew a lot about boxing, but this time John wasn't able to agree. "You sure?" he asked nervously. "That's his style," Dad reassured. Out in a suburb of Philadelphia, young Chuck Hasson watched as one of his favorite fighters, Benny Paret, was beaten senseless in the corner. For reasons he didn't understand, he stood up and yelled, "Kill him! Kill him!" as Griffith whacked away, as if on "a punching bag." "I don't think I've ever said that again." In another living room, boxing enthusiast Bert Sugar watched the spectacle with his pregnant wife. She told him she was never watching another fight again.

Benny Paret was administered last rites by a priest at the Garden before being rushed off to Roosevelt Hospital in an ambulance. A group of fifteen people waited in the hospital lobby for word about the fallen boxer. Among them was Emile Griffith, who told a reporter, "I'm sorry it happened. I hope everything is being done for him."[20]

At about one in the morning, the surgery began. After several hours of probing and drilling, doctors determined that Paret had suffered a cerebral laceration and had multiple blood clots in his brain. Manuel Alfaro said that his boxer's condition was "grave" but added, "I do not think he will die." Then he began to recast the event, removing himself from all complicity. "The referee," Alfaro explained with a tone of indignation, "should have stopped it sooner. I was shouting to him to stop it but he did not hear me. Paret was exhausted when the punch caught him and left him helpless." Sensing the criticism to come, he added, "I do not think tonight's result was any carryover from Paret's fight with Gene Fullmer."[21]

The reports from the hospital were bad. One doctor gave the Kid a one in ten-thousand chance of making it. Emile Griffith seemed utterly stricken. "I didn't mean him any harm," he told reporters. When Ruby Goldstein had dragged him off of Paret, Griffith recalled thinking that the referee was just breaking a clinch. "I wanted to keep punching and punching. My manager (Gil Clancy) told me to keep hitting when I saw I had him hurt so that's what I did." He also admitted to something else. "You know, he called me bad names at the weigh-in. I told Gil that if he did the same thing this time, I'd hit him. He did it again and I was burning mad." At this point, Gil Clancy saw the interview heading south and jumped in. "That's right," Clancy said. "But I told Emile the fight would be called off if he did anything like that. He wanted this title more than anything in the world. He was so excited at the end that I don't think he knew what he was doing."[22]

Gaspar was in the Garden at ringside that night as well, sitting next to his wife, Ida. When he saw Paret go down, he could see Benny's eyes and was horrified. "I looked into his face. His eyes were wide open, but there was no vision. His eyes were all white." Gaspar stood and told Ida, "Let's get out of here." He knew Paret was not going to make it. He could not bear to watch the corner work on a dead man.

Others reacted differently. Photos of the audience at the final, macabre scene show some people still cheering and at least one woman with her hands flat over her mouth in horror. After Paret sank, a ringside reporter leaned over to another and said, "I think we just saw a gay murder."[23]

The worst of it happened minutes after Griffith took back his title. Dunphy, standing in the ring with the new champ, says, "Benny, uh, rather, Emile, I want you to take a look at our screen here and we're going to replay the knockout in slow motion videotape and I'd like you to sort of describe what happened if you can remember." They look down, presumably at a monitor that has been brought in. The TV switched to what they are seeing. And so it would be that the first use of slow motion replay in sports history was of a killing.

Dunphy later learned that the networks were playing the slow-mo repeatedly after the fight. The ratings actually spiked just *after* the bout, due to people calling their friends and telling them to watch. The post-fight show ratings had beaten out the actual event.[24]

"There it is. That did it, that did it," says Dunphy to Griffith as they both watch him connect with the right that stunned Paret and opened him up to the horrific volley that followed.

Benny Paret died ten days later. He never regained consciousness. Lucy came up from Miami with Benny Jr. to stay with him in the hospital while the world waited. She had seen the fight on TV with a neighbor. Supposedly, her son had yelled, "Papa! Papa! Papa!" at the screen as Paret slid to the mat. Lucy didn't like to see his fights in person because she thought the sport was too brutal. Now she told reporters that the night before the bout, her husband had called to tell her that he didn't feel well. She had told him not to fight, but Benny had said that Manuel insisted that he must. Too much money had been already spent, his manager had said. Now here she was at her husband's side, leaning over his still form, watching the tubes going into his throat. Adding to the tragedy, reporters wrote, was that Lucy was three months pregnant.[25]

Gaspar visited Benny in the hospital about three days into his coma. He shook when he saw Benny's face covered with a mask of bandages. He squeezed his fallen rival's hand, leaned over and whispered, "I'm Gaspar Ortega, do you know me? You were a wonderful fighter." But Paret could not talk. And then, a miracle. "He squeezed my hand twice, very, very slowly. Not hard squeezes. Like he was saying, 'okay.'" Gaspar left the hospital very upset. He told his wife what had happened in the hospital room. He could scarcely focus on anything else.

Referee Ruby Goldstein was asked again and again why he hadn't stopped the fight. He began to look haggard and worn, found himself unable to sleep at night. He thought about visiting Paret in the hospital, but was advised not to. "I knew Paret as a tough fellow," Goldstein tried to explain to the press. Everyone knew Paret had an "iron chin." Most observant fans would have agreed, must have known that Paret was prone to "playing possum" and then suddenly exploding to life. He had actually done just that in the sixth round of this same fight and had floored Griffith as result. "Sometimes, in the first part of a round, he doesn't do too well," explained Goldstein. "Then he comes out of it and starts fighting." And of all people, Goldstein knew what he was talking about. He had refereed some five hundred fights over his nineteen-year tenure and was long considered one of the top refs in the business. He had even been criticized in the past for stopping fights too soon. Ed Sullivan had once praised him personally on his TV show for knowing when to call a battle before serious harm was done. "I thought he might roll away from the ropes in the twelfth round," Goldstein now said limply. "Lots of fighters do that."[26]

Heat also came down on Manuel Alfaro. Why had he put Paret in the ring so soon after the Fullmer beating? Gene Fullmer himself was telling reporters, "I never hit a guy so many times before he went down." Alfaro appeared to have forgotten what he had said just days earlier about Paret's readiness. Now he said that he personally had never wanted this fight, that he had really wanted his man to rest longer. But the New York

State Athletic Commission "kept after me." To hear Alfaro tell it, he was all but forced to relent. (The Commission promptly denied Alfaro's allegations).[27] Alfaro then took a different tack, deflecting the blame onto referee Ruby Goldstein. After Paret died, Alfaro added a new title to his repertoire: reformer. He began arguing for mandatory headgear.

Inevitably, the sport came under fire. Arthur Daley of the *New York Times* asked, "Is It Worth the Price?" As Paret lay in his coma, Daley reflected that in other sports, injury is "accidental." In boxing, it is the objective. Television had made the troublesome aspects of the sport infinitely worse. The evil lay in the "inexorable eye of the camera, particularly the rerun in slow motion." Watching Griffith pound away at the end made the fight into a "horror movie." Daly ended by indicating that the sport should be abolished. Trying to make it safer with bigger pads and headgear would not satisfy the "sadists who scream for blood and punishment." Other writers were even more strident. Wrote one, America would be "better-off" if the sport "were to die with Benny."[28]

Even before Paret stopped breathing, the critics had renewed their calls to abolish boxing. New York governor Nelson A. Rockefeller was reported to be "deeply concerned and disturbed." A commission was put on the case to investigate. From Cuba, the country that Paret had publicly disowned, radio announcers barked that the beating only illustrated the evils of professional boxing. It was "run by real gangsters who are interested only in filling their bags with dollars and do not have the least regard for the lives of the fighters."[29]

In the wake of Paret's death, the trickle of criticism opened into a full-blown flood. "Seldom," reported *Time* magazine, "had a nationwide TV audience been treated to so shocking a reminder of boxing's basic brutality." The *New York Times* editorialized, "Is this the pastime of a civilized people?" The *New York Post* called boxing "organized primitivism." *Life* magazine, the periodical that framed so many national discussions with its vivid true-life photographs, printed an image of Paret slumped in the corner, his face visibly ruined, a man pulling his mouth guard out of a frozen and contorted maw. The caption underneath: "$50,000 A fearful price for a fight." Explained *Life*, "The sickening thump of a fighter near death made the whole world wonder how far a man could go to make money." Officials in Tampa, Florida, suspended all pending matches. The state legislature of New York introduced a bill to ban the sport.[30]

Significantly, *Time* magazine's report of the fight was not in the sports pages but the "Medicine" section. Its discussion took on a disturbing, scientific quality as readers were treated to a detailed, stomach-turning description of Paret's demise. As Griffith pummeled away, "different parts of Paret's brain were hit by the overlying skull with enough force to break blood vessels between the middle (arachnoid) and outermost (dura mater) layers of the brain's covering (meninges). The resulting accumulations of blood and clots (called hematomas), together with multiple bruises and severe swelling, exerted inexorable pressure on several parts of Paret's brain and cut the elaborate circuitry of the nervous system." But scientific data was not the catalyst for the public outrage. It took no doctor to explain what Mailer knew: "His brain was smashed." The real source of outrage was that TV had brought death into the living room. Women and children had watched a man get beaten to death.[31]

The national Catholic weekly journal *America* focused on the role of TV in telescoping the horror. The editors noted that "15 million television fans watched challenger Emile Griffith scramble the brains of welterweight champion Benny Paret beyond repair, and then saw a rerun of the climactic moments of this state-supervised slaughter in slow motion." *America* warned that more carnage was to come, until finally "outraged public opinion demands the abolition of civilized man's most atavistic sport." The writers praised the pulpit for finally focusing on the immorality of the sport. Echoing much enlightened opinion, the editors looked to a glorious future "when the American people finally reject professional boxing for good, and inter it by the side of cockfighting, bearbaiting and the public execution of criminals."[32]

An international chorus joined in the condemnation. The British Parliament heard critics demand an end to the sport in the empire. The *London Daily Sketch* leaned that way too, calling the Paret-Griffith battle "the most murderous world title fight in history." The *Vienna Kurier* was outraged at the "unprecedented boxing scandal." Even the pope seemed to have lost faith. Vatican radio now called boxing "a morally objectionable sport."[33]

Boxing was wobbling under withering fire. *Ebony* magazine published a piece that summarized a common sentiment: "With the moans of the mother mingled the indignant outcries of thousands, who decreed that because Paret had died, professional boxing, too, had forfeited its right to live."[34] Such demands, of course, predated the Paret incident. Ever since the Kefauver Commission's airing of boxing's dirty laundry, journalists had publicly predicted the demise of the sport. A 1961 piece by W. C. Heinz in the *Saturday Evening Post*, titled "The Twilight of Boxing," reported sadly on that bellwether of fisticuffs, Stillman's Gym. Lou Stillman had sold the gym in July 1959 to Walter Scott and Company, and it had been renamed The Eighth Avenue Gym. Irving Cohen, the new gym operator, glumly reported, "I'm losing a hundred dollars a month not counting my time." Of 350 paying boxers, only 33 were left. Cohen offered the club to other managers but got no takers. "Boxing," he announced, "is dying of natural causes." Heinz agreed. Fight clubs in the country had diminished in number by 90 percent over the previous ten years. Gross gate receipts for boxing matches in the United States had declined from $14 million in 1946 to just over $4 million in 1959. The twelve thousand registered boxers in the early fifties had gone down to forty-two hundred in the early sixties, only three thousand of whom were American citizens.[35]

When Paret died, a perfect storm of disaster seemed to have struck boxing. The boxing clubs, the wellsprings from which talent had been drawn, were drying up. Schools were discontinuing their boxing teams, thus cutting away a key nursery for up-and-coming amateurs. Rising affluence was doing the same thing, many said, robbing America of the gritty desperation that bred the sport. The suburbs certainly were being built not with boxing in mind but rather with parks, pools, and baseball diamonds within their confines. The clusters of white, urban, working-class people who traditionally supported many of the city clubs were dispersing out to the stucco countrysides with the aid of the GI Bill. Plus, Estes Kefauver had exposed the public to the mob's role in the sport; the smell of corruption seemed to drift right through the TV sets and persuade many to change the channel. Other disappointed viewers pointed out that the champions were less heroic (and often less "American") than in days of old. The heavyweight champ, the man who traditionally bore most of the sport's popularity on his shoulders, was the unimpressive Floyd Patterson. In September 1962, Patterson would be replaced by a thug named Sonny Liston, a man who had already been brought forth by Senator Kefauver as an insider to mob corruption.

And, finally, there was the damage wrought by television, damage that had been traced out by critics since the early 1950s, damage that was now showing itself in the form of boxers who did not fight the Sweet Science of ring generalship and careful strategy but rather flailed away, heedless of their own safety. Paret, after all, was the perfect TV boxer. He was the kind of fighter who could last long enough to sell ten rounds worth of commercial time while giving the home audience a thrilling show. His demise seemed to prove horrifically just how far adrift the TV had cast the sport. For our entertainment, people were putting themselves into harm's way. They were dying for us.

But boxing continued on, just as it had always managed to do. Its defenders rose up to halt the negative stampede. *Ring* magazine pointed out that while nine boxers met their demise in 1961, forty-seven football players had died that same year. Said boxer Archie Moore, the violence of the sport offered "the only channel through which [underprivileged youths] can express this violence in a non-criminal manner and at the same time use it as a shortcut to an otherwise unattainable security." Ruby Goldstein warned that if the sport were banned, it would go underground in the form of criminal-infested "punch-easies." Widow Lucy Paret even said that the sport should not be banned. "If he hadn't gotten hurt, he would have continued to fight," she said of her late husband. "He knew no other business. And that's true of many fighters." Sportswriter Red Smith was the most abrasively indignant. The attacks, he claimed, were coming primarily from "part-time bleeding hearts, the professional sob sisters of press and politics and radio, who seize these opportunities (Paret's death) to parade their own nobility, demonstrate their eloquence, and incidentally stir the emotions of a few readers, voters or listeners."[36]

Smith was unfair, and he and the other defenders probably added little to the end result. Boxing was to go on, but it was more because of money than counter-punches from angry sportswriters. Or perhaps boxing went unabolished due to the fact that it had never entirely shucked its dangerous allure, so the audience's shock over the result of the Paret fight was not completely convincing. Despite what its defenders so vigorously argued, boxing ever remained, in the words of one writer, "the dark prince of sports." Of course it was dangerous. Of course the aim was to maim. People liked to see that. Gaspar's career continued to count on it.

On April 23, 1962, Indio faced a Chicano named Joey Limas in Albuquerque, New Mexico. It was not good. Perhaps the loss to Charley Scott had dispirited him. Perhaps the hand injury kept him from doing his best. Or perhaps he was, in his own word, "lazy" in that fight. Gaspar lost on decision to a man destined to win only eight more times over the next decade (though one of those victories would be against Don Jordan).

Then it was down to Sonora for a knockout victory against a local named Bernardo Velez. They fought next to a swimming pool surrounded by desert. A week later, Gaspar decisioned another poor Mexican in Sonora. And so the tour continued. Indio fought in bullrings, on tennis courts, in sweaty arenas, even in a Mexican prison yard ("the gate wasn't that good"). For one match at a bullring, Gaspar was actually talked into fighting a bull. He did three passes with a young bull to the delight of the crowd a day or so before thrashing the local hero. It was all good as far as Indio was concerned. He didn't care what local Golden Boy was thrust into the ring with him. He demolished nearly every one of them. By the end of 1962, Gaspar had logged an incredible twenty-two fights, and nearly all of these were after the month of April. Most incredibly, four of these battles were held on consecutive days. Gaspar won all four by knockout.

His reputation as the Gypsy of Boxing grew. Jimmy Breslin would soon call him "the last old-fashioned prize fighter the business has left."[37] Another sportswriter was impressed that Gaspar still looked so fresh faced: "you expect to see a beetle-browed, twisted nose character." Lest readers think Gaspar was untested, Nick Corby added, "He has fought with a bad leg, with a bad rib, with a bad hand, and with a bad foot. And not easy fights, unless you consider Emile Griffith, Benny Paret, Florentino Fernandez, and Federico Thompson easy." Corby would tell another reporter, "I think he does more to keep boxing alive than any of the current champions. He travels more miles, and fights in more different clubs, than any fighter boxing today, and he never puts on a poor show."[38]

Across Mexamerica people came to watch the busiest man in the sport. Some of his fights were locally advertised by men barking into loudspeakers mounted on trucks. Gaspar would show up, beat some poor pug senseless, collect his four or five hundred dollars, and then move on to the next town. He noticed that in Mexico, fans did not wave Mexican flags for him. When both fighters were Mexican, of course, flags from his fans wouldn't make sense. But their absence reminded him comfortingly of his roots. He fought a couple battles up north too. He battled Charley "Tombstone" Smith in Butte, Montana. Smith was a tough slugger whom Indio ended up facing three times and beating twice. After Gaspar KO'd Tombstone at their third matchup at the Butte Civic Center, Nick Corby hoisted him into the air and triumphantly carried him about. Then Corby put him down and just walked off. Gaspar noticed that Corby was missing and asked around. He found out later that his manager had had a mild heart attack and was taken to the hospital (Corby recovered).[39]

Heading into 1963, Gaspar had no illusions. He knew he'd never get back into the big time, would never have another title shot or even get near one. His mom started telling him to quit and get a nice job in Tijuana. His dad told him it was time to find real employment. Aniseto admitted to his son, "I worked all my life for nothing. You must be careful and do the best you can." Boxing, his parents told him, had become a dead end street. Of course Gaspar knew that they were right, but boxing was all he had, and he was still making good money from it. In Honolulu in October 1962, Gaspar got four thousand dollars to fight Stan Harrington (he won). In November that year, he received three thousand to fight Mel Barker in Albuquerque. Sometimes, he would pull in big, ego-boosting crowds, up to eight thousand people in some cases. Plus, when Indio showed up at those little Mexican towns for a fight, they all adored him. They packed into gyms just to watch him train. They fawned all over him in the streets. No, the game was not through with Indio. Not yet.

As Gaspar pummeled his way across Mexamerica and fewer people tuned in to watch the fights on TV, other events kept Americans glued to the tube. The world seemed to be getting less safe, and television was bringing the troubles right into American living rooms. On April 17, 1961, Kennedy gave the go-ahead for a CIA-organized invasion of Castro's Cuba, with exiles landing at the island's Bay of Pigs. Everything that could have gone wrong did. Not least was the fact that Castro knew all about the invasion beforehand. As Kennedy would later complain, "All he [Castro] has to do is read our papers. It's all laid out for him."[40] In August of that year, the Soviet Union sealed off the border between East and West Berlin and then ordered guards to check the passports of U.S. officials. Kennedy responded by sending fifteen hundred troops to West Germany, triggering a tense, sixteen-hour standoff. In October 1962, six months after Benny Paret's death, the world watched in terror as Kennedy put the military on high alert. The president went on television and told America that the Kremlin was testing our "courage and commitments." The Soviets were building nuclear missile bases in Cuba. Soviet subs were spotted in the Caribbean. Kennedy ominously told the home audience, "I have directed the armed forces to prepare for any eventualities." Then came the Soviet freighters, steaming toward Cuba, presumably carrying deadly loads. Had Armageddon finally arrived? At almost the last second, some of the freighters started to turn around. JFK's secretary of state famously said to National Security Advisor McGeorge Bundy, "We're eyeball to eyeball, and the other fellow just blinked."[41]

If 1962 was bad, 1963 would be even worse for the country and for the sport of boxing. In the second fight of a novel triple-title card set up by Parnassus and Eaton in Dodger Stadium in March, twenty-six thousand fans watched titleholder Davey Moore lose badly to Cuban expatriate Ultiminio "Sugar" Ramos. Moore, a popular fighter called the "Springfield Rifle" (he fought out of Springfield, Ohio), started the fight ahead, but by the third round he was being routed by his younger, faster adversary. In the tenth (and final round of his career, as it turned out), a series of blows sent Moore stumbling back from the middle of the ring all the way down to the edge. He fell back, his neck catching the bottom rope. Moore stayed there a moment, pushed his mouthguard back in, and then got back up, slowly and deliberately. The referee counted eight and allowed the fight to continue. There were thirty seconds left in the round. But Moore was no longer there. Ramos fired away, sending his opponent awkwardly bent over the middle rope, his upper body leaning over towards the audience. Ramos stepped back, unsure of how to handle the situation. Moore returned, wobbly, and Ramos pumped left after left into his skull, sending him bent over the same rope. The bell rang before Moore could extricate himself. His corner men had to help him to his stool. Between rounds, Moore's manager called the fight, giving the title to Ramos on a technical knockout.

Moore made it to his dressing room under his own power as the third fight of the evening, a junior welterweight title match between Roberto Cruz of the Philippines and Battling Torres of Mexico, got underway. From his dressing room Moore told gathered reporters, "Sure I want to fight him [Ramos] again. And I'll get the title back." He seemed to accept the loss. "It just wasn't my night." Later, after the reporters left, Moore put his hand on his head and complained of a fierce headache. He slumped over. He never regained consciousness. He died seventy-five hours later in a hospital. Explained the attending nurse, "He just stopped breathing."[42]

The outrage over Moore's death resurrected the whirlwind that had followed Paret's demise hardly a year earlier. Governor Pat Brown of California demanded an end to this "barbaric spectacle." His political opponent, former vice president Richard Nixon, exclaimed that boxing "should be kicked out or cleaned up, one or the other." Bills were immediately introduced in California, Oregon, Texas, Maryland, and Ohio to ban the sport. Three lawmakers in Ohio added, "The legislation has seen fit to outlaw dogfights, bearfights and cockfights. The least they could do is the same for humans." Reports surfaced that several boxers were quitting the sport, afraid for their lives. For the first time, the pope personally spoke out; John XXIII announced that boxing was "barbaric" and that "fist fights are contrary to natural principles."[43]

In its April 5, 1963, issue, *Life* magazine asked, "Why was the ring becoming a death chamber?" Sixteen boxers had died in the past fifteen months. The chilling answer to *Life*'s question was television itself. The magazine reported that "today's frenzied race to put anybody wearing gloves into the ring" had undercut the old traditions of rigorous journeymanship, when fighters had to fight many opponents and develop their skills before getting a chance at a title. Today's fighters, *Life* explained, "don't belong in the same ring with the fighters of 25 years ago."[44] The magazine did have an excellent point, but in this case it was misapplied. Moore was the one with experience here. Ramos was the kid getting rushed to the top.

Once again, the calls for abolition did not go unanswered. When a Massachusetts state representative called for a motion to ban the sport in the Bay State, he was defeated. Another representative called his motion "stupid" and asked why he didn't try and outlaw "motor scooters, bicycles and cars since these, too, were dangerous." Anthropologist Margaret Mead offered up a more philosophical defense. Society, she pointed out, is "robbing males of a robust mastery over their own bodies." Boxing helped retard "the emasculation of the modern male."[45]

As the boxing debate wore on, other events swamped it on the front pages. April 1963 was also the month that civil rights leader Martin Luther King Jr. launched a new phase in the struggle for American freedom with a series of demonstrations in Birmingham, Alabama. In the streets of the city, TV cameras captured for the first time the brutal tactics used by the defenders of Jim Crow in the Deep South. Audiences watched children get slammed with high pressure fire hoses and accosted by police clubs and snapping dogs. Kennedy watched, too, and felt "sick." He went on TV on June 11 with a stunning announcement: the time had come, he declared, "for this nation to fulfill its promise." He offered up a comprehensive civil rights bill intended to do away with discrimination in public places, to help African Americans vote freely, and to support schooling for blacks in the South.

But Kennedy's proposal did not settle things. One day after he went on the air, a sniper's bullet struck NAACP's Mississippi field secretary, Medgar Evers, as he got out of his car in front of his house. He died en route to the hospital, inflaming those who had hoped that a corner had just been turned. Then Kennedy's bill was criticized as not having teeth. Activists planned a major march on Washington, D.C., in August to protest the glacial pace of social change. Behind the scenes, Kennedy worked to tone down the event, which initially was planned to include a protracted sit-in on the Capitol steps until Congress passed a decent civil rights bill. On August 28, 1963, 250,000 Americans peacefully marched to the Lincoln Memorial. They listened to Martin Luther King's dream. Again, the world seemed on the verge of a new dawning of peace and freedom. At a press conference in November, Kennedy told reporters that he was optimistic about seeing a strong civil rights bill coming out of Congress. He told them, "However dark it looks now, I think that 'Westward, look the land is bright.'" About a week later, the president went to Dallas to help smooth over Democratic in-fighting before the next election cycle.

Gaspar did not pay much attention to the escalating civil rights wars. The year 1963 was not one of progress for him. It was a year of unrelenting, brutal combat. Day after day, week after week, he took on all comers.

Indio started off the year in Baltimore, fighting Charley Scott for the second time. It was a cold winter, and Gaspar elected to minimize his roadwork to stay out of the frigid weather. Just before the fight, a guy with an unusual-looking ID came into Gaspar's dressing room and told him that the Mexican consul had come to watch him. Corby lit right up. He told Gaspar, "You have to show these people who you are!" He seemed to still hold out hope for a bright future. Scott was currently the seventh-ranked welterweight in the world and favored 7–5 to beat Indio. Gaspar felt inspired. He wore his sombrero into the ring, to the cheers of many in the mixed crowd of nearly fifty-five hundred. Clustered around the ring was a retinue of Mexican nationals from the embassy. They were bursting with enthusiasm. They exhorted, "*Chinga lo! Chinga lo!*" ("Fuck him up!") He took a unanimous decision. The Mexican guy with the ID told him, "I'm so proud. You showed them that Mexicans have big balls." Nick Corby also seemed more proud than ever.[46]

The Scott fight was impressive, but it didn't get Gaspar any closer to the Garden. Over the next five months, he fought a series of opponents in Mexico. In Cananea, Sonora, he fought in front of five hundred people under a circus tent against a nobody named Pedro Torres. Nick Corby was working a day job in San Diego again and had to take off time to be in his corner. The paydays were shrinking now; Nick didn't take any money for the fight. A friend from Tijuana joined Indio's corner, a guy with jutting teeth they nicknamed Tiburon (Shark). After watching Torres in round one, Nick told Gaspar to watch when he put his head down. "Wait for him to throw a right uppercut, then hit him." Gaspar did, and knocked Torres out in round two. It was another of those times when Gaspar's opponent was still cognizant, but just sat there timidly on the mat until the ref counted to ten.

After that, Gaspar fought a highly ranked Mexican boxer named Beto Gerardo in Juarez. Gerardo gave him a good, close fight for the first four rounds. Corby told Gaspar to start throwing more body punches. Down Gerardo went in round seven. If Gaspar was off the American radar, in Mexico his star was still bright. His next opponent was the Mexican welterweight titleholder, Alvaro Guttierez. Gaspar fought him in front of a huge crowd at a bullring. Smartly, Alvaro did not put his title on the line. It was a tough fight: "He was a bull. No fighter, he was a bull." Alvaro charged in and kept on coming. Gaspar used his speed to avoid most of the onslaught, but by the end, exhausted, he settled in to trade punches with the rugged brawler, much to Nick Corby's chagrin. The fight was ruled a draw. Gaspar was happy with the decision.

By June 1963, Gaspar had knocked out five straight opponents, each in under four rounds. His opponents were small-time locals who let themselves be battered for a paycheck. Gaspar began to get lazy. He'd jump rope in the afternoons and do a few short exercises, but that was about it. He thought the constant fights were workout enough.

About this time, *Ring* magazine featured Gaspar in a big, two-part article ostensibly written by his wife (a writer came over to the apartment and they talked it out), titled "Fear Is My Companion." Ida commented on what it was like being married to the busiest man in the sport. He "is a gypsy fighter," she explained; always gone, sometimes for months at a time. She talked about the nervousness of being the wife of a man in a deadly sport, recalling how painful it was to hear about the deaths of Paret and Moore, men who left behind widows and children of their own. "But I am a deep believer in a higher power, and I don't question the whys and wherefores of life." Indeed, the widows of Paret and Moore both placed the deaths of their husbands not in their opponents' hands but in God's. Ida would, of course, be happier if her husband didn't box, she wrote, happier if he'd hold down a "comparatively quiet 9-to-5 job." But she knew that that wasn't him. "Boxing is my husband's life. . . . It would be terrible selfish for me to attempt to compel him to give it up." Besides, if not for boxing, the two would have never met; how else would she, a New Yorker, be married to an uneducated soldier's son from Tijuana? Plus there was the money to consider. He made more of it by boxing than he would at a "workingman's job."

Ida recounted their romance. She wrote how, after Gaspar had been beaten by Logart in the fight he "dedicated" to her, she had tried to cheer him up by not mentioning boxing. She told how he had come out of his shell and shared his childhood experiences with her. She talked about their children, of which there were now four. Michael, the boy born in the seventh round of the Galivan fight, was most like dad. He "already has an ambition, to be a bullfighter," which apparently thrilled Gaspar. Ida recalled how Michael was delivered by the resident physician of the hospital because both her Los Angeles obstetrician and the doctor who had come up from Tijuana to assist were at the fight that night.

Reading the article, one gets a sense of the enormous reserve of quiet strength and determination Ida possessed. For instance, when Gaspar demanded to know, "Where's all the money I sent you?," she would pull out her "little black book," brimming with detailed accounts of all of the family's expenses and deposits. "Argument's over then and there." She went on to say that while he's quiet in public, Gaspar is no "angel." "Underneath his generally kind disposition," she wrote, "there's a volcano if someone takes advantage of him." She told the story of his once bashing in the trash can at Orchard Beach in response to being hassled by a group of Puerto Ricans. "On the few occasions when he loses control, the aftereffect is deep. He becomes violently ill, and sometimes will throw up."

Pictures accompanying the article paint the dualities of Gaspar's life and profession. Images of the "happy family" were lined up in the living room: Gaspar getting a kiss on the cheek from little daughter Martha, images of Ida cooking and paying the bills. And then the images of brutality: Gaspar's face covered in welts, Gaspar falling back in the ring, Gaspar connecting a hard straight right to Mickey Crawford's face. ("Note effect of blow as Crawford's face becomes distorted," reads the caption.)

Out of the blue in the summer of 1963, Gaspar got word from Jimmy Stinson that he had landed another TV fight. Indio was to report to New York City for a fight with a kid named Billy Bello. It didn't take long for Gaspar to figure out what was going on.

Billy Bello was just twenty years old, barely old enough to be permitted to fight in ten-round bouts by New York State law. In fact, his fight with

Gaspar would be only his second ten-round battle. Bello was a quietly confident, religious kid from the Bronx who still lived with his parents. When not training, Billy sold Catholic artifacts in a small shop in the neighborhood. He had a stellar amateur record and was being groomed by his management to go forth and do great things. He was good-looking, naturally talented, and oft predicted to be a title contender. They said he was the next Billy Conn (once his weight filled in and he moved into the middleweight and light heavyweight ranks, of course). Bello's manager, Cy Crisci, even grandly told a reporter, "I think he's going all the way. I think he'll be the biggest boxing attraction in the country in another two years." Billy also seemed confident in his own abilities. When asked about the other welters, he shrugged, "They're not bad—some of them."[47]

The Indian was to be Bello's launching pad. As an over-the-hill ex-contender, Gaspar seemed the perfect foil to showcase Bello's acumen and rocket him up the ranks. Though Gaspar was favored to win and was still ranked number ten by *Ring* magazine among welters and a surprising number four by the World Boxing Association as a junior middleweight (the 154-pound division), he was considered a dinosaur.[48] Bello told the *New York Times* that he dreamed he would knock out Gaspar in round one. "He's standing between me and the big purses, the international matches," Bello said. "And I've been watching him, he's rough and he's a fighter but he isn't a very smart boxer. He gets hit a lot. And I'm a hitter." Although he had scarcely been boxing professionally for two years, Bello assured *New York Times* journalist Robert Lipsyte that he was ready. "I been watching Ortega since I was a little kid," he said. "And I'm ready for him. I been ready for him for years." An image comes to mind of a young boy dancing in a darkened family room, throwing tightened fists to the tune of tiny on-screen figures. Now, Bello was ready to walk through to the other side. "Beat Ortega good on national television," Bello said dreamily, "and I'm ready for a shot at the junior welterweight title, ready for the really big time."[49]

Don Dunphy introduced the battle as being between "a rising young-ster and a well-tested veteran," a kid's first TV shot against a man whose many opponents "read like a who's who of the welterweight division." After they touched gloves, they both went to their corners, knelt, and crossed themselves. It was about the only thing they did equally. Gaspar brutalized Bello all over the ring that night, especially early on in the fight, bloodying the youngster's nose in the first round and opening another cut under his right eye in the third with, as the *Times* would report it, one of his "long, obvious punches that the 20-year-old should have slipped." Gaspar tired towards the end, giving Bello an opportunity to finally get in some good exchanges, and Bello did manage to stagger Gaspar with a solid straight left in the ninth, making the decision closer than it probably should have been. But Gaspar won the split.[50]

Bello just shouldn't have been in the ring with Ortega that night. It represented the worst of what critics said was happening to the sport. Promising young fighters were getting thrown into the big time way too early, without ever having the chance to hone their craft against a variety of club opponents. In only his second ten-rounder and seventeenth professional fight, Bello faced a twelve-year ring veteran, a man once ranked number one in the world, a man who had knocked out more than twice as many men as Bello had ever even faced as a pro. At one point in the fight, Dunphy noticed Bello looking to his corner "for instruction."

The Bello victory didn't boost Gaspar's chances for progress up the ranks—he was clearly less a viable contender than a headdress-wearing hurdle for rising stars—but it certainly set back Bello's career. Although he was soon training for what he believed would be a rematch with Gaspar, demons that had not been discussed in newspaper columns revealed themselves. Two weeks after the fight, a tenant in Bello's apartment building noticed a man lying on the fifth floor landing stretched on his right side, his right arm extended straight over his head. The tenant assumed that the man was a drunk sleeping off a bender and ignored him. Ten hours later, another tenant saw the figure and checked. It was Billy Bello, and he was dead. Next to the body were three envelopes, the "type used to package powdered narcotics."[51] Doctors arrived and declared him deceased, locating the track marks on his left arm. A heroin overdose had ended Billy Bellos's once-promising career. Even today, Gaspar cannot forget the kid. He needed more refining, "but he had heart."

Gaspar plowed through the rest of 1963 a boxing wanderer. The day Bello's body was discovered, Indio knocked out Alberto Perez in Ensenada. A week later he fought Al Mendez in Nogales. Tiburon told Gaspar he was tired the night of the Mendez fight. Earlier in the day, their bus had broken down in the desert and, at Tiburon's suggestion, they had rented bikes to make it to the rodeo venue on time. Gaspar felt sorry for his sweaty, exhausted friend. Come to think of it, he was tired himself. So he went Old School on the clearly outclassed Mendez. He crouched down and looked at the floor. When Mendez paused to see what Gaspar was looking at, the wily battler leveled him with a devastating overhand punch. Fight over. It was just forty-five seconds into the first round.

In August 1963, Gaspar fought three more locals along the border. In September, he fought five. How does he describe these foes? "Another piece of shit" is how he describes one of them. By late September, Gaspar hadn't lost in twenty-three straight matches against a parade of paychecks with gloves. Then Tiburon got a message to call Nick Corby. "What's going on, Nick?" asked Tiburon. Pack your things, Corby told him. We're going to Rome.

Gaspar's role as stepping-stone was going international. Nick Corby and Jimmy Stinson had managed to arrange a battle against Nino Benvenuti, an Italian wunderkind who had fought thirty-seven opponents and had beaten them all. Benvenuti was a star in Italy ever since he had won the welterweight gold medal at the 1960 Rome Olympics. He had gone pro in 1961 and become a middleweight, annihilating opponent after opponent, picking up the Italian middleweight title along the way. He had imported and defeated an aging Isaac Logart in 1962 at the Palazzetto dello Sport in Rome. Now he aimed to do the same thing with Gaspar.

Gaspar had to cancel a string of projected fights in America to do this, but it was an offer he just couldn't pass up. He grabbed a visa in San Diego and hopped on a plane to Europe for the first time in his life, arriving there a little under a week before fight night. He knew no Italian, so he used his very limited English to get around. At the hotel, the man at the desk asked if he could help him. Gaspar pulled out an ID card and handed it over. "You're here to fight Nino!" the man enthused, in accented English. Gaspar began to get an idea that he was about to become famous in Italy, at least briefly. The guy handed Gaspar a key and said, "*nono piano*." Gaspar figured the guy was still using English. He tried to tell him that he was not here to play the piano. The guy said it again, "*nono piano*." Gaspar stared at him. As if repetition would do the trick, the guy said it several more times, getting more excited each time. Finally, another fellow who may or may not have worked there grabbed the key and indicated to Gaspar to follow him. *Nono piano*, Gaspar soon figured out, meant ninth floor.

The Palazzetto dello Sport was unlike anything Gaspar had ever been in. Built for the 1960 games, it held over ten thousand people and struck a modern pose with its unique ribbed, concrete dome. Inside, the place was packed. Gaspar played it up, entering the ring with a big sombrero on his head. He knew of course that he was fodder, set up to add credibility to the boxing hero of Italy. He gave away an astounding eighteen pounds to

Nino, but he didn't mind. Once the battle was underway, Gaspar learned that his style violated Italian boxing rules. The ref kept telling him not to bend or move his head so much. Against the rules. So he did the best he could, brought the fight to Benvenuti, slugging inside against his much bigger opponent. Incredibly, Gaspar went the distance, despite a hostile crowd and an enormous cut that opened atop his head and sent a small river of blood down his pate. The blood actually seemed to scare Benvenuti, who backed off a bit when he noticed it. The cut wasn't really Nino's fault. Turning up Fifth Avenue for a jog through Central Park a few days before he'd left America, someone had hurled a beer can out an apartment window, and it struck him atop his head. He had to get eighteen stitches at the emergency room. When bloody Gaspar came hurtling towards a wary Nino, he heard some in the crowd chant "Gaspar! Gaspar!" The Italians liked this.

Gaspar lost the Benvenuti bout on points, returning to the States bloodied and exhausted. The year 1963 had been a rough one thus far, and he decided to lay low for a while, to collect himself. He was recuperating in the living room of their three-bedroom apartment one day, listening to his favorite New York station (one that alternated between Spanish and English songs), when he heard the announcement. He yelled to his wife in the kitchen to come in quick. She ran in and he told her, and she turned on the TV. The president had been shot. They kept the TV set on for most of their waking hours over the next four days.

Every TV station had coverage of the event. It started at 1:40 P.M. on Friday, when Walter Cronkite broke into *As the World Turns* on CBS with an audio announcement: "In Dallas, Texas, three shots were fired at President Kennedy's motorcade in downtown Dallas. The first reports say that President Kennedy has been seriously wounded by this shooting." Minutes later Cronkite was reporting from the network's New York studios that Kennedy was dead. By now, every television network offered nonstop, commercial-free coverage from Dallas. Two days later, viewers watched the man accused of the murder, Lee Harvey Oswald, get shot and killed on live TV. "He's been shot! He's been shot!" hollered the broadcast announcer. Throughout the rest of the day, networks deployed video replay technology to show Oswald's death over and over again. Ratings shot through the roof. The *New York Times* called it "easily the most extraordinary moments of TV that a set-owner ever watched." From the time Cronkite made his first announcement until Kennedy was buried at Arlington National Cemetery four days later, Americans remained glued to their sets. Never had television so knitted the country together.[52]

A few days after Kennedy's funeral, Gaspar got a call from Nick Corby. Another fighter, this one a Mexican middleweight titleholder named Aristeo Chavarin, wanted a piece of him.[53] Gaspar was ready. Chavarin wouldn't be putting his precious title on the line. Gaspar came out to Ciudad Juarez only a day or so before the fight and beat Chavarin in a unanimous decision. A week later, the borderlands tour now fully back on, Gaspar took down Kid Rayo in Phoenix, Arizona, in his fifth match against the fast Nicaraguan. Rayo was the last opponent for the Indian in the year 1963. He was number twenty-three.

Two days before Christmas, buried away on the back sports pages of the country's newspapers, was a report. ABC had just announced that it would be taking boxing off the air. The plan was to cancel *Saturday Night Fight of the Week* after ABC's contract with Gillette ran out the following September. It might leave the air even sooner if the network could find another sport to co-sponsor with the razor company.

No other network was interested in picking up the show. It was all over.

Gaspar Ortega's parents, Aniseto and Sebastiana Benitez.
Personal Photo. Gaspar Ortega Scrapbook #2.

Early photo (left to right) of Nick Corby, Sapo Ortega,
Gaspar Ortega, Unidentified Man. Gaspar Ortega Scrapbook #2.

Gaspar Ortega. *Double KO Magazine*, October 16, 1957.

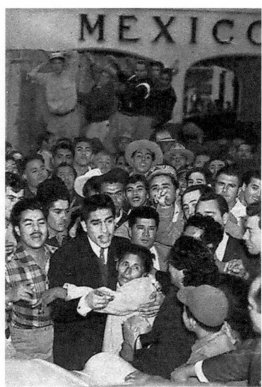

Gaspar hailed by adoring throngs in Tijuana, ca. 1957. *Ring* Magazine, December 1962.

Gaspar Ortega headlines
a Mexican boxing
magazine in one of several
headdresses made for him.
K.O. Semanario Deportivo,
August 27, 1960.

Gaspar Ortega and Emile Griffith, along with hats from Howard
Albert Millinery, at Gilhuly's restaurant in New York City before their
first fight. February 8, 1960. Promotional Photo. Gaspar Ortega.

Frankie Carbo, aka "Mr. Gray," the underworld commissioner of boxing. *Bluebook Magazine,* March 1955.

Gaspar Ortega "serenades" Carmen Basilio prior to their fight in 1962. Gaspar did not play the guitar in real life, nor did he like the outfits his management insisted he wear. But he valued self-promotion. *Ring* Magazine, December 1962.

Gaspar Ortega headlines a Mexican boxing magazine.
K.O. Semanario Deportivo, March 9, 1963.

Gaspar, Ida, and their growing family, as featured in a
boxing magazine, ca. 1962. Gaspar Ortega Scrapbook #2.

GASPAR
ORTEGA

Gaspar Ortega with sombrero for promotional photo.
Domenica Sport (Guida Dello Spettatore Sportivo—Omaggio).
Undated photo, Gaspar Ortega Scrapbook #2.

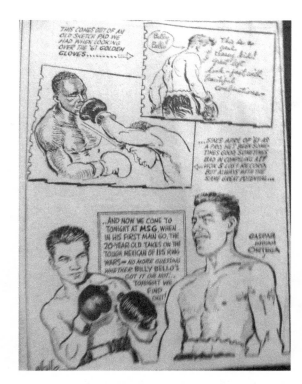

This cartoon, titled "Graduation," tells the story of up-and-comer Billy Bello and his first shot at the big time against Gaspar Ortega. Uncited, 1963, by Bill Gallo. Gaspar Ortega Scrapbook #1.

Gaspar connecting with Mickey Crawford, the fighting artist, 1958.
Gaspar Ortega Scrapbook #2.

Gaspar Ortega and referee son Michael, 2011. Photo by the author.

CHAPTER 13

Changing Times

Were they really going to kill the fights? Weren't there still millions of faithful viewers? When word first leaked to the *New York Times* on Sunday, December 22, 1963, Gillette denied it as a rumor. Garden publicist F. X. Condon quickly warned that if the show was indeed dropped, the Garden might have to cancel its weekly fight shows altogether and stop funding local boxing programs around the country. The president of Madison Square Garden Boxing, Inc., said the rumor of the show's demise was "not true as far as I know."[1]

But it *was* true. The official announcement, from an unnamed representative, was terse: "ABC has no plans to continue its boxing show next season. By next season, I mean 1964. I can't say more than that at this time." The decision had been made by the higher-ups at the network, apparently without the knowledge of affiliates and advertisers. Of course, talk of decline had been ongoing for years. ABC's switch from Saturdays back to Fridays in October 1963 had seemed more an act of desperation than a calculated move to recover lost viewers. In the void of official explanation, the *Times* tried to summarize ABC's rationale for dropping the show: "Waning interest in boxing, the lack of enough competent fighters to sustain a regular TV series, [and] unsavory publicity for the sport and the economics of television" were at the root of it.[2] Other reports concurred, dredging up the litany of problems like an Unholy Trinity of Doom. Viewership was down. Fighting skills were on the decline ("dance contests," criticized "many viewers").[3] It was corrupt; Kefauver had proven it.

In this context, the press reported positive reactions to ABC's decision. Explained former TV fighter Joey Giardello, "At first a lot of guys are going to starve. But then the little clubs will spring up again, boxing will get to be a neighborhood thing again, and promoters will have to come up with good fights to pack a house." There was nothing, Giardello explained, "creepier for a fighter than to fight in a half-empty arena. All those people may be watching you on television, but you can't hear them cheer or boo, or get behind you and scream." Public criticism for ABC's move, what there was of it, appeared to come from those who believed that the boxers would suffer financially. The Garden, explained publicist Condon, paid fighters much higher rates than they could ever earn at the clubs.[4]

What would fill the TV boxing void? In February 1964, an obvious choice got official recognition. Football would be taking boxing's place. According to an ABC spokesman, starting September 25, just after boxing left, the network would begin playing a series of five NFL games on Friday nights. Yes, Friday night was boxing night in America. But it was also football night.

By the early sixties, professional football, with the help of TV, had truly taken off. Some columnists were already declaring that it had replaced baseball as America's national pastime. It was on TV just about every day of the week. In Washington, D.C., for instance, one could watch the Redskins game on Sunday, clips of the match on Tuesdays, an official *Redskins Review* show on Wednesdays, a scouting report show on Thursdays, and a regular chat with Coach Bill McPeak on Fridays. Uniforms had already been changed to better show contrast on television. Football players now hawked electric razors, aftershave lotion, and clothing. The quarterback for the New York Giants, Charlie Conerly, had become the first Marlboro Man. There were new "TV timeouts" to give the sponsors more opportunity to sell, and halftimes had been shortened to allow TV networks more scheduling flexibility.[5] CBS had recently paid the NFL $14.1 million per year to broadcast games for the next two years, triple over its last bid. Fueled with Gillette's cash after NBC initially dropped the *Friday Night Fights* in 1960, ABC also had big plans. Its *Wide World of Sports* was well underway, establishing itself as the new standard in sports broadcasting. There were even rumors that the network would be doing something with its Monday night lineup. Perhaps baseball, or even more football.[6]

Yet there were also fears. Would TV "kill" football the same way it had boxing? More than one journalist noted the eerie "coincidence" between the demise of TV boxing and the rise of TV football. In fact, some football franchises were already seemingly going the boxing route, playing some games not for home viewers but for closed-circuit television in movie houses.[7]

The Garden, meanwhile, was desperately working out its own way of saving TV boxing. In early January, Condon suggested that the venue might form its own network. In February the Garden confirmed that it was currently working to sell a brand-new boxing network to stations around the country. Gillette, it was claimed, would continue to sponsor the Garden's TV fights, which would begin just days after the show left the air in September. Said Garden boxing director Harry Markson, "We don't know how many TV stations we'll have yet."[8]

Gaspar Ortega would spend 1964 carrying out an epic campaign to become the busiest boxer in history. The motto, "anywhere, anyplace," became his creed. He mainly fought along the border in Mexico, but he also trotted the globe. He fought Stan Harrington twice more in Honolulu. He battled Willie Ross at the Castaways Hotel in Vegas. He took on undefeated welter contender François Pavilla in Paris and lost, but he made it to the base of the Eiffel Tower, a wide-eyed tourist amidst the visiting throngs.

Against a parade of local unknowns, Gaspar posted an incredible schedule in 1964, fighting twenty-nine times. May 1964 should be recorded as a record-setting moment in sports history. Gaspar fought on the 4th, the 6th, the 8th, the 11th, the 13th, the 14th, the 16th, the 19th, the 23rd, the 25th, and the 30th. Eleven opponents in twenty-six days. He beat them all, knocking out eight of them in five rounds or less. "Sometimes," he would later tell a reporter, "I didn't know where I was when I woke up in the morning."

On September 11, 1964, ABC aired the last Friday Night Fight. Madison Square Garden had been unable to secure major markets for its own boxing network and retired its big idea in August.[9] So this was it. "TV Boxing Dies Friday," ran one headline. The battle was between Dick Tiger and Don Fullmer at the Cleveland Arena. It was an appropriately symbolic match for the sport. Dick Tiger had appeared on TV more than any other fighter in history (with Gaspar having the second most TV appearances, according to the media). He was from Nigeria, had been brought into the orbit of the sport through his native land's connection with British colonialism. His opponent, Don Fullmer, was a white kid from Utah, the brother of Gene Fullmer.[10]

Fewer than two thousand people showed up at the Cleveland Arena to watch a fight which was so bad that the referee had to instruct the two men to "get going" amidst a riot of boos in the sixth round. Something important was coming to an end, and everyone seemed to sense it. Don Dunphy would recall, "To me, the bout, which was not a rouser, seemed secondary as I spent the evening saying goodbyes and thanking the multitude of sportswriters, radio and TV people, promoters, boxing officials, and others who contributed to making that program so vital and important." The last thing Dunphy did after the fight ended was to thank the viewers and listeners. Without them, he said, none of this would have been possible.[11]

The end of regularly televised network boxing inspired a small wave of reflection. Gillette's show had been on the air just shy of twenty years, the longest-running broadcast in history up to that point. Although the final fight proved an unceremonious end, there was a sense that an era had just passed, and a significant one at that. Robert Lipsyte of the *New York Times* astutely observed that boxing embodied the entertainment commodity of an older generation. It represented a bygone class of male amusement, one characterized by gruff urban types and ethnic rivalries. But "progress" had unraveled it. New rules smoothed the edges of the old conflicts, such as the banning of wearing of the Star of David or the Harp of Erin on one's trunks. "Assimilation" had made ethnic conflict less resonant. New, family-oriented activities like bowling leagues eroded the former appeal of the Sweet Science. Of course, television had also played its part, annihilating the clubs that had bonded men together in sweaty arenas. Now, better shows on air outcompeted it. If boxing had once seemed perfect for TV, now it was not particularly good TV. "Much of boxing is dull" these days anyway, Lipsyte wrote. The old skills were gone. Besides, fans were no longer "bloodthirsty." Still, a moment of silence was in order. "A generation grew up seeing boxing for free, in its living room, without the tangy smells and spattered gore of ringside," said Lipsyte: "It demanded national names, and got 20 years of Gaspar Ortega and Tiger Jones. Then it got bored and turned on more predictable and colorful violence."[12]

Bored is a word associated with youth. It is perhaps as apt an explanation as any for what happened to the TV fights. Suggests historian Randy Roberts, the major reason for ABC's decision to drop the show was not a simple question of ratings or even of bad publicity. It had to do with demographics. In 1964 the largest age segment in America was seventeen-year-olds. Raised as a generation of abundance, teenagers in 1964 represented the "pig in the python," a massive population bulge entering into its prime spending years, the biggest wave of mass consumers in American history. Those in the advertising business took notice, and TV programmers began to look at not just the number of people watching a particular show but also the makeup of those numbers. The Boomers were not children anymore; and they were beginning to tell dad what they wanted to watch. Programming schedules started to change. Family sitcoms began to center their plotlines on youths. TV parents increasingly became inept cardboard foils for adolescent jokes rather than the drivers of plot. TV Westerns took a sudden, sharp nosedive off the air. Notes Roberts, "The most popular horse on television in the 1960s was Mr. Ed."[13]

Although the fights still gathered a regular home audience of 5 million viewers, marketers thought advertising money could be better spent appealing directly to younger buyers. "The problem," as Roberts explains, "was not boxing's ratings, it was boxing's audience." Raised in the Depression, World War II vets were simply not as eager to part with their dollars as was the first generation brought up on TV, a cohort that often failed to differentiate between commercials and regular programming. As for TV sports, ABC's programming visionary, Roone Arledge, recognized that newer fare such as college football attracted more big-spending, college-educated fans than did boxing. In many ways, Arledge led the revolution. He turned the cameras onto the fans in the stands, onto the back stories, onto the inside action. He brought Americans exotic offerings like ski races and wrist wrestling. Boxing did not vanish completely, but it merged into the background.

To fully grasp the causes of prime-time TV boxing's demise is to understand a major rupture in the fabric of American society. On April 12, 1963, a young folk singer who called himself Bob Dylan played a show in New York and debuted a new song, "Who Killed Davey Moore?" In the number, Dylan repeats the question of the title and role-plays various people who all deny their culpability: the referee, the crowd in the stands, the boxing writers, even Sugar Ramos himself (though not called by name). Each suspect has an answer that exonerates him. The referee is pressured by the crowd. The crowd just wants to see a good fight. The manager was never told by Moore that there were any health issues. The gambler "never touched him none" and bet money on Moore to boot. The sportswriter says that football is also dangerous and that boxing is "just the old American way." Ramos simply did what he was paid to do—hit the other guy. What is most telling in Dylan's song is that, with the exception of Ramos, all of the people he role-plays (who are clearly guilty as a group) represent what Norman Mailer, in his Paret essay, referred to as the Establishment. The Establishment, every hip youngster knew, was the insidious power that maintained the status quo. The Establishment kept boxing alive, wrote Mailer, because boxing served its interests. The sport was like a pressure-release valve on urban discontent and gang violence. The Establishment fed off the corruption that thrived in boxing. For Mailer, the Establishment included the police and the mob, as well as "the labor unions and the colleges and the newspapers and the corporations."[14]

Ramos is the only sympathetic figure in Dylan's song. He's the man most obviously responsible, but he's also clearly another victim of the Establishment. At one point in the live recording (Dylan never released a studio recording of the song), Dylan sings of Moore's opponent as a man

> Who came here from Cuba's door
> Where boxing ain't allowed no more.

You can hear the audience cheer at this part. They are cheering the outlaw Castro and his apparently humane decision to ban a barbaric profession. They are cheering the rebel who defied the Establishment.

While Dylan's hip New York audience was clearly unrepresentative of America at this time, its response to the Castro reference hinted at a great tide about to overwhelm the nation. The generation raised by the veterans of World War II was coming into its own. There seemed to be, all at once, a sudden, broad-based recognition that the parents didn't have all the answers. That dad could be a drag. The year 1964, which saw the end of TV boxing, marked a clear break with the past. In that year, a chain of disconcerting events tumbled over each other in rapid succession. The Beatles invaded. The civil rights wars escalated with the Mississippi Freedom Summer and the passage of the Civil Rights Act. Free speech battles in Berkeley set university police officers against college students. Radical activists electrified young people, and Malcolm X called Martin Luther King Jr. a "traitor" to his race. Race riots erupted in Harlem and Rochester in New York, Paterson and Elizabeth in New Jersey, and Philadelphia. A boxing riot nearly destroyed the Olympic Auditorium in Los Angeles after a Japanese fighter won an unpopular decision against a Mexican in the ring. (Wrote the *Los Angeles Times*: "Only a bombing raid could have wreaked so much havoc.") Escalation in Vietnam also began that year, with Congress's issuance of the Gulf of Tonkin Resolution in August. One might even say that 1964 heralded the true start of what became known as "the Sixties."[15]

The change involved more than simply youthful rebellion and demographics. With the rising of the youth, older categories of masculine identity that anchored Gillette's show underwent bombardment. The stolid, stand-alone father figure archetypical of the movie and TV Western genre began to seem outdated and unrealistic. When David Brinkley commented on his TV show in the spring of 1964 that "many think televised boxing is an ugly brontosaurus that has somehow survived beyond its time," he might have well been talking about the fathers. The sons seemed to be pulling away all at once, recognizing the artifice of television and the obsolete manliness of cowboys. Once dominant, by the mid-sixties gunslingers had nearly left television completely.[16] As for the TV producers, it was clear that new heroes were required to keep adolescents in family rooms. Spacemen, super spies, and clever kids came to the fore. Movie Westerns took a violent and realistic turn. As the war in Vietnam escalated, the most revered place for proving manhood for the "Greatest Generation"—the battlefield—was dragged through the mud, dismantled. Boys raised on John Wayne and the *Friday Night Fights* would be shockingly disabused of combat's romanticism via the rice paddies of Southeast Asia. The Vietnam War itself would become TV fare of a decidedly unromantic variety.[17]

The end of regular boxing on TV, then, needs to be hooked into the sea change happening in American culture, the coming of age of the Baby Boom generation. Boys who had watched the fights with dad increasingly looked at him as a product of a bygone era, ignoring him just as advertisers did. They went to college in record numbers and began to assemble a new vision of manhood, one forged not in combat but in the eerie landscape of Cold War plenty, compounded by a sense that the Establishment had betrayed them. Dylan's 1964 hit song "The Times They Are a-Changin'" spoke to the issue. Key Establishment figures are called out: the "writers and critics," "senators, congressmen," and lastly and most poignantly, the "mothers and fathers." To the parents, Dylan warned,

And don't criticize
What you can't understand

> Your sons and your daughters
> Are beyond your command

The media seemed to agree.

But boxing was not down for the count. When critics wrote of its demise, they mistakenly conflated TV boxing with the sport in toto. It was *Dad's* boxing that was on the way out. Boxing would survive. But it would look different. There would be more focus on back stories, more theatricality, and new "paying" formats (like high-profile TV "specials" and closed-circuit screenings) The new face of the sport symbolized the change. He was a boxer who was the polar opposite of Rocky Marciano and Joe Louis. He knew how to market himself and how to shake up the Establishment. His name was Ali.

Starting his fighting career as Cassius Clay, Muhammad Ali was a TV fighter par excellence. He would appear on ABC's *Saturday Night Fight of the Week* twice in 1961 and twice in 1962. Unlike the other TV fighters, the Louisville Lip quickly grasped the benefits of self-promotion and theater inherent in electronic media. For his televised battle against Alex Miteff, he announced to shocked reporters that he would knock out his opponent in the sixth round. And then he did. He loved the spotlight, appearing on Johnny Carson's show and reciting poetry in beat cafés. He pushed the envelope, mimicking not Joe Louis but the outlandish wrestler Gorgeous George, whom he had met a month before his first TV appearance. Sportswriter Jimmy Cannon saw what was going on:

> Clay is part of the Beatle movement. He fits in with the famous singers no one can hear and the punks riding motorcycles with iron crosses pinned to their leather jackets and Batman and the boys with their long dirty hair and the girls with the unwashed look and the college kids dancing naked at secret proms held in apartments and the revolt of students who get a check from Dad every first of the month and the painters who copy the label off soup cans and the surf bums who refuse to work and the whole pampered style-making cult of the bored young.[18]

The Age of Ali looked much different than the Age of the *Friday Night Fights* that the fathers had supported. Television and youth culture made Ali. He marketed himself in unheard-of ways and then, in a stunning turn of events that seemed to mirror the turbulence of the decade, he rejected the Establishment completely, changing his name and refusing to be inducted into the U.S. Army. "I ain't got no quarrel with them Viet-cong," he said. The decision temporarily wrecked his career, but it also cemented him into the counterculture and added indelibly to the mosaic of the period.

The forces that propelled Ali to stardom also helped blast away at the scaffolding that supported the old structure of the sport. Television drove managers to push promising fighters into the limelight too fast. Fighters who could perform on cue managed to parlay the hype into well-promoted, if infrequent, battles. Those who could not plunged into obscurity. The long-term consequence would be the careful choreographing of the early careers of promising fighters, getting them a series of inferior "tomato can" (has-been or second-rater) opponents in a short buildup for a big-time "money" fight on closed-circuit TV. The number of fights a champ needed on his resume decreased. According to research conducted by boxing scholar Mike Silver, the average number of professional fights to a title was seventy in 1955 but only thirty-eight by 1965.[19] Rocky Marciano fought forty-three opponents before getting his shot at the title. Ali faced a mere nineteen as a pro before he took Sonny Liston's belt.

Other things also contributed to the transformation of the sport. Ali merely capitalized on the shift. For example, the dream of a federal boxing czar who would clean up and systematize the sport died in the early sixties. Its death was sad but perhaps inevitable. Boxing reform had rooted itself not in creating leagues and rules like baseball and football but rather in extricating the sport from the mob's grasp. When Robert Kennedy became attorney general in 1961, Estes Kefauver discovered that one of his staunchest early supporters now did not feel that a boxing commission was necessary. Rather, Kennedy went after the mob in his own way, quadrupling the number of attorneys dealing with racketeering and co-ordinating the various departments under his command.[20] Bobby did finally put away Carbo, but one thing he didn't want was another regulatory commission tacked on to his Justice Department. Estes Kefauver's bill to establish a federal boxing commission never even made it to the floor for a vote.

Kefauver plugged on, though, still hopeful that something could be done at the federal level to specifically address the sport's problems rather than just an enlarged federal effort against the Mafia in general. On August 8, 1963, he was in the midst of arguing for an amendment to a bill that he felt gave private industry too much power in creating America's satellite system when he visibly blanched. He announced, "Mr. President, I yield the floor," and then left. He went to a nearby office, telling those around him that he had heartburn from some Mexican food he'd eaten the night before. Finally talked into seeing a doctor, Kefauver was told that he'd had a mild heart attack. But it was much more serious than that. He was dead a day later.[21]

Kefauver's replacement as chairman of the Senate Subcommittee on Antitrust and Monopoly did not give up the fight for boxing reform, and in the wake of the dubious victory of Cassius Clay over Sonny Liston on February 25, 1964, a new congressional investigation was scheduled. Again a bill for a federal boxing commission was proposed, and again Robert Kennedy refused to grant Justice Department support. An even more dubious Clay rematch victory in May 1965 (marked by a mysterious first-round knockout punch immortalized in a *Sports Illustrated* photo of Ali standing over a felled Liston, yelling, according to ringsiders, "Get up and fight, you bum! You're supposed to be so bad! Nobody will believe this!") sparked yet another investigation. The House bill that emerged from this was a much watered-down version of the Kefauver bill, and it focused on broadcasts of "fraudulent" fights. The bill sailed through the House with an overwhelming 346 to 4 vote. Yet once again, it died in the Senate without reaching the floor. The next time Congress broached the subject of boxing reform would be 1979, and again legislation would not even come to a vote. In 1983 and again in 1992, proposed bills failed. Finally, in 1996 a Senate bill called the Professional Boxing Safety Act was proposed by Senators John McCain and Richard Bryan, and it passed. This act focused on safety in the ring, and it was followed by the successful passage in 1999 of the Muhammad Ali Act, which aimed to provide some structure to the process of sanctioning. The legislation passed, though critics note that it is a far cry from Kefauver's dream, that it is essentially toothless.[22]

From out of the void left by the collapse of the IBC and the death of federal regulation emerged a new boxing regime. In 1962 the National Boxing Association was grandly renamed the World Boxing Association (WBA). Finally recognizing the global nature of the sport, the WBA assigned each commission under its purview a single vote, which as *The Boxing Register* points out, gave New Hampshire the same power as Mexico. The WBA went on to preside over yet more dubious title fights, the stripping of Ali of his heavyweight title (twice), and the further alienation of much of the sports world.[23]

George Parnassus recognized the problems of the WBA and saw opportunity in an unregulated, post-Octopus world. In 1963 the Greek formed the World Boxing Council (WBC), aimed ostensibly at providing better representation for international fighters. As might have been foreseen, both the WBA and the WBC saw themselves as preeminent institutions, and neither felt compelled to synchronize their rankings. The era of multiple titleholders had begun. Inevitably, more sanctioning bodies took root, with the International Boxing Federation breaking away from the WBA in 1983 and the World Boxing Organization following the lead in 1988. Today, these four are joined by a host of other "legitimate" sanctioning organizations. No single legislative structure controls or regulates them. "Contender" seems to define almost anyone, and most people today couldn't name any one of the sixty-or-so "world champions" of the sport. Couple this with the declining number of registered boxers, and boxing begins to look like a farce. As Jim Brady writes, "With just the major sanctioning bodies and not counting the whackos, you have about one 'world champion' for every sixty-nine pros. It's ridiculous."[24]

The upheaval that finally annihilated the glory days of TV boxing passed above Gaspar Ortega like a mid-ocean wave over a fish. By late 1964 El Indio was simply boxing for the paycheck, putting on the headdress for the crowds who handed over cash to watch him batter local talent or, less likely, spruce up the records of hopeful contenders. But then something happened. Almost as if an internal clock wound down along with the demise of TV fights, Gaspar started losing. On September 10, 1964, the day before the last of the televised *Friday Night Fights*, Gaspar lost to Stan Harrington in Hawaii. A few weeks later, he faced a welterweight named Gabe Terronez in Fresno, California, and was uncharacteristically knocked down in the second round. He lost the unanimous decision. A California newspaper reported, "Gabe Trounces Fading Gaspar."[25]

Then things got worse. Gaspar traveled again to Italy to battle WBC and WBA light middleweight champion Sandro Mazzinghi at the Palazetto dello Sport in a nontitle match. Here, in front of ten thousand screaming Italians, Gaspar received the worst beating of his career. Mazzinghi was a big man, and when he struck Gaspar, it felt as though he had something packed in his gloves. "Everywhere he hit me it hurt," Gaspar remembers. Indio was knocked down in the fifth and sixth rounds. Nick Corby refused to let him come out in the seventh. For the second time in his career, he had been stopped, not lasting to the end of the final round.

Gaspar's first fight of 1965 was another debacle, though of a different sort. He faced a mediocre welterweight named Marshall Wells in Corpus Christi and left the arena thinking he had won on points. It was later determined that a judge had made a scorecard error, and Indio's win turned into a draw.

The end was near. For the first time in his career, Gaspar was beginning to get worried about getting hurt in the ring. He started to think about it all the time. In February 1965, he lost dismally against a decent, if light-hitting, British fighter named Brian Curvis, in a match held at Royal Albert Hall (and apparently televised in England). A United Press report sadly noted this was a battle "ranked by British boxing fans today as one of the most forgettable fights of their lives." As a full audience of five thousand English fans watched on, Gaspar seemed unwilling to get in there and trade blows. It was possibly his worst performance. Wrote one journalist, "Ortega, 148-½, hopped on his bicycle at the opening bell and stayed on it until the final gong. At times he fought like a novice, throwing punches while off balance and far out [of] range."[26]

Still he kept going. Gaspar faced off next with a seasoned veteran named Manuel Gonzalez in Houston, a man who hoped that beating the Indian would position him for a title shot against Emile Griffith. Gonzalez had in fact just beaten Griffith in a nontitle match and saw a match with Ortega as an opportunity to gather further momentum for his campaign. A poster for the fight asked, "Can the 'Indian' Scalp Manny?" The answer was no. Gaspar lost on points. Gonzalez would go on to get his title match, after three more fights, and lose.[27]

Next, Gaspar was in the Boston Garden facing a local undefeated boxer trying to move up the ranks. Gaspar, after all, was still the eighth-ranked fighter in his division, and he was still a good bet for a "game" match. After this fight, held on May 25, 1965, the arena was darkened and the Clay-Liston heavyweight rematch was shown on a big screen. A live Gaspar was usurped by a big TV screen. Gaspar lost his fight on points and then watched the mysterious "phantom punch" that felled Liston. Like everyone else, he thought that Liston threw the match.

The tour schedule had slowed considerably by this point. Gaspar felt sluggish, fatigued, nervous, *wrong*. It was almost an out-of-body feeling: "I wasn't Gaspar Ortega anymore." In August 1965, he was in San Jose, California, looking across the ring at Henry Aldrich, another undefeated kid looking for a big break. Aldrich had just beaten a tired-looking Isaac Logart and aimed to do the same against Gaspar. He did.

A month later, Gaspar was in the Uptown Arena in Modesto, California. His opponent was another campaigner, Oakland's Charlie Shipes. A reporter observed that "an impressive showing against Ortega will give the Oakland boxer a spot in the World Boxing Assn. ratings thus far denied." Shipes held the California state welterweight belt, but as was routine these days, would not put it on the line against Gaspar. Just in case.[28]

Shipes beat Gaspar on points (though he would later lose his title fight). In his dressing room afterward, Gaspar made a decision. It was all over. A strange sense of peace followed. The next day, he took a bus downstate to San Diego. At the station, he called Nick Corby, who lived across town, and told him, "I'm not fighting anymore." Corby did not put up a fuss. "Whatever you think is best for you," Corby said.

Sapo picked Gaspar up at the bus station. When Gaspar told his brother that it was over, Sapo made no attempt to disguise his happiness. He drove Indio to the new cinderblock house that Gaspar had bought for his parents up on the hillside in Colonia Morelos, near the old Army base. The roads were still mostly dirt, but the neighborhood was changing now. It had electricity, for instance. Gaspar got out of the car and went in and told Jefa the news.

"*Gracias a Dios!*" she hollered. Thank God.

Then she paused, suspicious. "I hear that many fighters retire and then come back. Are *you* going to come back?"

Gaspar shook his head with grave certainty. "*No más,*" he said.

Jefa smiled. Her baby was safe.

A week later, Gaspar returned to New York City to be with his wife and family full-time, for the first time. It was time to start a new chapter. But what would that be? Gaspar got an offer to train kids to box at the YMCA on First Avenue. One day as he was preparing for this new job, a big black guy showed up at the apartment. Gaspar had seen him before. He introduced himself as John Hicks, and in his poor Spanish he reminded Indio of their first acquaintance. It had been back in Mexico. Hicks had gone to see Gaspar fight one day on his tour of Mexamerica and had found that he didn't have enough cash to get back to New York. Gaspar, a generous man by nature, loaned the young man money, never expecting to see him again. But here he was, in the boxer's New York living room. Now Hicks wanted to pay him back, but not in a way Gaspar would have expected.

"I want you to move to Connecticut," Hicks said.

"Where is that place?"

"It's nearby! It's between here and Boston."

"Oh. Why?"

Hicks told him that New York was not for him. It was too busy, there were too many people. In Connecticut, he would find a quieter situation where he could raise his kids. Hicks wanted to set up his favorite fighter with a new life. He told Gaspar that he would find him a job and a place to live, too. Hicks's attitude was infectious: "He can *talk*," Gaspar recollected.

Gaspar agreed to let this fast-talking fellow take him up to Connecticut for a look around. Hicks drove him to a quiet suburb outside of New Haven called Branford. Here Gaspar was in for another surprise: John Hicks's white wife. That was a rarity in those days.

Hicks was as good as his word. He let Gaspar and his family stay at the Hicks's home. Hicks found him a job at a social work agency in New Haven called Community Progress Incorporated. The old fighter came to enjoy it. The slow pace suited him. After a few months, they brought Ida up to look for an apartment. Gaspar's English was still very poor, but Hicks was there to help with that, too. He got a tutor to come into Community Progress every day for an hour or so. Gaspar focused as intensely on this as he had in preparing for his fights. After a few months, he was amazed at his progress. "I was speaking English already! Not fluent, but much better than before." At Community Progress, Gaspar found a new sense of purpose. He helped out people in need. In another year, he had his first green card.

About six months into his New England life, Nick Corby called. He'd been getting lots of offers from all over the world. Promoters in America, Mexico, Canada, Australia, and Italy were begging for matches. After all, Gaspar had left not at the bottom of the ladder, like many others, but merely on his way down. He could still help boost young careers, still make a wad of cash in the process. Corby told him that if he just trained for a few months, "You could make a comeback." "*No más*," said Gaspar. He would never fight again. Corby took it well. He was never pushy.

The next step for Gaspar was not a belt but a paper. One day a West Haven policeman who happened to be another big fan told Gaspar that he should join the force. Gaspar thought about this. He had always possessed a strong sense of purpose, and the cop was so flattering. Indio started to consider it. In order to be a cop, of course, he would have to become a U.S. citizen. So Gaspar started to study, filed all the paperwork with the policeman's help, and in the early 1970s took the oath, getting his citizenship papers. Soon after this, he got a call from the cop's wife. The policeman was dead. Gaspar is not sure today how it happened, but at that moment, he had a change of heart. He decided not to enter the Police Academy. Citizen Gaspar continued on as a social worker and served the community in some form or another for the next half century.

The year that Gaspar quit boxing was the year that he turned thirty. This was the same age that the bullfighter Manolete died. It was the year that the Immigration and Nationality Act abolished the old restrictions that had formerly held back non–Western European immigrants and changed the demographic face of the nation. It was the year that Malcolm X perished in a hail of gunfire. It was the year that the first official American combat troops shipped out to Vietnam. It was the year that students started burning draft cards.

In 1965 the Boomers knew their place, and it wasn't in front of the TV with dad.

In 1965 Gaspar "Indio" Ortega waved goodbye to the ring, the lighted square that had sold so many televisions, that had made him a star.

Nightmares

The nightmares began soon after he retired. They were always the same. A voice would whisper, "Kill him." He knew the voice. It belonged to Benny Paret. "Kill him," Benny would say. "Don't worry. I will be in your corner." Kid Paret wanted Gaspar to exact his revenge against Emile Griffith. "No, I can't," Gaspar would tell the specter. "I'm retired now." Then he would jolt awake, slicked in sweat. Night after night, Benny's disembodied voice would come and offer its grave request. After a week it got so bad that Gaspar didn't want to go to sleep. He went to a doctor in New York who gave a thin plastic envelope containing three tiny pills. "Take one of these before you go to bed," said the doc. That night, Gaspar took a pill and slept the sleep of the dead. Benny did not come. The next night, he took another, and again, no Benny. With one pill left, Gaspar elected to go it without help, just to see what happened. The ghost did not come. He would never take the third pill, and Benny would never haunt his dreams again.

It was not so easy for Emile Griffith. Sleep became a playground for his fears. For years, Kid Paret would return at night, again and again. Sometimes Emile would be walking down the street in his dream and would reach to extend a handshake to a fan only to realize he now clasped the clammy dead hand of the Kid. Other times, he would be in an arena to watch a fight and would find an empty seat. He'd ask if the seat was taken and a voice would tell him no. He'd sit down before realizing that it was Benny's voice that was talking. Even when awake, the neutral corner in which he had demolished the Kid became spooky. He would admit privately that he didn't want to hurt anyone else in the ring. Emile's style became more conservative. The press noticed. But he still won. In fact, Griffith would go on to become a legend. When he finally retired in 1977, he had won welter and middleweight titles a stunning six times and had fought more times at the Garden than anyone in history. Later, he would be considered one of the greatest boxers of any era. When the fourth (and current) iteration of Madison Square Garden opened in 1968, Griffith would be in its first fight event.

After he retired, Emile Griffith got a job at the Secaucus youth detention facility, helping troubled kids. One of them, a sixteen-year-old named Luis Rodrigo, moved in with Griffith, but such things were not allowed and the ex-champ was fired. Griffith went on to adopt Luis (who still lives with him) and to train boxers by day and work at a bar by night. The big money was long gone, but Emile managed to keep his positive attitude and still made friends easily. He had since divorced a young dancer named Sadie (whom he'd married in 1971 and separated from a few years later). Now, he simply struggled to make ends meet, occasionally making appearances and always shaking hands with fans. In 1992 he was leaving a gay bar in New York when a bunch of thugs dropped him. They beat him savagely with pipes or clubs. He fought back, felt a guy's nose go "pop" under his fist. These heavies had no idea who they were messing with—this wasn't some old queen ripe for abuse. This was the ex-champion of the world. But there were too many of them. Griffith stumbled to a subway and rode in a delirium for hours before finding his way back to the apartment. He was taken to a hospital, near death, but he recovered.

However, the mind is something that can't be repaired at a hospital. Soon after, Griffith felt he was losing his. They called it boxer's dementia. The past began to fog, the present slowed to a steady drift. He found that he couldn't remember things. The ring battles had taken their toll.

Research tells us that boxers suffer disproportionally from neurological damage. The scientific term for it is chronic traumatic brain injury (CTBI). The results are permanent and progressive. Symptoms include Parkinson-ism, dementia, personality changes, and cerebellum dysfunction. The data is not precise: the brain is complex, boxing rules vary across space and time, and long-term longitudinal studies of boxers are still incomplete and problematic. But it is clear that successive blows to the head can cause lasting damage. One researcher has equated a heavyweight punch to "a 13-pound mallet swung at 20 miles an hour." The brain rattles about like a water balloon in a box. A study of the brains of deceased boxers revealed significant tears and nerve damage. Other reports suggest that between 10 and 25 percent of boxers suffer from "postboxing neurological syndrome."[1]

Griffith would not be the only one of Gaspar's former opponents to exhibit brain damage. Don Jordan, the man from whom Paret originally took the title, lost his mind as well. In 1970 he gave a bizarre interview to journalist Peter Heller in which he explained that he had grown up in the Dominican Republic as "what you call hired assassin." "I was paid to kill people for a living," explained a clearly unhinged Jordan. "I did it. I was happy. It was a way of living. I was killing people when I was ten years old. What's wrong with it?"

How many people did you kill?

"I killed thirty people in one month. . . . And when I'd blow somebody's brains out, I used to watch his face. It used to bug the shit out of me. The expression and anxiety in their face, the structure of it. I knew what they meant by it. You cannot kill a human and forget his face. You never forget a man you kill." He talked about using poison darts in the neck. "The first time you kill someone, you throw up, you get sick as a dog. Your guts come out, you cry, you throw up. The second time, no feeling."

Jordan also talked about how, after coming to the United States, he had been put in prison for tying a man to the ground with wire and stakes and setting him on fire. "I tried to roast him like an animal." While incarcerated Jordan got to speak with a psychiatrist, who told him, "You have no business being here." Jordan replied, "I'm here, now let's discuss the point why I'm here." The shrink protested: "But you're too intelligent to be in a place like this." To which Jordan responded, "No. That's beside the point. Let's talk to the level. I'm not a fool. The problem is that I'm here."

At the end of the first paragraph of the interview, published in Heller's book *"In This Corner. . . !" 42 World Champions Tell Their Stories*, there is an asterisk. At bottom of the page the reader finds: "*Although Jordan told of a life growing up in the Caribbean and working as an assassin, none of this is true. Jordan grew up in Los Angeles."[2]

What *is* true? I asked Gaspar. "Man, that guy was crazy," Indio replied, shaking his head.

One thing that is true is that in 1996 Don Jordan was robbed and beaten by two assailants in a Southern California parking lot. He slipped into a coma and never regained consciousness. His heart stopped five months later.

Denny Moyer, who defeated Gaspar at the Garden in 1959, went into real estate after he retired from the ring. Later, he lived in a Portland nursing home, suffering from acute ring-related dementia, until he passed away in June 2010 at age seventy.[3]

Hardy "Bazooka" Smallwood, the man who first faced Gaspar in St. Nick's for his second TV fight, became a Pentecostal minister in the Bronx and dedicated his life to working for peace and positive change. In 1988 he was featured in *New York* magazine for working with a Hasidic rabbi to bring peace to racially tense Crown Heights. In 1991 he received the first Citizen of the Month award from the New York City Police Department for cleaning up a crime-ridden apartment building he had moved into.

Mickey Crawford retired six months after his last fight with Gaspar, in February 1959, and followed his dream of becoming a full-time painter. He was inducted into the Saginaw Boxing Hall of Fame in 2008. He still lives in the house he grew up in, spending his days in front of an easel. Carmen Basilio retired from the ring in 1961 after losing to Paul Pender in Boston. He died in November 2012 at the age of eighty-five.

Tony DeMarco had a rough time transitioning out of the ring. He had been on the *Ed Sullivan Show* and on *Masquerade Party* (Carmen Basilio was on with him, and they had dressed Basilio up in drag as Carmen from the famous opera). His life to come would have its share of hardships, but he managed to stay financially comfortable and even live to see the mayor of Boston name a street after him in the old neighborhood.

Joe Cortez, the kid who had befriended Gaspar when he first moved to New York, remains a good friend to Indio. Cortez became a fighter himself and won several Golden Gloves tournaments before going pro in 1962. He even occasionally sparred with Gaspar in the first part of the 1960s, though once he gave Gaspar such a hard time in the ring that Gaspar grabbed him in the dressing room afterwards and scolded him. The next day, Cortez just covered up and let Gaspar whack away. Joe fought professionally until 1970. He moved to Puerto Rico in 1969 with his wife and two daughters before returning to the U.S. mainland in 1976. He became a hotel manager but found that he couldn't leave the sport Gaspar had taught him to love. He decided to become a referee. He's since become one of the most famous and respected referees in the business, presiding over some 156 title fights in eleven countries and refereeing fights with Mike Tyson, Oscar De La Hoya, Evander Holyfield, Lennox Lewis, and many others. In 2011 Cortez was inducted into the International Boxing Hall of Fame

Other Friday Night Fighters now rest with Paret, Basilio, and Jordan among the dead. Willie Pep, the first Friday Night Fighter, battled pugilistic dementia for years, dying in a Connecticut nursing home in 2006. His first TV opponent, Albert "Chalky" Wright, whose career hit the skids swiftly, died mysteriously in the bathtub in 1957. Stan Harrington, who battled Gaspar in Honolulu, succumbed to inoperable cancer in 1997. Luis Federico Thompson died in 2010. Ralph Dupas, who fought Gaspar in 1958, suffered such severe brain disease later in life that in his final five years he was completely bedridden. In the end, said his brother, "He just couldn't breathe anymore." He died at age seventy-two in 2008.[4] The man who faced Gaspar in his very first TV match, Isaac Logart, died in 1988 in New York City, aged fifty-five years. Kid Gavilan stayed in Miami, but he fell on hard times. By the 1980s, "the Keed" was selling sausages on the streets. A few years later, he began to exhibit symptoms of brain disease—he became disoriented, forgot simple things. He died in 2003, aged seventy-seven, broke and completely estranged from his family. After Kid Gavilan was buried under a simple plaque in Miami's Our Lady of Mercy Cemetery, the fight world once again took notice of him. A group of fighters and fans, headed by ex-champ Ray Mancini, chipped in under the aegis of the Ring 8 Veteran Boxers Association, exhumed his remains, and placed him under a large granite headstone in a higher-profile section of the cemetery.[5]

Frankie Carbo, aka Mr. Gray, would rot away in prison until 1976, when he was released for health reasons. He died that same year in Miami Beach. Blinky Palermo was paroled after ten years. He tried unsuccessfully to get back into the boxing business in the late 1970s and died in Philadelphia in 1996, aged ninety-one. Frank Norris left boxing for good after the Kefauver hearings, much despised by many in the boxing world. When he died of a heart attack in 1966, Red Smith wrote an obituary describing Norris as "the rich ogre, the playboy associate of mobsters, the promoter who did business with the underworld and let boxing fall into the wrong hands." Norris was fifty-nine years old and worth an estimated $250 million at the time. Just as he had always said, he never needed boxing to make ends meet. Truman Gibson, Norris's compatriot and the man who briefly took over the IBC empire until he was convicted of extortion and received two concurrent five-year sentences (both were suspended), moved back to Chicago and resumed his private legal practice. He died in December 2005, aged ninety-three.[6]

George Parnassus would become famous as the man who brought "big-time boxing to southern California." He passed away in 1975, aged seventy-eight.[7] Gaspar lost touch with Nick Corby over the years. According to the U.S. Social Security Death Index, Corby died in 1993, aged seventy-five.

Gaspar Indio Ortega went on to live a quiet life in the Nutmeg State, his adopted home. He worked for a while for Community Progress Incorporated and then at the Skill Center in New Haven, helping troubled kids. He became close to these tough cases, bringing them home, feeding them. He was the first person the kids would call when they got arrested. Gaspar also started working nights with an ambulance service in New Haven. In addition, he served as an interpreter at Yale–New Haven hospital ("And with *his* English!" Ida says in disbelief). Later, he was a counselor for youths getting out of jail. One night he came home with a little old lady in tow. He had found her wandering out in the street, disoriented. Gaspar asked Ida if she could stay with them. She agreed, and the lady stayed for a week, then just left. Ida had to get used to the unfortunates who always seemed to show up in need. Once Gaspar asked his wife if he could bring someone over who used to be a counselor and now needed help after serving some time. "What did he do?" asked Ida. "He killed his wife."

One day Gaspar was asked to help keep troubled kids off the street in a way familiar to him; teaching them how to box. He started training kids at the Silver City Boxing Club in Meriden, Connecticut. The *New York Times* found him there and did a piece on him in 1999. "Even if he weren't a famous former fighter," explained the Silver City director, "I'd still want him here because of his personality and the way he relates to the kids." His New Haven boss told the *Times*, "Gaspar has a knack of reaching people, including hard-core criminals." The reporter also interviewed Gil Clancy, who told him that "Emile always said he was the toughest he ever fought." The reporter ended on a wistful note: "Hardly any boxing fans in the New Haven area are aware that Ortega—one of the best fighters of his time—has been in their midst for more than three decades."[8]

In Tijuana, Gaspar's place in history is on much firmer ground. A gym was built in his honor right near the place where he once crossed over illegally to work in the fields near San Diego. He is still recognized on the streets of Tijuana, if mainly by older residents. Musician Carlos Santana would also keep Indio's memory alive. He would later reflect that Gaspar and his other boxing hero, Sugar Ray Robinson, taught him how to "really apply intense prayer." Watching these fighters on TV gave him an "emotional investment" that he needed to address when his favorites were taking a beating. He would get on his knees and pray in front of the screen for his man to prevail. He felt, for the first time, as though he was "pulling God's coat."[9] He'd later offer tickets and backstage passes to Gaspar and his family when he toured Connecticut.

The brain damage that wiped the joy out of the golden years of so many of this boxing cohort did not strike Gaspar. He attributes this to his defensive, slippery style. Though he is occasionally off balance when he walks, that is minor compared to the devastation that brought such misery to so many other retired fighters.

In the early 1980s, his son by Dalila, Gaspar Jr., then aged sixteen, moved out to Connecticut to live with them. He had been getting in trouble in school, and Dalila did not know what to do with him. When he arrived in Connecticut, Gaspar Jr. scarcely knew his father—he had seen him only four times up until this point. Ida warmly accepted the youngster into their house. She met him at the door and said, "This is your new home." She served him a fruit salad she made special, and Gaspar Jr. never forgot it. He stayed in America long enough to learn English, but family tensions made the experience rough, and he returned to Mexico. Today, he owns a successful cleaning service.

Gaspar's other kids all did well for themselves, getting jobs, building families. Michael, the boy born in the seventh round of Gaspar's battle at L.A.'s Wrigley Field with Kid Gavilan, decided to follow his dad into the business. He grew up going to boxing gyms with his dad. The ring felt like "my playpen," he said. Whitey Bimstein was the "sweet nice one"; Freddie Brown was "always grouchy." It was the classic "good cop–bad cop" routine, and Michael loved them both. "Any time I smell a cigar, I think of those guys." Nick Corby was his godfather. First, Michael had wanted to be a matador; his dad would press his knuckles to his temples and charge low at him with index-finger horns. Michael even got a matador cape for Christmas one year, his all-time favorite present. In the eighth grade, Michael thought seriously about becoming a fighter. Unfortunately, boxing was banned in Connecticut at the time. When he did get his first fight—his dad entered him in New York's Golden Gloves tournament in the early 1970s—he lost to an experienced opponent.

Joe Cortez, who was like another dad to Michael, first piqued his interest in becoming a boxing referee. It started unintentionally—Joe had Mike tape his refereed fights from TV so he could critique himself. The next thing he knew, Mike was giving him some pretty smart advice. Joe told him he could be good at this and talked Mike into going to some seminars in the early 1990s.

The real push happened late one night. Mike was flipping through the channels when he caught an old fight on TV. It was the infamous Paret-Griffith III battle, a fight Mike had only heard about. "It was one of the worst things I saw in my life." He couldn't get to sleep afterwards. He kept thinking, "What if it was my father trapped in that corner?" He felt as if God was trying to tell him something. Maybe he could save some-body's life and save somebody's family a lifetime of grief. "That's when I decided to become a ref." After getting past some local politics, he got a Connecticut license and started to officiate. The best kind of fight? "One where nobody gets badly hurt." Before every fight, he prays for both men. "When I go into the ring," he explains, "I literally have the lives of two people in my hands." Today he's considered among the top referees in the business. (Explains boxing enthusiast LeRoy Neiman, "It is with great understanding of the many facets of the sport and compassion that Gaspar Ortega's son is well respected as the 3rd man in the ring.")[10]

Ida started working again when her kids were old enough to go to school. She got a cosmetology license in New York City and was employed in an upscale beauty salon, washing hair and polishing nails. After they moved to Connecticut, Ida landed a job at Yale University in the Commons Dining Hall, checking the IDs of freshmen and keeping track of their guests. She did this for four years. It was a good job, giving her summers off to be with her children. She also worked evenings as a reception-ist at the University of New Haven. She later became the branch manager of a bank and worked there for twenty-six years, until the bank merged with a larger one and offered her an acceptable retirement package. She went on to manage a different bank for a while before finally slowing down, but Ida always remained active in her community, volunteering with various organizations.

In 1995 Gaspar was diagnosed with throat cancer. After he'd quit box-ing in 1965, Gaspar picked up a pack-a-day habit, and it had taken his toll. But Gaspar always was a fighter, and he survived, albeit with a new, gravelly voice. In 2010 he was diagnosed with prostate cancer. He under-went surgery and recovered. In 2011 he caught pneumonia while shoveling snow, and at the hospital his carotid artery ruptured. He recovered again. Today he lives with his wife in East Haven, Connecticut, in a house they bought with both of their earnings.

The Friday Night Fighters, as a whole, met sad ends.. Typically, retiring after long, steady declines, they would afterward discover that their managers had been using them, that the mob had taken its slice up front, and that the government, after everybody else had taken what they needed, now wanted its cut. Later, many would endure the experience of losing their minds.

Unlike athletes in other major sports, boxers had no union to turn to. There was no systematization, no regulation, no health care. They were simply battered shells cast adrift. Most did not have skills that translated in the emerging technologically oriented economy. Saddest of all, the mass TV audience that had elevated their status to household names had moved on, forgetting Friday's Heroes completely. Those of us raised by the Boomers do not know about the men who presented our parents a singular model of Cold War manhood. We don't know about the show that brought folks together. We don't know the whole story about the beginning of television.

One organization that does give a damn about boxers is Ring 8. It was established in New York City in 1954, the eighth (hence the name) branch of the National Veteran Boxers Association. Its official motto is "Boxers Helping Boxers," and it provides a network of care and resources for indigent fighters, mainly from the Golden Age—the 1940s and 1950s. Among many other contributions, the organization paid for a decent tombstone over Kid Gavilan's unmarked grave and currently provides money for Emile Griffith's dementia medication while helping out with other aging fighters' bills and care.

A few years back, I had an opportunity to attend a Ring 8 dinner and say a few words about my research and about Gaspar, who received a ceremonial belt that evening. I found a warm group of gentlemen eager to share their stories. At my table, I sat between Emile Griffith and Gaspar Ortega. Griffith, whom I had met once before, was all smiles. Sadly, his mind was so wiped out by his disease that I was not able to retrieve any stories from him. I asked if he remembered the TV fights. He beamed a big smile and told me he did, but that was about it.

Later that night, we were out in the parking lot. Gaspar and I were getting ready to head back up to Connecticut, and Emile was with us, awaiting his ride home. Griffith pulled out his pack of cigarettes and retrieved a smoke. Gaspar leaned over and asked for one. Griffith smiled his big smile and handed over the pack. Gaspar took one, used his own lighter to light them both up.

"You remember me?" Gaspar asked.

"Yes, yes," Emile replied.

"You kicked my ass in the ring."

"No, no," said Emile.

"Yes you did."

There was a moment of silence as Emile scanned his memories, ciga-rette dangling between his middle and index fingers. Something seemed to pass over his face. Then he shook his head, laughed, and said, "Well, you win some, you lose some."

A Note on Sources

Personal interviews, conducted between 2005 and 2011, form the core of this book. It all started, of course, with Gaspar Ortega, whom I interviewed countless times. Other Golden Age boxers have also been of great help. They include Hardy "Bazooka" Smallwood, Tony DeMarco, Carmen Basilio, Emile Griffith, Joe Miceli, Bill Tate, and Chico Vejar (whom I spoke with at a Connecticut Hall of Fame Banquet). In Tijuana, I interviewed Ramon "Kid Irapuato" Perez Pazuelgo, Jose Luis Diaz, Bernardo "Gordo" Zuniga, and Manuel "Jilguerillo" Cruz. Gaspar's family—especially Ida, Michael, Rene, Torito, Sapo, Fausto, Felix, Gaspar Benitez Jr., Lupita, Eulala, and Cathy—and friends Ben Rendon, Joe Cortez, Victor Bernal, and Raymond Solis all provided insightful interviews. Baby Boomer interviews have also been extremely helpful—Joseph Rondinone, Rochelle Rondinone, Jon Purmont, Brenda Sullivan Miller, Dr. Harold Levy, Bob Jirsa, Chuck Hasson, Milton Hernandez, John O'Connor, Dr. Alan Miller, and Bob Hink all kindly shared their memories with me. Gil Clancy, Bert Randolph Sugar, and LeRoy Neiman were also helpful with their personal recollections of the *Friday Night Fights*.

Collections also provided a wealth of information. The New Jersey Boxing Hall of Fame, the International Boxing Hall of Fame, the Papers of Jack Barrett at the Brooklyn College Archives, Rosario Marinez at Tijuana's periodical collections, and Rick Kaletsky's Muhammad Ali collection all provided treasure troves of old newspapers, boxing magazines, and memorabilia. Boxrec.com is an unparalleled resource for boxing records. Gaspar's personal collection of clippings, noted as Gaspar Ortega Scrapbook #1–3, also provided vital, impossible-to-find pieces in English and Spanish.

Contemporary periodicals were essential to recovering the story of the *Friday Night Fights*. Thanks to wonderful online databases such as ProQuest and NewspaperArchive, plus the electronic databases of the Buley Library at Southern Connecticut State University and the Sterling Library at Yale, I have been able to track down numerous articles. Of course, paper and microfilm also have been helpful, and the Buley and Sterling Libraries have plenty of these as well.

Friday Night Fights films also shaped this work. Watching the footage gives one a strong sense of the limits and possibilities of early TV boxing. Gaspar's personal fight collection, plus some bouts I located myself, provided a good feel for what Cold War audiences saw.

Key boxing histories include Jeffrey Sammons, *Beyond the Ring: The Role of Boxing in American Society* (1990); Kasia Boddy, *Boxing: A Cultural History* (2008); Arne K. Lang, *Prizefighting: An American History* (2008); Kevin Mitchell, *Jacobs Beach: The Mob, The Fights, The Fifties* (2010); and Mike Silver, *The Arc of Boxing: The Rise and Decline of the Sweet Science* (2008). Randy Roberts's essay, "The Wide World of Muhammad Ali: The Politics and Economics of Televised Boxing," in *Muhammad Ali, the People's Champ* (1998), edited by Elliot J. Gorn, was pivotal in shaping my understanding of the fights, as was Jeff Neal-Lunsford's "Sport in the Land of Television: The Use of Sport in Network Prime-time Schedules 1946–1950," *Journal of Sport History*, 19 (Spring 1992). Period boxing biographies, such as Nick Tosches, *The Devil and Sonny Liston* (2000); Gary B. Youmans, *The Onion Picker: Carmen Basilio and Boxing in the 1950s* (2007); and Russell Sullivan, *Rocky Marciano: The Rock of His Times* (2005), also provided solid context. Key autobiographies include Willie Pep, with Robert Sacchi, *Willie Pep Remembers . . . Friday's Heroes* (1973); Tony DeMarco, *Nardo: Memoirs of a Boxing Champion* (2011); and Don Dunphy, *Don Dunphy at Ringside* (1988).

In terms of the federal government's challenge to the IBC's monopoly, the most important source is "Professional Boxing," *Hearings before the Subcommittee on Antitrust and Monopoly of the Committee on the Judiciary*, United States Senate, Parts 1–4 (Washington, DC, 1960–64). Secondary works such as Stephen R. Lowe, *The Kid on the Sandlot: Congress and Professional Sports, 1910–1992* (1995), and Edmund P. Edmonds and William H. Manz, eds., *Congress and Boxing: A Legislative History, 1960–2003*, vol. 1 (2005), include some good analysis.

On corruption in the sport, see Thomas Myler, *The Sweet Science Goes Sour: How Scandal Brought Boxing to Its Knees* (2006); Teddy Brenner and Barney Nagler, *Only the Ring Was Square* (1981); Jim Brady, *Boxing Confidential* (2003); and many others.

On Latinos in the sport during this time, see Gregory S. Rodriguez, "*Raza* Boxing: Community, Identity, and Hybridity in the 1960s and 1970s in Southern California," in *Mexican Americans and Sports: A Reader on Athletics and Barrio Life*, ed. Jorge Iber and Samuel O. Regalado (2006).

Essential works for understanding the hypermasculine culture of the Cold War include K. A. Cuordileone, "'Politics in the Age of Anxiety': Cold War Political Culture and the Crisis in American Masculinity, 1949–1960," *Journal of American History* 87, no. 2 (2000): 515–45; Margot A. Henrikson, *Dr. Strangelove's America: Society and Culture in the Atomic Age* (1997); Elaine Tyler May, *Homeward Bound: American Families in the Cold War* (2008); and Richard Slotkin, *Gunfighter Nation: The Myth of the Frontier in Twentieth-Century America* (1998).

Notes

Preface. Boxing Lessons

1. Jack Gould, "Television Network Will Drop Boxing from Weekly Programming in 1964," *New York Times*, December 23, 1963.
2. David Halberstam, *The Fifties* (New York: Random House, 1993).

Introduction. Fight Night

1. Ronald K. Fried, *Corner Men: Great Boxing Trainers* (New York: Four Walls Eight Windows, 1991), 274.
2. Elliot J. Gorn, *The Manly Art: Bare Knuckle Prize Fighting in America* (Ithaca, NY: Cornell University Press, 1989), 225, 207.
3. Quoted in Kasia Boddy, *Boxing: A Cultural History* (London: Reaktion Books, 2008), 188.
4. Elliot J. Gorn and Warren Goldstein, *A Brief History of American Sports* (New York: Hill and Wang, 1993), 105.

Chapter 1. "And the Winner—Television!"

1. Theodore Roosevelt, *Theodore Roosevelt: An Autobiography* (New York: Macmillan, 1913), 49.
2. Arne K. Lang, *Prizefighting: An American History* (Jefferson, NC: McFarland, 2008), 50, 54.
3. Kasia Boddy, *Boxing: A Cultural History* (London: Reaktion Books, 2008), 113.
4. During Prohibition, for example, Al Capone and Lucky Luciano had been "secret owners" of a number of boxers. See Selwyn Raab, *Five Families: The Rise, Decline, and Resurgence of America's Most Powerful Mafia Empires* (New York: St. Martin's Press, 2006), 37, 103.
5. Ibid. 104.

6. Jack Cuddy, "'Fight a Week' Says Jacobs," *Nebraska (Lincoln) State Journal*, August 23, 1944.

7. Thomas Patrick Doherty, *Cold War, Cool Medium: Television, McCarthyism, and American Culture* (New York: Columbia University Press, 2005), 1.

8. Jeffrey T. Sammons, *Beyond the Ring: The Role of Boxing in American Society* (Urbana: University of Illinois Press, 1990), 131.

9. Eric Barnouw, *Tube of Plenty: The Evolution of American Television* (New York: Oxford University Press, 1990), 78; Sammons, *Beyond the Ring*, 131; "All London Toys With Television," *New York Times*, March 19, 1939. You can go back even farther if you are looking at the history of motion pictures. According to one film historian, "boxing created cinema." The first boxing film was made in August 1894, depicting six one-minute rounds between Mike Leonard and Jack Cushing. Charlie Chaplin, a fan of boxing himself, starred in several boxing-themed comedies in 1914 and 1915. See Boddy, *Boxing*, 154, 152, 156.

10. Jeff Neal-Lunsford, "Sport in the Land of Television: The Use of Sport in Network Prime-time Schedules 1946–1950," *Journal of Sports History* 19, no. 1 (Spring 1992): 58; "Sports Shows, Radio vs. Video," *New York Times*, June 13, 1946.

11. Philip Lopate, ed., *Writing New York: A Literary Anthology* (New York: Library of America, 1998), 914

12. Jack Cuddy, "Chalky Wright Faces Severe Test in Friday Battle," *Ogden (UT) State Examiner*, September 27, 1944.

13. Willie Pep, with Robert Sacchi, *Willie Pep Remembers . . . Friday's Heroes* (New York: Frederick Fell, 1973).

14. "50 Bouts to Be Televised to Wounded Service Men," *New York Times*, September 27, 1944.

15. "Washington to See Bout by Television," *New York Times*, June 15, 1946.

16. Barnouw, *Tube of Plenty*, 126–27.

17. Neal-Lunsford, "Sport in the Land of Television," 61.

18. Ibid., 59–60.

19. Given the limits of demographic data from this period, these numbers are ballpark figures. See Jack Gould, "Television Network Will Drop Boxing from Weekly Programming in 1964," *New York Times*, December 23, 1963.

20. "Coexistence or Else," *Newsweek*, March 14, 1955.

21. Randy Roberts, "The Wide World of Muhammad Ali: The Politics and Economics of Televised Boxing," in *Muhammad Ali, the People's Champ*, ed. Elliot J. Gorn (Urbana: University of Illinois Press, 1995), 30.

22. Gordon McKibben, *Cutting Edge: Gillette's Journey to Global Leadership* (Boston: Harvard Business School, 1998), 50, 38.

23. Neal-Lunsford, "Sport in the Land of Television," 62.

24. McKibben, *Cutting Edge*, 51, 49.

25. One cannot escape the anti-Semitic overtone of this description. "The Boxing Racket," *Life*, June 17, 1946.

26. Red Skelton quoted in Randy Roberts and James Olsen, *Winning Is the Only Thing: Sports in America since 1945* (Baltimore: The Johns Hopkins University Press, 1989), 95; "On Television This Week," *New York Times*, January 20, 1952; Roberts, "The Wide World of Muhammad Ali," in *Muhammad Ali, the People's Champ*, 28–29.

27. Neal-Lunsford, "Sport in the Land of Television," 61.

28. "Kids in the Ring," *Life*, May 16, 1949.

Chapter 2. "The Regular Friday Coaxial Bloodbath"

1. K. A. Cuordileone, "'Politics in the Age of Anxiety': Cold War Political Culture and the Crisis in American Masculinity, 1949–1960," *Journal of American History* 87, no. 2 (2000): 521.

2. Bill Bryson, *The Life and Times of the Thunderbolt Kid: A Memoir* (New York: Random House, 2006), 197.

3. Jonathan Shay, *Odysseus in America: Combat Trauma and the Trials of Homecoming* (New York: Scribner, 2002), 109; "Hurtling Suicide Injures Woman," *New York Times*, January 26, 1947; "Woman Critically Hurt by Empire State Building Suicide," *Naugatuck (CT) Daily News*, January 26, 1947.

4. William Styron, "My Generation," quoted in Margot A. Henrikson, *Dr. Strangelove's America: Society and Culture in the Atomic Age* (Berkeley: University of California Press, 1997), 25.

5. Suzanne Mettler, *Soldiers to Citizens: The G.I. Bill and the Making of the Greatest Generation* (Oxford: Oxford University Press, 2005), 15.

6. Styron, "My Generation," quoted in Henrikson, *Dr. Strangelove's America*, 25.

7. Arthur G. Neal, *National Trauma and Collective Memory*, 2nd ed.(Armonk, NY: M. E. Sharpe, 2005), chaps. 4 and 5.

8. Lynn Spigel, *Make Room for TV: Television and the Family Ideal in Postwar America* (Chicago: University of Chicago Press, 1992), 39–40.

9. Bryson, *The Life and Times of the Thunderbolt Kid*, 176; "What TV Is Doing to America," *U.S. News and World Report*, September 2, 1955.

10. The metaphor of containment is one that historian Elaine Tyler May finds a fitting descriptor of the postwar family as well. See her *Homeward Bound: American Families in the Cold War* (New York: Basic Books, 1999).

11. Bryson, *The Life and Times of the Thunderbolt Kid*, 69.

12. Richard Slotkin, *Gunfighter Nation: The Myth of the Frontier in Twentieth-Century America* (Norman: University of Oklahoma Press, 1998), 352

13. William Boddy, "'Sixty Million Viewers Can't Be Wrong': The Rise and Fall of the Television Western," in *Back in the Saddle Again: New Essays on the Western*, ed. Edward Buscombe and Roberta E. Pearson (London: British Film Institute, 1998), 119, 122.

14. Reverend Samuel H. Lowther, "God Makes a Champion," *Boxing and Wrestling*, August 1957; "Vicious Basilio Flattens Saxton for Second Round KO," *Newport (RI) Daily News*, February 23, 1957.

15. Ted Carroll, "TV Title Bouts Prime Bargains," *Ring Annual Magazine on TV Fights*, 1954.

16. Personal interview with Carlos Santana, September 9, 2012.

17. Neal Shine, *Life with Mae: A Detroit Family Memoir* (Detroit: Wayne State University Press, 2007), 41; Christopher Buckley, *Sleepwalk: California Dreamin' and a Last Dance with the '60 s* (Spokane, WA: Eastern Washington University Press, 2006); Jack Niece, *The Side-Yard Superhero* (Austin, TX: Synergy Books, 2009), 73; Spencer Nadler, *The Language of Cells: A Doctor and His Patients* (New York: Vintage, 2002), 51; Binnie Klein, *Blows to the Head: How Boxing Changed My Mind* (Albany: State University of New York Press, 2010), 43; Lyn Cryderman, *Glory Land: A Memoir of a Lifetime in Church* (Grand Rapids, MI: Zondervan, 1999), 24; J. L. Normandin, *Write of Passage: A Journey from Darkness to Light* (Victoria, BC: Trafford Publishing, 2003), 4.

18. James Spada, *Streisand: Her Life* (New York: Crown Publishers, 1995), 28; Jack Carew, *You'll Never Get No For An Answer* (New York: Simon and Schuster, 1987), 132–33; Lynne Cheney, *Blue Skies, No Fences: A Memoir of Childhood and Family* (New York: Simon and Schuster, 2007), 181; John McCain, with Mark Salter, *Faith of My Fathers* (New York: Random House, 1999), 144; Kate Buford, *Burt Lancaster: An American Life* (Cambridge, MA: Da Capo Press, 2001), 217; Richard O. Davies, *Rivals!: The Ten Greatest Sports Rivalries of the Twentieth Century* (West Sussex, UK: John Wiley and Sons, 2010), 157.

19. Joe Tiller, with Tom Kubat, *Tiller: Not Your Average Joe* (Champaign, IL: Sports Publishing, 2006), 5.

20. Ronald Wallace, "The Friday Night Fights," in his *The Uses of Adversity* (Pittsburgh: University of Pittsburgh Press, 1998), 23.

21. Kasia Boddy, *Boxing: A Cultural History* (London: Reaktion Books, 2008), 218.

22. Stanley Weston, "Where Is Vejar Going?" *Boxing and Wrestling*, July 1955.

23. Joan Loubet, "As the Women See It," *Ring—Annual Magazine on TV Fights*, 1954.

24. On the origins of this new primitive masculinity, see Gail Bederman, *Manliness and Civilization: A Cultural History of Gender and Race in the United states, 1880–1917* (Chicago: University of Chicago Press, 1995), 168–69; Edgar Rice Burroughs, *Tarzan of the Apes* (1912; repr., Fairfield, IA: 1st World Press, 2005). Gladiator movies, coincidentally, also proved a financial success in the 1950s and early 1960s.

25. Bederman, *Manliness and Civilization*, 234.

26. Susan Faludi, *The Terror Dream: Fear and Fantasy in Post-9/11 America* (New York: Henry Holt, 2007), 282–86.

27. Al Buck, "TV Talent Big Problem," *Ring—Annual Magazine on TV Fights*, 1954.

28. John Lardner, "So You Think You See the Fights on TV!" *Saturday Evening Post*, April 5, 1953.

29. *Ring—Annual Magazine on TV Fights*, 1955.

30. Mettler, *Soldiers to Citizens*, 7.

Chapter 3. The Friday Night Fighters

1. Current Population Reports: Consumer Income, November 1956. Table C. Median Income of Men and Women, By Color and Extent of Employment, For the United States, By Regions: 1955, accessed at http://www2.census.gov/prod2/popscan/p60–023.pdf. In the heavyweight title fight between Marciano and Ezzard Charles on June 17, 1954, Marciano received $250,000. See Russell Sullivan, *Rocky Marciano: The Rock of His Times* (Urbana: University of Illinois Press, 2005), 273.

2. Malcolm X, with Alex Haley, *The Autobiography of Malcolm X* (New York: Random House, 1999), 295.

3. Professional football had integrated earlier than baseball, but this was "a decidedly second tier sport at the time." Dave Zirin, *A People's History of Sports in the United States* (New York: The New Press, 2008), 107.

4. Michael T. Isenberg, *John L. Sullivan and His America* (Urbana: University of Illinois Press, 1994), 293.

5. Benjamin G. Rader, *American Sports: From the Age of Folk Games to the Age of Televised Sports*, 4th ed. (Upper Saddle River, NJ: Prentice-Hall, 1999), 151.

6. Henry Louis Gates Jr., *Colored People: A Memoir* (New York: Knopf, 1994), 20.

7. As cultural historian Kasia Boddy points out, "Boxing fans (and therefore TV networks) . . . wanted to see interracial fights." See Kasia Boddy, *Boxing: A Cultural History* (London: Reaktion Books, 2008), 323.

8. Malcolm X and Haley, *The Autobiography of Malcolm X*, 25.

9. David Margolick, *Beyond Glory: Joe Louis vs. Max Schmeling, and a World on the Brink* (New York: Knopf, 2005).

10. Boddy, *Boxing*, 169.

11. Douglas Century, *Barney Ross* (New York: Random House, 2006), 29.

12. Boddy, *Boxing*, 170. Wearing the Star is still seen by some as a symbol of fighting prowess. I watched Roman Greenberg fight at Madison Square Garden on March 10, 2007, and he wore the Star of David proudly on his trunks.

13. S. Kirson Weinberg and Henry Around, "The Occupational Culture of the Boxer," *American Journal of Sociology* 57, no. 5 (March 1952): 460.

14. Paul Magno, "Legends of Mexican Boxing (Part 1): Baby Arizmendi," *Boxing Tribune*, August 3, 2011, accessed at http://theboxingtribune.com/2011/08/legends-of-mexican-boxing-part-1-baby-arizmendi; Weinberg and Around, "The Occupational Culture of the Boxer," 460; "Classy Bantams," *Life*, March 21, 1955.

15. Carlos E. Cortes, "Chicanas in Film: History of an Image," in *Latin Looks: Images of Latinas and Latinos in the U.S. Media*, ed. Clara E. Rodriguez (Boulder, CO: Westview Press, 1998), 121–41; Mae M. Ngai, *Impossible Subjects: Illegal Aliens and the Making of Modern America* (Princeton, NJ: Princeton University Press, 2004).

16. S. Robert Lichter and Daniel R. Admundson, "Distorted Reality: Hispanic Characters in TV Entertainment," in Rodriguez, *Latin Looks*, 59.

17. Roger Kahn, *A Flame of Pure Fire: Jack Dempsey and the Roaring 20s* (San Diego, CA: Harcourt, 2000), 334.

18. Russ J. Newland, "Mexican Fighter Is Eager to Fight Kid Chocolate," *Reno (NV) Evening Gazette*, January 23, 1933.

19. "Rudy Garcia, Boxing's Two-Fisted Tamale," *Boxing and Wrestling*, September 1955.

20. "Asaltador de Gigantes," *Time*, May 26, 1952.

21. John Lardner, "So You Think You See the Fights on TV!" *Saturday Evening Post*, April 5, 1953.

22. Ibid.

23. Fred Eisentadt, untitled article, March 1957, Gaspar Ortega Scrapbook #1, Ortega's personal collection.

24. "A Punch Is Not Enough—Today's Boxer Must Be a Character," *New York Times*, October 25, 1959.

25. Charles Einstein, "TV Slugs the Boxers," *Harper's Magazine*, August 1956.

26. Lardner, "So You Think You See the Fights on TV!"

27. John Lardner, "They Hate Self-Defense," *Newsweek*, February 22, 1954.

28. "Coexistence, Or Else," *Newsweek*, March 14, 1955.

29. Einstein, "TV Slugs the Boxers."

30. Quoted in Lardner, "So You Think You See the Fights on TV!"

31. Robert Coughlan, "How the IBC Runs Boxing," *Sports Illustrated*, January 17, 1955.

32. Kay Thompson, *Eloise* (New York: Simon and Schuster, 1983), 60.

33. Parke Cummings, "The Rule Clearly States," *Saturday Evening Post*, January 1, 1955.

34. Gibson K. Gibson Jr., with Steve Huntley, *Knocking Down Barriers: My Fight for Black America* (Evanston, IL: Northwestern University Press, 2005), 251.

35. "Murder on TV," *Newsweek*, May 4, 1953.

36. "Boston Massacre," *Time*, May 4, 1953.

37. Einstein, "TV Slugs the Boxers."

38. Jersey Jones, "Boon or Bane?" *Ring—Annual Magazine on TV Fights*, 1954.

39. Lewis Eskin, "Studio Fights," *Ring—Annual Magazine on TV Fights*, 1954.

40. Mike Silver, *The Arc of Boxing: The Rise and Decline of the Sweet Science* (Jefferson, NC: McFarland, 2008), 36–37.

41. Murray Goodman, "Boxing—The World Sport," *Ring—Annual Magazine on TV Fights*, 1954.

42. John Duncan, *In the Red Corner: A Journey into Cuban Boxing* (London: Yellow Jersey Press, 2000), 234–39.

43. Willie Pep, with Robert Sacchi, *Willie Pep Remembers . . . Friday's Heroes* (New York: Frederick Fell, 1973), chap. 9; E. C. Wallenfeldt, *The Six-Minute Fraternity: The Rise and Fall of NCAA Tournament Boxing, 1932–60* (Westport, CT: Praeger, 1994), 155–61.

44. "Fallen Idol," *Time*, February 23, 1953.

45. Einstein, "TV Slugs the Boxers"; Lardner, "So You Think You See the Fights on TV!"

Chapter 4. The Mexamerican

1. The magnet of Tijuana pulled in both directions, of course; Mexicans long trekked there from the hinterlands to capitalize on the influx of greenbacks. See Ramon Eduardo Ruiz, *On the Rim of Mexico: Encounters of the Rich and Poor* (Boulder, CO: Westview Press, 1998), 38; Gaspar Benitez Jr., interview with the author, August 7, 2005.

2. Raymond Chandler, *The Long Goodbye* (New York: Random House, 1988), 37.

3. Humberto Felix Berumen, *Tijuana La Horrible: Entre la Historia y el Mito* (Tijuana: El Colegio de la Frontera Norte, 2003), 153–56.

4. Ernest Hemingway, *The Sun Also Rises* (New York: Simon and Schuster, 1954), 18.

5. Cota Leon, "Quien es Nick Corby," *K.O. Semanario Deportivo*, May 27, 1961.

6. The now long-retired referee of this bloodbath told me that he sensed greatness in Gaspar and that's why he didn't stop the fight. But perhaps it had more to do with the sheer, audience-pleasing force of will displayed by the young Tijuanan who refused to stay down.

Chapter 5. The Discovery of New York

1. A. J. Leibling, "The University of Eighth Avenue," in his *A Neutral Corner: Boxing Essays* (New York: North Point Press, 1990), 21.

2. W. C. Heinz, "The Twilight of Boxing," *Saturday Evening Post*, January 7, 1961.

3. Ronald K. Fried, *Corner Men: Great Boxing Trainers* (New York: Four Walls Eight Windows, 1991), 38.

4. Ibid., 31–32.

5. Ibid., 37.

6. Ibid., 33.

7. Ibid., 275.

8. William J. Briordy, "Ward Knocks Out Portuguez in 5th," *New York Times*, August 26, 1954.

9. Joseph C. Nichols, "Basilio Gains Unanimous Decision over Fiore in 10-Round Garden Bout," *New York Times*, September 11, 1954.

10. "Patterson Beats Slade at Garden," *New York Times*, November 20, 1954.

11. Deane McGowen, "Drake Outpoints Giovanelli Here," *New York Times*, August 25, 1955. Again Gaspar is "Caspar" here.

12. "Eye Cut Forces Henry out of GG Final Match," *Monessen (PA) Daily Independent*, February 20, 1952.

13. Joseph C. Nichols, "Logart Gains Split Decision Over Fuentes in Welterweight Bout at Garden," *New York Times*, February 11, 1956.

14. Ibid.

15. Murray Rose, "Logart to Get Test on Friday," *Ogden (UT) Standard-Examiner*, March 16, 1958.

16. *Ring Annual Magazine on TV Fights*, 1954.

17. Jersey Jones, "Successful Invasion by Cubans," *The Ring*, December 1959; Roberto Gonzalez Echevarria, *The Pride of Havana: A History of Cuban Baseball* (New York: Oxford University Press, 1999), 299–300.

18. "Logart Wins Garden Bout," *Titusville (PA) Herald*, March 17, 1956.

19. Murray Rose, "Logart Beats Ortega, Set for DeMarco," *Corpus Christi (TX) Times*, March 17, 1956.

Chapter 6. Climb

1. Undated, untitled articles and images, Gaspar Ortega Scrapbook #1, Ortega's personal collection.

2. "Ortega Gains Decision Over Poirier," *Provo (UT) Daily Herald*, June 12, 1956 ; "Ortega Wins Close Fight; Plan Rematch," *Waterloo (IA) Daily Courier*, June 12, 1956.

3. "Ortega Upsets Logart in Surprising Split Decision," *Walla Walla (WA) Union Bulletin*, October 18, 1956.

4. Dave O'Hara, "Logart Still Top Threat, Despite Loss," *Lima (OH) News*, October 18, 1956.

5. Joe Phelan, "Gaspar Ortega Cops Upset over Favored Isaac Logart with Split in Boston Main," *Nevada (Reno) State Journal*, October 18, 1956.

6. "Ortega Upsets Logart," *New York Times*, October 18, 1956.

7. O'Hara, "Logart Still Top Threat."

8. Tony DeMarco, interview with the author, December 19, 2006.

9. "DeMarco to Box Ortega Tonight," *New York Times*, November 23, 1956.

10. Jack Cuddy, "Former Champ Out-Fought By 4–1 Underdog," *Bridgeport (CT) Telegram*, November 24, 1956.

11. Tony DeMarco, interview with the author, December 19, 2006.

12. Cuddy, "Former Champ Out-Fought."

13. "Ortega Wins over Tony DeMarco," *Provo (UT) Daily Herald*, November 25, 1956.

14. "Ortega Takes Upset Nod over DeMarco," *Reno (NV) Evening Gazette*, November 24, 1956.

15. "Tony DeMarco Favored over Mexican Star," *Nevada (Reno) State Journal*, December 21, 1956.

16. United Press, "Tony Demarco Picked to Win," *Gettysburg (PA) Times*, December 21, 1956.

17. "Tony DeMarco Favored over Mexican Star," *Nevada (Reno) State Journal*, December 21, 1956.

18. United Press, "Tony Demarco Picked to Win."

19. "Gaspar Ortega Wants Shot at the Title; Thumps Demarco," *Zanesville (OH) Signal*, December 22, 1956.

20. Jack Cuddy, "DeMarco Split Verdict Victim Again," *Lowell (MA) Sun*, December 22, 1956.

21. Tony DeMarco, interview with the author, December 19, 2006.

22. "Gaspar Ortega Wants Shot at the Title," *Zanesville (OH) Signal*, December 22, 1956.

23. Cuddy, "DeMarco Split Verdict Victim Again," *Lowell (MA) Sun*, December 22, 1956.

Chapter 7. The Tournament

1. Fred Eisenstadt, untitled, undated article, in Gaspar Ortega Scrapbook #1, Ortega's personal collection; Gene Ward, "Gaspar Ortega: Busiest Boxer Around"; "Gaspar Ortega Gets No. 2 Ranking in Latest Ratings," *Lowell (MA) Sun*, January 6, 1957.

2. Undated, untitled article in Gaspar Ortega Scrapbook #1.

3. "Bout Signed," *Humboldt (CA) Standard*, January 10, 1957; "DeMarco to Meet Ortega for Third Time in Hub Feb. 9," *Lowell (MA) Sun*, January 9, 1957.

4. "Sport Shorts," *Gettysburg (PA) Times*, February 9, 1957.

5. "Gasper [*sic*] Ortega Picked to Beat Tony DeMarco," *Daily (Connellsville, PA) Courier*, February 9, 1957.

6. "Tony DeMarco Outslugs Gaspar Ortega," *Nevada (Reno) State Journal*, February 10, 1957.

7. "Beat Him Because I Kept My Head—Tony," *Lowell (MA) Sun*, February 10, 1957.

8. "Weighs Offer: Basilio Studies Pro Bout," *Ogden (UT) Standard-Examiner*, March 4, 1957.

9. Billy Shaw, "In Syracuse Rings," August 1957 article, Gaspar Ortega Scrapbook #1; Jack Chandler, "Gaspar Ortega 7–5 Pick Over Isaac Logart," *Nevada (Reno) State Journal*, May 10, 1957.

10. Jack Chandler, "Gaspar Ortega 7–5 Pick"; "Ortega Outpoints Logart on Rally," *New York Times*, May 11, 1957.

11. "Ortega Outpoints Logart on Rally"; "Ortega Decisions Logart," *Pacific Stars and Stripes*, May 12, 1957.

12. Gary B. Youmans, *The Onion Picker: Carmen Basilio and Boxing in the 1950s* (Syracuse, NY: Syracuse University Press, 2007), 179.

13. "Top Welters to Get Fight Offer," *Oakland (CA) Tribune*, October 17, 1957.

14. Jeffrey T. Sammons, *Beyond the Ring: The Role of Boxing in American Society* (Urbana: University of Illinois Press, 1990), 169.

15. Don Cusic, *Baseball and Country Music* (Madison: University of Wisconsin Press/Popular Press, 2003), 36.

16. "Tab Gavilan 9–5 Tonight Over Ortega," *Press-Telegram (Long Beach, CA)*,

October 22, 1957; "Kid Gavilan Faces Ortega in 12-Round Wrigley Field Match," *Fairbanks (AK) Daily News-Miner*, October 22, 1957.

17. Dave Lewis, "Ortega Wins Split Decision" and "Once Over Lightly," *Independent (Long Beach, CA)*, October 23, 24, 1957.

18. "Five Welters Named for Title Tournament," *Post-Standard (Syracuse, NY)*, November 2, 1957.

19. "World Fight Group Names Six to Vie for Welter Title," *European Stars and Stripes*, November 3, 1957.

20. "Akins Tells Helfand He's Champion Now," *New York Times*, November 6, 1957; "Akins Agrees to Box in Title Tournament," *New York Times*, November 13, 1957.

21. "Six Welterweights Agree to Enter Tournament to Find New Champ," *Newport (RI) Daily News*, November 13, 1957.

22. "World Fight Group," *European Stars and Stripes*, November 3, 1957.

23. "Aussie Turns Down Fight with Akins," *Morgantown (WV) Post*, January 23, 1958.

24. "Lighter Boys in Spotlight in Week's Boxing Schedule," *Titusville (PA) Herald*, December 2, 1957.

25. "Logart 7–5 Choice Over Ortega," *Times (Troy, NY) Record*, December 6, 1957.

26. "Logart Gains Unanimous Decision Over Ortega in 12 Round Bout," *New York Times*, December 7, 1957.

27. "DeMarco, Akins in Rematch of Pier Six Slugfest Tonight," *Bennington (VT) Evening Banner*, January 21, 1958.

28. "Virgil Akins Stops DeMarco in Boston," *Ogden (UT) Standard-Examiner*, January 22, 1958.

29. "Martinez Gets Bye in Welter Tourney Elimination Draw," *Logansport (IN) Press*, February 4, 1958.

30. Jack Cuddy, "Grand Jury Summons Akins, Logart," *Times (Troy, NY) Record*, March 22, 1958.

31. Ibid.

32. Oscar Fraley, "Disregard Odds—Underdog Martinez Picked by Fraley to Capture Title," *Oxnard (CA) Press-Courier*, June 6, 1958; "Akins, Martinez Fight for Title," *Ogden (UT) Standard-Examiner*, June 1, 1958.

33. "Akins TKOs Martinez for Crown," *Times (Troy, NY) Record*, June 7, 1958.; Jack Hand, "Akins Stops Martinez in Fourth to Annex Vacant Welter Title," *Billings (MT) Gazette*, June 7, 1958.

34. "Akins Seeks Basilio after Shellacking Vince Martinez," *Huronite and the Daily Plainsman (Huron, SD)*, June 6, 1958.

35. "Dupas 7–5 Pick to Beat Ortega," *Raleigh (WV) Register*, February 5, 1958.

36. "Dupas Defeats Gaspar Ortega," *Bridgeport (CT) Post*, February 6, 1958.

37. Gay Talese, "Here a Jab, There a Dab and That's Mickey Crawford," *New York Times*, July 9, 1958.

38. Ibid.

39. Gordon S. White Jr., "Ortega Triumphs over Crawford," *New York Times*, July 12, 1958.

40. "Gaspar Yells for Akins Title Bout," *El Paso (TX) Herald-Post*, July 12, 1958.

41. Martin Cane, "Artist on the Canvas," *Sports Illustrated*, July 7, 1958.

Chapter 8. The Secret Government

1. Howard M. Tuckner, "Ortega Counts Cash and Calories," *New York Times*, August 12, 1958.

2. U.S. Department of Commerce, *Current Population Reports: Consumer Income*, Ser. P-60 No. 28, May 1958.

3. Ed Corrigan, "Gaspar Ortega, Crawford Draw," *Stevens Point (WI) Daily Journal*, August 14, 1958.

4. Deane McGowen, "Crawford Fights Ortega to Draw," *New York Times*, August 14, 1958.

5. "Don Jordan Is Upset Winner Over G. Ortega," *Gettysburg (PA) Times*, September 18, 1958; "Jordan Is Victor in Ortega Fight," *New York Times*, September 18, 1958.

6. Bob Myers, "Ortega and Jordan Fight," *Port Angeles (WA) Evening News*, October 22, 1958; Hank Hollingworth, "Jordan, Ortega in L.B.," *Independent (Long Beach, CA) Press-Telegram*, October 19, 1958; "Boxing" Ad, *Independent (Long Beach, CA) Press-Telegram*, October 22, 1958.

7. Hollingworth, "Jordan, Ortega in L.B.," *Independent (Long Beach, CA) Press-Telegram*, October 19, 1958. Gaspar took the picture home to Tijuana but has since lost it.

8. "Jordan Gains Split Decision in Twelve-Round Fight on Coast," *New York Times*, October 23, 1958.

9. Robert K. Christenberry, "My Rugged Education in Boxing," *Life*, May 26, 1952.

10. W. C. Heinz, "So He's Going to Clean Up Boxing!," *Saturday Evening Post*, February 16, 1952.

11. Christenberry also wanted to make the sport safer. He gave all New York boxing clubs thirty days to put in shock-absorbing safety mats and required KO'd fighters put on a thirty-day "ill and unavailable" list. Ibid.

12. Christenberry, "My Rugged Education."

13. Dan Parker, "Rover Boy in the Jungles of Boxing," *Sports Illustrated*, November 15, 1954.

14. Jeffrey T. Sammons, *Beyond the Ring: The Role of Boxing in American Society* (Urbana: University of Illinois Press, 1990), 151.

15. Other Carbo pseudonyms include Frank Martin, Frank Fortunato, Frank Tucker, Frank Russo, Dago Frank, The Ambassador, The Uncle, The Man, The Traveling Salesman, The Southern Salesman, Jimmy the Wop, Mr. Fury, Mr. Big, The Superintendent, The Gray Haired Guy, and "She" when he was spoken of on wiretapped phones.

16. Russell Sullivan, *Rocky Marciano: The Rock of His Times* (Urbana: University of Illinois Press, 2005), 56; Jim Brady, *Boxing Confidential: Power, Corruption and the Richest Prize in Sport* (Lytham, UK: Milo Books, 2002), chaps. 2–4; David Remnick, *King of the World: Muhammad Ali and the Rise of an American Hero* (New York: Random House, 1998), 59–62. Also seen spelled as Fratianno.

17. John Field and Earl Brown, "The Boxing Racket," *Life*, June 17, 1946.

18. Nick Tosches, *The Devil and Sonny Liston* (Boston: Little, Brown, 2000), 113–14.

19. Dan Parker, "The Killer Who Controls the Fights," *Bluebook*, March 1955.

20. Kevin Mitchell, *Jacobs Beach: The Mob, The Fights, The Fifties* (New York: Pegasus Books, 2010), 184.

21. Brady, *Boxing Confidential*, 97.

22. Tosches, *The Devil and Sonny Liston*, 110.

23. Thomas Myler, *The Sweet Science Goes Sour: How Scandal Brought Boxing to Its Knees* (Vancouver, BC: Greystone Books, 2006), 22–24; Brady, *Boxing Confidential*, 102.

24. "Events and Discoveries," *Sports Illustrated*, October 5, 1959.

25. Tony Demarco, interview with the author, December 19, 2006; Carmen Basilio, interview with the author, October 28, 2010.

26. Tony DeMarco, interview with the author, December 19, 2006.

27. Selwyn Raab, *Five Families: The Rise, Decline, and Resurgence of America's Most Powerful Mafia Empires* (New York: St. Martin's Press, 2006), 156.

28. Gibson K. Gibson Jr., with Steve Huntley, *Knocking Down Barriers: My Fight for Black America* (Evanston, IL: Northwestern University Press, 2005), 274; "Professional Boxing," *Hearings before the Subcommittee on Antitrust and Monopoly of the Committee on the Judiciary*, United States Senate, Parts 1–4 (Washington, DC, 1960–64), 417.

29. Gibson, *Knocking Down Barriers*, 273, 271; "Professional Boxing," 302.

Chapter 9. Trouble

1. Volker Skierka, *Fidel Castro: A Biography* (Cambridge: Polity Press, 2004), 69; Martin Gilbert, *A History of the Twentieth Century*, vol. 3, *1952–1999* (New York: William Morrow, 1999), 196–97.

2. Nixon quoted in John M. Murrin et al., *Liberty, Equality, Power: A History of the American People*, compact 4th ed. (Belmont, CA: Thompson Wadsworth, 2006), 1017; Skierka, *Fidel Castro*, 69.

3. Quote from Arthur Schlesinger Jr., cited in Gilbert, *A History of the Twentieth Century*, 197.

4. John Sugden, *Boxing and Society: An International Analysis* (Manchester, UK: Manchester University Press, 1996), 135.

5. John Duncan, *In the Red Corner: A Journey into Cuban Boxing* (London: Yellow Jersey Press, 2000), 89.

6. Tom Gjelten, *Bacardi and the Long Fight for Cuba: The Biography of a Cause* (New York: Penguin, 2008), 16, 170.

7. Al Warden, "Thumbnail Sketch of Benny 'Kid' Paret," *Ogden (UT) Standard-Examiner*, November 19, 1961; Hans J. Massaquoi, "Should Boxing Be Abolished?" *Ebony*, June 1962.

8. "Indio Ortega Abre hoy en E. U.," *El Heraldo (Tijuana)*, January 2, 1959; "Ortega Favored to Down Young Moyer Tonight," *Brownwood (TX) Bulletin*, January 2, 1959; Jack Cuddy, "Decision Amazes Writers: Ortega Batters Moyer But Loses," *Chronicle Telegram (Elyria, OH)*, January 3, 1959.

9. Cuddy, "Decision Amazes Writers."

10. Jack Hand, "Denny Moyer Winner Over Gaspar Ortega," *Port Angeles (WA) Evening News*, January 3, 1959; Cuddy, "Decision Amazes Writers."

11. "Ring Verdict Approved," *New York Times*, January 10, 1959.

12. "Gaspar Ortega Pelea Hoy Contra Ruddel Stich [*sic*] en N.Y.," *El Heraldo (Tijuana)*, February 6, 1959.

13. Byron Crawford, "Boxer Made 'The Greatest' Sacrifice of All," *Courier-Journal (Louisville, KY)*, November 25, 2005.

14. "Drowning Takes Life of Boxer Rudell Stitch," *Ellensburg (WA) Daily Record*, June 7, 1960.

15. *Jet* magazine, May 28, 1959.

16. "Ortega's Luck Has Changed," *Lowell (MA) Sun*, February 7, 1959.

17. Ibid.; "Wounded Eye Healed—Ortega Faces Stitch in Rings War Return," *Arizona (Phoenix) Republic*; "Ortega Gano Decision A Stitch," *El Heraldo (Tijuana)*, February 7, 1959; Deane McGowen, "Ortega Outpoints Stitch on Split Decision in Ten-Round Bout at the Garden," *New York Times*, February 7, 1959.

18. "Stitch Easily Wins Fight with Ortega," *New York Times*, May 9, 1959.

19. "Stitch Had Date to Sign Pact with a Contender," *New York Times*, June 7, 1960; "Stitch Drowns Fishing," *Tucson (AZ) Daily Citizen*, June 6, 1960.

20. "Facil Decision Gano Ortega a Terrazas," *El Heraldo (Tijuana)*, July 14, 1959.

21. "Ortega Fights Paret in Garden Tonight," *Logansport (IN) Pharos-Tribune*, August 7, 1959.

22. "Undefeated Cuban Trounces Experienced Ortega," *Nevada (Reno) State Journal*, September 12, 1959.

23. Ibid.

24. Bob Allison, "Ortega Big Exception to Boxing Generalities," untitled news clipping, December 10, 1963, Gaspar Ortega Scrapbook #2, Ortega's personal collection.

25. Al Buck, "Fullmer Asks for Downes-Pender Winner," *Ring*, October 1961.

26. David Marabiss, *Rome 1960: The Olympics that Changed the World* (New York: Simon and Schuster, 2008), 77, 282.

27. Michael O'Brien, *John F. Kennedy: A Biography* (New York: St. Martin's Press,

2005), 753; David Remnick, *King of the World: Muhammad Ali and the Rise of an American Hero* (New York: Random House, 1998), 14

28. Johnny Salak, "TV and Boxing," in Gaspar Ortega Scrapbook #1, Ortega's personal collection.

29. "Fans Boo as Ortega Gets Verdict over Harrington," *Milwaukee Sentinel*, January 9, 1960; "Harrington Will Be Given Second Shot at Ortega," *Modesto (CA) Bee*, January 10, 1960.

30. "Griffith and Ortega Fight," *Sheboygan (WI) Journal*, February 12, 1960.

31. Ron Ross, *Nine . . . Ten . . . And Out!: The Two Worlds of Emile Griffith* (New York: DiBella Entertainment, 2008), 4.

32. Ibid., chap. 2.

33. Ibid., chap. 3.

34. Ibid., 24.

35. "Griffith and Ortega Fight"; "Welters to Vie Wednesday," *Ogden (UT) Standard-Examiner*, February 8, 1960; "Welterweights Top Week's Ring Slate," *Aiken (SC) Standard and Review*, February 8, 1960; Jack Cuddy, "Ortega and Foe Battle Called a Draw," *Anderson (IN) Daily Bulletin*, February 13, 1960; Ross, *Nine . . . Ten . . . And Out!*, 38.

36. Cuddy, "Ortega and Foe Battle Called a Draw."

37. "Ebbets 'Feeled' TV Winnah Was Da Bum," *Long Beach (CA) Press Telegram*, February 13, 1960.

38. "Ortega Loses to Griffith," *Racine (WI) Journal Times*, February 13, 1960; Al Buck, "All in Step—All But the Fighter and the Ref," newspaper article, Gaspar Ortega Scrapbook #3, Ortega's personal collection; Jack Cuddy, "Decision Win Ires Griffith," *San Mateo (CA) Times*, February 13, 1960.

39. "Red Smith: The 100th Fist Fight," *Pacific Stars and Stripes*, January 27, 1977.

40. Buck, "All in Step—All But the Fighter and the Ref"; Ross, *Nine . . . Ten . . . and Out!*, 39.

41. Robert M. Lipsyte, "A Title for a Fighting Choir Boy," *New York Times*, April 3, 1961; Ross, *Nine . . . Ten . . . and Out!*, 42.

42. Lipsyte, "A Title for a Fighting Choir Boy."

43. In January 1961, the *New York Times* wondered what would happen to men such as Florentino Fernandez, Luis Rodriguez, and Benny Paret when Castro officially deep-sixed their lucrative livelihoods. "Boxing Also Involved," *New York Times*, January 5, 1961.

44. Duncan, *In the Red Corner*, 150, 151.

45. Richard Goldstein, "Kid Gavilan, 77, Welterweight Champion in the Early 50's," *New York Times*, February 15, 2003; Duncan, *In the Red Corner*, 251–55.

46. Noted the *Times*, he then lived in New York City, though he "recently went to Cuba to visit his mother." In "Boxing Also Involved," *New York Times*, January 5, 1961.

47. Dan Barry, *City Lights: Stories about New York* (New York: St. Martin's Press, 2007), 178.

48. Deane McGowen, "Cuban Suggested as Jordan Rival," *New York Times*, March

26, 1960. According to fight doctor Ferdie Pacheco, Paret got the title fight because he was controlled by Carbo, and his corner did not object to handing over 50 percent to Mr. Gray. See Ferdie Pacheco, *Blood in My Coffee: The Life of the Fight Doctor* (Champaign, IL: Sports Publishing, 2005), 100.

49. "Castro Rejects 'Threats,'" *New York Times*, May 28, 1960; "Castro Message Bids Paret 'Win Your Battle,'" *New York Times*, December 9, 1959.

50. "Hart Is Ring Foe of Paret Tonight," *New York Times*, July 12, 1960.

51. "Paret and Moyer to Box Here Aug. 16," *New York Times*, July 31, 1960.

52. Deane McGowen, "Paret Outpoints Thompson at Garden and Keeps World Welterweight Title," *New York Times*, December 11, 1960.

53. "Ortega Easily Outpoints Paret in Nontitle Contest on Coast," *New York Times*, February 26, 1961.

54. "Ortega, Campeón sin Corona," undated issue of *Puños y Llaves*, Gaspar Ortega Scrapbook #1, Ortega's personal collection.

Chapter 10. The Shot

1. This story appeared in a 1952 article that circulated widely, and it also currently appears on the Web site of the International Boxing Hall of Fame (http://www .ibhof.com/pages/about/inductees/nonparticipant/parnassus.html). In a 1971 *Sports Illustrated* interview, Parnassus said, "If one of the boys in the place was fighting, I bet a few dollars on him. If he won, I give him a free meal ticket. Before I knew it, if anybody asked them who was their manager, they would say Parnassus." In Roy Blount, "Out of This I Am Getting Not a Nyickl," *Sports Illustrated*, May 31, 1971.

2. "Mr. Parnassus Learned Life the Hard Way," *Winnipeg (MB) Free Press*, January 3, 1952; Gregory S. Rodriguez, "*Raza* Boxing: Community, Identity, and Hybridity in the 1960s and 1970s in Southern California," in *Mexican Americans and Sports: A Reader on Athletics and Barrio Life*, ed. Jorge Iber and Samuel Regalado (College Station, TX: Texas A & M University Press, 2007), 177–79; Mark Kram, "The Lady Is a Champ," *Sports Illustrated*, November 6, 1967.

3. "Parnassus Eyes Halimi-Macias Go," *Pasadena (CA) Independent*, July 9, 1957.

4. Gilbert Rogin, "Capital of the World," *Sports Illustrated*, September 8, 1958.

5. "Brawling Marks Los Angeles Bout," *New York Times*, January 18, 1958; Rogin, "Capital of the World."

6. Rogin, "Capital of the World"; "LA Promoter Miles Ahead," *Miami News*, August 16, 1959.

7. Al Warden, "The Sports Highway," *Ogden (UT) Standard-Examiner*, September 12, 1960.

8. Carmen Basilio, interview with the author, October 28, 2010.

9. Rudyard Kipling, "The Ballad of East and West," in *The Collected Poems of Rudyard Kipling* (Ware, UK: Wordsworth Editions, 1994), 245.

10. "Griffith Signs to Meet Ortega," *Janesville (WI) Daily Gazette*, April 15, 1961.

11. "Griffith Favored, 2–1," *San Antonio (TX) Light*, June 3, 1961.

12. "Ortega Y Griffith Estan Listos," *El Heraldo (Tijuana)*, June 1, 1961.

13. Frank Harvey, "Griffith Holds Firm at 2–1 in Title Match," *Long Beach (CA) Press-Telegram*, June 3, 1961; Frank Harvey, "Griffith, Ortega in Title Tiff," *Long Beach (CA) Independent*, June 3, 1961; "Griffith 2–1 Pick to Keep Title over Ortega Tonight," *Abilene (TX) Reporter-News*, June 3, 1961.

14. "Sports of Sorts," *Daily Mail (Hagerstown, MD)*, October 2, 1939.

15. "Ortega Not Satisfied," *New York Times*, February 27, 1961; "Ortega May Get Title Go," *Eugene (OR) Register*, February 27, 1961.

16. "Ortega Set for Training," *New York Times*, May 7, 1961.

17. "Griffith-Ortega Bout Set Back," *New York Times*, May 15, 1961.

18. "Griffith Ligero Favorito Sobre Gaspar Ortega," *El Heraldo (Tijuana)*, June 3, 1961; *K.O. Semanario Deportivo*, May 27, 1961; "Ortega Y Griffith Estan Listos" and "Sere Campeon: Dijo G. Ortega a la Prensa en Los Angeles, Cal.," *El Heraldo (Tijuana)*, June 1, 1961.

19. "Ortega to Have Strong Backing," *Redlands (CA) Daily Facts*, June 2, 1961.

20. Frankie Goodman, "Boxing Biz," *Valley News (Van Nuys, CA)*, May 28, 1961; "Ortega Battles Griffith in Title Fight Saturday," *Valley News (Van Nuys, CA)*, June 1, 1961. Was Stable put in to narrow the odds by highlighting Ortega's drive and toughness? For possible evidence of this, see "Griffith 2–1 to Retain Welter Title Tonight," *Nevada (Reno) State Journal*, June 3, 1961; *New York Times*, June 3, 1961.

21. Bill McCormick, "Griffith Is Relaxed Puncher," *Pacific Stars and Stripes*, June 13, 1961; Ron Ross, *Nine . . . Ten . . . and Out!: The Two Worlds of Emile Griffith* (New York: DiBella Entertainment, 2008), 45; Tod Trent, "Sports Standard," *Evening Standard (Uniontown, PA)*, June 9, 1961; "Champ Won't Try for KO?" *Charleston (WV) Daily Mail*, June 2, 1961.

Chapter 11. Bloodying the Sport

1. Edmund P. Edmonds and William H. Manz, eds., *Congress and Boxing: A Legislative History, 1960–2003*, vol. 1 (Buffalo, NY: William S. Hein, 2005), 2.

2. Quoted in David Remnick, *King of the World: Muhammad Ali and the Rise of an American Hero* (New York: Random House, 1998), 63. This is, of course, true enough, although the fact that Logart and Akins were both top-ranked welters could not have been overridden by the underworld commissioner. Then again, Carbo's role in positioning the top contenders in the first place certainly adds to the case against him.

3. Selwyn Raab, *Five Families: The Rise, Decline, and Resurgence of America's Most Powerful Mafia Empires* (New York: St. Martin's Press, 2006), 108–16. As an ABC correspondent would later reflect, "there was a time . . . when you did not become a judge, or anybody of significance in New York City politics, without getting Frank Costello's OK." Quoted in Jim Brady, *Boxing Confidential: Power, Corruption and the Richest Prize in Sport* (Lytham, UK: Milo Books, 2002), 128.

4. See Anthony Summers, *Official and Confidential: The Secret Life of J. Edgar Hoover* (Hingham, MA: Wheeler, 1993), and Thomas A. Reppetto, *Bringing Down the Mob: The War against the American Mafia* (New York: Henry Holt, 2006), 32–33, for representative arguments of different views of Hoover.

5. Brady, *Boxing Confidential*, 107.

6. Ibid., 90–91, 102.

7. Tom Wicker, "Norris Involved, Senate Body Told," *New York Times*, December 6, 1960.

8. Charles L. Fontenay, *Estes Kefauver: A Biography* (Knoxville: University of Tennessee Press, 1980), 11; Thomas Reppetto, *American Mafia: A History of Its Rise to Power* (New York: Henry Holt, 2004), 255–57.

9. Thomas Patrick Doherty, *Cold War, Cool Medium: Television, McCarthyism, and American Culture* (New York: Columbia University Press, 2005), 109, 113, 115; Fontenay, *Estes Kefauver*, 171.

10. Doherty, *Cold War, Cool Medium, 107–115*; James L. Baughman, *Same Time, Same Station: Creating American Television, 1948–1961* (Baltimore: The Johns Hopkins University Press, 2007), 227.

11. Stephen R. Lowe, *The Kid on the Sandlot: Congress and Professional Sports, 1910–1992* (Bowling Green, OH: Bowling Green University Popular Press, 1995), 62; "Senate Boxing Inquiry Set," *New York Times*, March 22, 1960.

12. "La Motta Called to Boxing Inquiry," *New York Times*, June 30, 1960. Preparing for his upcoming election, Kefauver had to put Senator Philip Hart in charge of the first round of testimony.

13. Because he stood to make only nineteen thousand dollars from the Cerdan fight, LaMotta testified, he bet ten thousand dollars on himself to eke out a profit from the match.

14. "LaMotta Confesses He Threw '47 Garden Bout with Billy Fox," *New York Times*, June 15, 1960.

15. "Professional Boxing," *Hearings before the Subcommittee on Antitrust and Monopoly of the Committee on the Judiciary*, United States Senate, Parts 1–4 (Washington, DC, 1960–64), 299, 272; "Norris Links Carbo with Title Fights," *Pasadena (CA) Star-News*, December 10, 1960.

16. "Professional Boxing," 661–90, 477–78.

17. Ibid., 761.

18. Ibid., 1576, 1251–52, 1261.

19. Lowe, *The Kid on the Sandlot*, 67–68.

20. "Professional Boxing," 1266–70, 1276, 1299, 1418, 1408.

21. "Heavyweights Duel over Ingo's Health," *Ogden (UT) Standard-Examiner*, June 3, 1961.

22. Quoted in Elliott J. Gorn, *The Manly Art: Bare-Knuckle Prizefighting in America* (Ithaca, NY: Cornell University Press, 1989), 59.

23. "Janiro 5–6 Choice to Defeat Roach," *New York Times*, January 16, 1948; Joseph

C. Nichols, "Cerdan 1–2 Favorite Over Roach in 10-Rounder at Garden Tonight," *New York Times*, March 12, 1948.

24. Joseph C. Nichols, "Cerdan Knocks Out Roach in 2:31 of Eighth Round before 16,905 Spectators," *New York Times*, March 13, 1948.

25. "Roach Advised to Retire," *New York Times*, February 24, 1950.

26. Joe Kelly, "Between the Lines," *Lubbock (TX) Evening Journal*, February 24, 1950.

27. "Ten and Out," *Time*, March 6, 1950; James P. Dawson, "Roach in Hospital after Fight Here," *New York Times*, February 23, 1950; Arthur Daley, "Death Scores a Knockout," *New York Times*, February 24, 1950.

28. Dawson, "Roach in Hospital after Fight Here," *New York Times*, February 23, 1950.

29. Kelly, "Between the Lines," *Lubbock (TX) Evening Journal*, February 24, 1950; Jack Cuddy, "Boxing Commission, DA Probe Ring Death," *Olean (NY) Times Herald*, February 24, 1950; Daley, "Death Scores a Knockout," *New York Times*, February 24, 1950.

30. "Comprehensive Plan to Eliminate Serious Ring Injuries Announced," *New York Times*, March 2, 1950.

31. "Roach Death Brings Two N.Y. Probes," *San Antonio (TX) Light*, February 24, 1950; "Death of a Fighter," *Life*, March 6, 1950.

32. "Sonny Boy West Dies as Result of Ring Injury," *St. Petersburg (FL) Times*, December 22, 1950.

33. "Boxer Succumbs to Injury in Bout," *New York Times*, December 13, 1954; "Heavyweight Dies after Knockout," *Dixon (IL) Evening Telegraph*, December 12, 1954.

34. "The Manly Art of Murder," *Time*, January 24, 1955.

35. Kasia Boddy, *Boxing: A Cultural History* (London: Reaktion Books, 2008), 322, 321; Jack Gould, "TV: Requiem For a Heavyweight," *New York Times*, October 12, 1956.

36. Robert Coughlan, "How the IBC Runs Boxing," *Sports Illustrated*, January 17, 1955.

37. "Heavyweight Bout," *Time*, June 18, 1956.

38. *Mike Wallace Interview*. Originally aired October 26, 1957, from Harry Ransom Center Archives, at http://www.hrc.utexas.edu/multimedia/video/2008/wallace/basilio_carmen_t.html.

39. Boddy, *Boxing: A Cultural History*, 322; Jack Gould, "Television Network Will Drop Boxing from Weekly Programming in 1964," *New York Times*, December 23, 1963.

40. Remnick, *King of the World*, 12–13.

41. Gene Ward, "What's Wrong With Boxing," *Boxing and Wrestling*, October 1961.

42. A. J. Liebling, *A Neutral Corner: Boxing Essays* (New York: North Point Press, 1990), 4–5.

43. John Sugden, *Boxing and Society: An International Analysis* (Manchester, UK: Manchester University Press, 1996), 40.

44. "Prizefighting: Quantity Is Down but Some Quality Is Coming Up," *Newsweek*, December 10, 1951.

45. Al Buck, "TV Talent a Big Problem," *Ring—Annual Magazine on TV Fights*, 1954.

46. "Coexistence, or Else," *Newsweek*, March 14, 1955.

47. Eddie Borden, "This Doesn't Make Any Sense" and "What's Ahead," *Weekly Boxing World*, December 9, 1957, October 27, 1957.

48. Jersey Jones, "Boon or Bane?," *Ring—Annual Magazine on TV Fights*, 1954; Boddy, *Boxing: A Cultural History*, 319.

49. Mark Bowden, *The Best Game Ever: Giants vs. Colts, 1958, and the Birth of the Modern NFL* (New York: Atlantic Monthly Press, 2008), 86, 89, 112, 113.

50. Jim Kensil, "TV Boxing Moves to Saturdays," *Ada (OK) Evening News*, March 17, 1960; Jeff Neal-Lunsford, "Sport in the Land of Television: The Use of Sport in Network Primetime Schedules, 1946–1950," *Journal of Sport History* 19 (Spring 1992), 63.

51. William Leggett, "Friday—and No Fight," *Sports Illustrated*, July 11, 1960.

52. Quoted in Richard Worsnop, "Sports on Television," *Editorial Research Reports*, October 21, 1964, 778.

Chapter 12. The Ship Goes Down

1. "Fernandez Is Third in NBA Mit Ratings," *Ogden (UT) Standard-Examiner*, June 30, 1961; Ron Ross, *Nine . . . Ten . . . and Out! The Two Worlds of Emile Griffith* (New York: DiBella Entertainment, 2008), 48; *Lima (OH) News*, June 11, 1961; Bill McCormick, "Griffith Is Relaxed Puncher," *Pacific Stars and Stripes*, June 13, 1961. Parnassus offered him an astounding $150,000 to face the winner of the upcoming Gene Fullmer–Florentino Fernandez fight.

2. "Griffith Will Defend Title Here Next September against Paret," *New York Times*, June 5, 1961.

3. "Emile Says Foe Easier," *Billings (MT) Gazette*, June 4, 1961.

4. "Griffith May Seek Middleweight Title," *Corpus (TX) Christi Times*, June 5, 1961.

5. Red Smith, "Red Smith's Views of Sports," *Mansfield (OH) News Journal*, September 29, 1961; "Griffith, Paret Ready to Clash," *Pacific Stars and Stripes*, September 25, 1961.

6. William R. Conklin, "Griffith Beaten on Split Verdict," *New York Times*, October 1, 1961.

7. "Griffith's Manager Calls Paret's Victory Unfair," *New York Times*, October 2, 1961.

8. Harry Grayson, "Marciano Pilots Fighter," *Ogden (UT) Standard-Examiner*, October 17, 1961.

9. William J. Briordy, "Ortega, Busiest Man in Boxing, Ready for Scott Fight Saturday," *New York Times*, January 4, 1962.

10. Ibid.

11. Another sign of sports evolution was that between the rounds, Dunphy told viewers about all of the sports offerings on ABC, "America's number one network for sports." The next day, Sunday, would be the premier of ABC's newest sports offering, *The Wide World of Sports*.

12. "Paret Won't Drop His Crown If He Lifts Fullmer's," *Brainerd (MN) Daily Dispatch*, December 7, 1961.

13. Bob Myers, "Fullmer K.O.'s Paret in Tenth of Slugfest," *Post-Register (Idaho Falls, ID)*, December 11, 1961.

14. Bill Coltrin, "Fullmer Kayoes Paret in Vegas Title Battle," and "Paret 'Mad' at Gene's Rope Trick," *Salt Lake (UT) Tribune*, December 10, 1961.

15. *Ring of Fire: The Emile Griffith Story*, DVD, directed by Ron Berger (Troy, MI: Anchor Bay Entertainment, 2005); "Boxing Card," *Clearfield (PA) Progress*, March 19, 1962; "Griffith Favored Heavily to Beat Champion Paret," *Pacific Stars and Stripes*, March 24, 1962.

16. "Griffith Favored Heavily."

17. Don Dunphy, *Don Dunphy at Ringside* (New York: Henry Holt, 1988), 145–46.

18. Gary Smith, "The Shadow Boxer," *Sports Illustrated*, April 18, 2005.

19. Norman Mailer, "Death [of Paret]," in *Norton Book of Sports*, ed. George Plimpton (New York: W.W. Norton, 1992), 418.

20. Robert L. Teague, "Griffith Is Victor," *New York Times*, March 25, 1962.

21. "Paret Near Death after KO," *Oakland (CA) Tribune*, March 25, 1962.

22. "Says Griffith: 'Meant No Harm to Paret,'" *Oakland (CA) Tribune*, March 25, 1962.

23. *Ring of Fire*; Smith, "The Shadow Boxer," *Sports Illustrated*, April 18, 2005.

24. Dunphy, *Don Dunphy at Ringside*, 146, 163.

25. Hans J. Massaquoi, "Should Boxing Be Abolished?" *Ebony*, June 1962.

26. Robert M. Lipsyte, "Paret's Manager Says Goldstein Should Have Halted Bout Sooner," *New York Times*, March 26, 1962; *Ring of Fire*.

27. Massaquoi, "Should Boxing Be Abolished?"; "Paret's Mom Arrives," *Troy (NY) Record*, March 30, 1962.

28. Arthur Daley, "Is It Worth the Price?" *New York Times*, April 1, 1962; "One 'Sport' Too Many," *Valley Independent (Monessen, PA)*, April 5, 1962.

29. "Commission Clears Fight Officials," *Hutchinson (KS) News*, April 28, 1962.

30. "Magnified by TV," *Time*, April 6, 1962; *Life*, April 6, 1962.

31. "The Aim Is to Maim," *Time*, April 5, 1962.

32. "A Ring Requiem," *America: The National Catholic Weekly*, April 21, 1962.

33. "Magnified by TV."

34. Massaquoi, "Should Boxing Be Abolished?"

35. W. C. Heinz, "The Twilight of Boxing," *Saturday Evening Post*, January 7, 1961.

36. Massaquoi, "Should Boxing Be Abolished?"

37. Jimmy Breslin, "The Prize Fighter," *New York Herald Tribune*, 1963, in Gaspar Ortega Scrapbook #2, Ortega's personal collection.

38. Bob Allison, "Ortega Big Exception to Boxing Generalities," untitled newspaper, December 10, 1963, in Gaspar Ortega Scrapbook #2, Ortega's personal collection; Gene Ward, "Gaspar Ortega," undated, untitled article, in Gaspar Ortega Scrapbook #3, Ortega's personal collection.

39. "Corby Said Much Improved," *Billings (MT) Gazette*, September 12, 1962.

40. James T. Patterson, *Grand Expectations: The United States, 1945–1974* (New York: Oxford University Press, 1996), 494.

41. Melvyn P. Leffler, *For the Soul of Mankind: The United States, the Soviet Union, and the Cold War* (New York: Hill and Wang, 2007), 151; Patterson, *Grand Expectations*, 502.

42. Parnassus initially predicted thirty-eight thousand fans but scaled back his predictions as the event loomed. "Three Boxing Crowns at Stake on Card," *New York Times*, February 7, 1963; Bill Becker, "Big Ring Bill Set in Dodgers' Park," *New York Times*, March 6, 1963; "Paret and Rival Arrive for Fight," *New York Times*, March 23, 1962; Ferdie Pacheco, *Blood in My Coffee: The Life of the Fight Doctor* (Champaign, IL: Sports Publishing, 2005), 101; Morton Sharnik, "Death of a Champion," *Sports Illustrated*, April 1, 1963; Louie Robinson, "Penny-Wise Moore Buried; Left Wealth and 'Ban Boxing' Cries," *Jet*, April 11, 1963.

43. "The Aim Is to Maim."

44. "He Fought, Talked, Then Died . . . ," *Life*, April 5, 1963.

45. "Formal Inquiry of Ring Fatality Opened by Pennsylvania Board," *New York Times*, April 9, 1963.

46. "Ortega Upsets Charley Scott in 10-Rounder," *Galesburg (IL) Register-Mail*, January 29, 1963; "Late Staying-Power Wins for Ortega," *Simpson's Leader-Times (Kittanning, PA)*, January 29, 1963.

47. Walter Moran, "Is Billy Bello as Good as They Say?" *Boxing Illustrated*, October 1961.

48. "Bello Tests Ortega in Garden Bout," *Ogden (UT) Standard-Examiner*, July 6, 1963.

49. Robert Lipsyte, "Boxer Gets His Big Chance Tonight," *New York Times*, July 6, 1963.

50. "Bello Loses First Main Event on a Split Decision to Ortega," *New York Times*, July 7, 1963.

51. "Ortega, Bello May Be Re-matched," *Columbus (NE) Daily Telegram*, July 8, 1963; "Billy Bello Dies in Bronx Hallway," *New York Times*, July 21, 1963; "Bello Loses Final Fight," *San Antonio (TX) Express and News*, July 21, 1963.

52. Kennedy's assassination was also filmed by a man named Abraham Zapruder. That film would not make it to broadcast television until March 1975. "Kennedy, John F: Assassination and Funeral," in *Encyclopedia of Television*, 2nd ed., ed. Horace Newcomb (New York: Taylor and Francis, 2004), 1249–53.

53. "Gaspar Steps into Middle Class," *El Paso (TX) Herald-Post*, December 3, 1963.

Chapter 13. Changing Times

1. Robert Lipsyte, "Boxing Blackout Regarded as Bane and Benefit," *New York Times*, December 23, 1963.

2. Bob Green, "ABC Cancels Traditional Bouts," *Ada (OK) Evening News*, December

23, 1963; Jack Gould, "Television Network Will Drop Boxing from Weekly Programming in 1964," *New York Times*, December 23, 1963.

3. Lipsyte, "Boxing Blackout Regarded as Bane and Benefit."

4. Ibid.

5. Richard L. Worsnop, "Sports on Television," *Editorial Research Reports 1964*, vol. 2 (Washington, DC: Congressional Quarterly Service, 1964), 765–69.

6. "Pro Football Gets TV 'Treatment,'" *The News (Frederick, MD)*, February 12, 1964.

7. Worsnop, "Sports on Television," 777, 779.

8. "Garden Thinking of Network to Televise Fights," *New York Times*, January 3, 1964; "Garden Plans TV Network if ABC Cancels," *The News (Frederick, MD)*, January 3, 1964; "Own TV Network Formed by Garden," *Oakland (CA) Tribune*, February 18, 1964; "Garden to Televise Bouts on Own Chain," *New York Times*, February 18, 1964.

9. Val Adams, "Pro Boxing to End on TV Sept. 11," *New York Times*, August 8, 1964.

10. "TV Boxing Dies Friday," *Kingsport (TN) Times*, September 7, 1964; "Knockout Blow Aims at Weekly TV Fights," *Billings (MT) Gazette*, September 8, 1964.

11. "Dick Tiger Batters Down Don Fullmer," *Great Bend (KS) Tribune*, September 13, 1964; Don Dunphy, *Don Dunphy at Ringside* (New York: Henry Holt, 1988), 166.

12. Robert Lipsyte, "Sports of the Times: What's Next in Boxing?" *New York Times*, September 21, 1964.

13. Randy Roberts, "The Wide World of Muhammad Ali: The Politics and Economics of Televised Boxing," in *Muhammad Ali, the People's Champ*, ed. Elliot J. Gorn (Urbana: University of Illinois Press, 1995), 38.

14. Mailer, "Death [of Paret]."

15. Gregory S. Rodriguez, "*Raza* Boxing: Community, Identity, and Hybridity in the 1960s and 1970s in Southern California," in *Mexican Americans and Sports: A Reader on Athletics and Barrio Life*, ed. Jorge Iber and Samuel O. Regalado (College Station, TX: Texas A&M University Press, 2007), 160–61; Joshua Zeitz, "1964—The Year the Sixties Began," *American Heritage*, October 2006.

16. Roberts, "The Wide World of Muhammad Ali," 37; Steven D. Stark, *Glued to the Television: The 60 Television Shows and Events That Made Us Who We Are Today* (New York: The Free Press, 1997), 67.

17. See, for instance, Philip Caputo, *A Rumor of War* (New York: Henry Holt, 1996), 6. In Tim O'Brien's autobiographical *If I Die in a Combat Zone* (New York: Dell, 1973), a character says, "to avoid war is to avoid manhood" (37).

18. Roberts, "The Wide World of Muhammad Ali," 40, 41, 44. Jimmy Cannon quoted in Jeffrey T. Sammons, "Rebel With a Cause: Muhammad Ali as Sixties Protest Symbol," in Gorn, *Muhammad Ali, the People's Champ*, 166.

19. Mike Silver, *The Arc of Boxing: The Rise and Decline of the Sweet Science* (Jefferson, NC: McFarland, 2008), 51.

20. Thomas A. Reppetto, *Bringing Down the Mob: The War against the American Mafia* (New York: Henry Holt, 2006), chap. 4.

21. Charles L. Fontenay, *Estes Kefauver: A Biography* (Knoxville: University of Tennessee Press, 1980), 401–3.

22. Stephen R. Lowe, *The Kid on the Sandlot: Congress and Professional Sports, 1910–1992* (Bowling Green, OH: Bowling Green University Popular Press, 1995), 73–80; Edmund P. Edmonds and William H. Manz, eds., *Congress and Boxing: A Legislative History, 1960–2003*, vol. 1 (Buffalo, NY: William S. Hein, 2005).

23. James B. Roberts and Alexander Skutt, *The Boxing Register*, 4th ed. (Ithaca, NY: McBooks Press, 2006), 50.

24. Brady quoted in Silver, *The Arc of Boxing*, 203.

25. "Gabe Trounces Fading Gaspar," *San Mateo (CA) Times*, September 30, 1964.

26. "Ortega Loses to British Fighter," *Columbus (NE) Daily Telegram*, February 24, 1965; "Curvis Defeats Gaspar Ortega," *Arizona (Phoenix) Republic*, February 24, 1965.

27. "Gonzalez Guns for Title Shot in Houston Match," *The Post Dispatch (Syracuse, NY)*, March 23, 1965.

28. "Shipes to Face Ortega in Modesto," *Daily Review (Hayward, CA)*, September 22, 1965.

Epilogue. Nightmares

1. H. Clausen, P. McCrory, and V. Anderson, "The Risk of Chronic Traumatic Brain Injury in Professional Boxing: Change in Exposure Variables over the Past Century," *British Journal of Sports Medicine* 39, no. 9 (2005): 661; Barry D. Jordan, ed., *Medical Aspects of Boxing* (New York: CRC Press, 1993), 147–49; Manfred Oehmichen, Roland N. Auer, and Hans Gunter Konig, "Boxing Brain Injury," in *Forensic Neuropathology* (Tubingen, Germany: Springer, 2006), 207–8; Nathan D. Zasler, Douglas I. Katz, and Ross D. Zafonte, *Brain Injury Medicine: Principles and Practice* (New York: Demos Medical Publishing, 2007), 65–66; Robert P. Granacher Jr., *Traumatic Brain Injury: Methods for Clinical and Forensic Neuropsychiatric Assessment*, 2nd ed. (New York: CRC Press, 2008), 15.

2. Peter Heller, *"In this Corner…" 42 World Champions Tell Their Stories*, expanded ed. (New York: Da Capo Press, 1994), 356–65.

3. Adam Smith, "Saginaw County Sports Hall of Fame Inductee Mickey Crawford: A Portrait of Pugilism," *Saginaw News*, August 26, 2008, accessed at *Michigan Live*, http://www.mlive.com/sports/saginaw/index.ssf/2008/08/saginaw_county_sports_hall_of.html.

4. John Reid, "Hall of Famer Dupas Dies at 72," *Times-Picayune (New Orleans)*, January 27, 2008, accessed at http://www.nola.com/sports/t-p/index.ssf?/base/sports-35/1201446790307680.xml&coll=1.

5. Richard Goldstein, "Kid Gavilan, 77, Welterweight Champion in the Early 50's," *New York Times*, February 15, 2003; Vincent M. Mallozzi, "No Rest until Kid Gavilan Has Peace," *New York Times*, March 13, 2005.

6. Thomas Myler, *The Sweet Science Goes Sour: How Scandal Brought Boxing to*

Its Knees (Vancouver, BC: Greystone Books, 2006), 37–40; "Truman K. Gibson, Jr., Lawyer, Activist and First Black Boxing Promoter, Dies," *Jet*, January 23, 2006.

7. "George Parnassus Dead at 78," *New York Times*, February 26, 1975.

8. Jack Cavanaugh, "Ortega Is Still Making Contact in the Ring," *New York Times*, May 2, 1999.

9. Personal interview with Carlos Santana, September 7, 2012.

10. Email exchange, LeRoy Neiman and Troy Rondinone, June 21, 2011.

Index

TROY RONDINONE is an associate professor of history at Southern Connecticut State University and the author of *The Great Industrial War: Framing Class Conflict in the Media, 1865–1950.*

The University of Illinois Press
is a founding member of the
Association of American University Presses.

Composed in 11/13 Adobe Minion Pro
with Avenir display
by Jim Proefrock
at the University of Illinois Press
Manufactured by Sheridan Books, Inc.

University of Illinois Press
1325 South Oak Street
Champaign, IL 61820-6903
www.press.uillinois.edu